ROUTLEDGE LIBRARY EDITIONS: POLITICAL THOUGHT AND POLITICAL PHILOSOPHY

I0130587

Volume 23

J. A. HOBSON

J. A. HOBSON
A Reader

Edited by
MICHAEL FREEDEN

Routledge
Taylor & Francis Group
LONDON AND NEW YORK

First published in 1988 by Unwin Hyman Ltd

This edition first published in 2020
by Routledge
2 Park Square, Milton Park, Abingdon, Oxon OX14 4RN

and by Routledge
52 Vanderbilt Avenue, New York, NY 10017

Routledge is an imprint of the Taylor & Francis Group, an informa business

British Library Cataloguing in Publication Data
A catalogue record for this book is available from the British Library

ISBN: 978-0-367-21961-1 (Set)
ISBN: 978-0-429-35434-2 (Set) (ebk)
ISBN: 978-0-367-24624-2 (Volume 23) (hbk)
ISBN: 978-0-367-24626-6 (Volume 23) (pbk)
ISBN: 978-0-429-28355-0 (Volume 23) (ebk)

Publisher's Note
The publisher has gone to great lengths to ensure the quality of this reprint but points out that some imperfections in the original copies may be apparent.

Disclaimer
The publisher has made every effort to trace copyright holders and would welcome correspondence from those they have been unable to trace.

J. A. Hobson:
A Reader

edited by

MICHAEL FREEDEN

London
UNWIN HYMAN
Boston   Sydney   Wellington

Published by the Academic Division of
Unwin Hyman Ltd
15/17 Broadwick Street, London W1V 1FP, UK

Allen & Unwin Inc.,
8 Winchester Place, Winchester, Mass. 01890, USA

Allen & Unwin (Australia) Ltd,
8 Napier Street, North Sydney, NSW 2060, Australia

Allen & Unwin (New Zealand) Ltd in association with
the Port Nicholson Press Ltd,
60 Cambridge Terrace, Wellington, New Zealand

First published in 1988

British Library Cataloguing in Publication Data

Hobson, J. A.
    J. A. Hobson: a reader.
    1. Political science   2. Economics
    I. Title   II. Freeden, Michael
    320   JA66
    ISBN 0-04-445107-5
    ISBN 0-04-445110-5 Pbk

Library of Congress Cataloging-in-Publication Data

Hobson, J. A. (John Atkinson), 1858-1940.
    J. A. Hobson: a reader / edited by Michael Freeden.
    p. cm.
    Bibliography: p.
    Includes index.
    ISBN 0-04-445107-5 (alk. paper).
    ISBN 0-04-445110-5 (pbk.: alk. paper)
    1. Political science. 2. Economics.   I. Freeden, Michael.
    II. Title.
    JC223.H615 1988
    320—dc19

Typeset by Grove Graphics
Printed by Billing and Sons Ltd, London and Worcester

Contents

Contents

Acknowledgements

I would like to thank P. J. Cain for his helpful comments on the Introduction, and Jane Harris-Matthews of Unwin Hyman for her encouragement and assistance. For permission to reproduce material by J. A. Hobson, I would also like to thank the following publishers and organizations: The Estate of J. A. Hobson and The Bodley Head, Curtis Brown Group Ltd, Guardian Newspapers Ltd, James Nisbet & Co. Ltd, Longman, Macmillan Publishing Co. Inc., *New Statesman*, Oxford University Press and South Place Ethical Society.

Michael Freeden
Mansfield College, Oxford

Note on the Text

In the introduction, the bracketed numbers in bold type refer to the selections reproduced here.

Some of the footnotes in the selections from Hobson have been deleted. Those that are retained have been inserted in the text in square brackets.

A space between paragraphs, followed by an unindented paragraph, indicates that a section of the reproduced text has been deleted.

Introduction

I

If John Atkinson Hobson were to lay claim to nothing else, he would deserve to be remembered as one of the most prolific and versatile writers and publicists of late-nineteenth- and early-twentieth-century Britain. But he is also one of the most underrated of the many creative individuals – authors, journalists, theorists, academics, artists, politicians, scientists – who forged the ideas, constructed the frames of reference and prescribed the types of activity that determined the road Britain has taken over the past hundred years. True, on a restricted scale Hobson made a name for himself as a vociferous critic of imperialism. As an economist, too, he constitutes a bold footprint for those tracking the development of Keynesian and proto-Keynesian theories. Yet Hobson was far more than an economist or a student of imperialism. His interests also ranged over social philosophy, political theory, international relations and the political events of his day; and what he had to say on any of these fields invariably had bearing on each and every one. Hobson's acute analyses and his dedication to social reform must be appreciated in the context of a nation slowly coming to terms with the pressures that accompanied the extension of the franchise, growing urbanization, widespread dissatisfaction with the human costs of the Industrial Revolution and increased international competition. All this would suggest a justified interest in Hobson as a wide-ranging generalist and systematizer. In particular, social and political theorists could be rewarded by joining those historians and economists who have already focused their attention on his works.

The reason that Hobson has been late in attracting broad scholarly attention and has consequently not made the top ranks of British thinkers is a complex and arguably misguided one. It is not merely that many economists have short memories and few of them are concerned with intellectual ancestry. An answer to this puzzle has much more to do with the mode of discourse that Hobson

1

adopted and its distance from the language and ends of the academic disciplines he trespassed upon. Indeed, if Hobson is remembered for his economic analysis, it is precisely because he achieved in that field a degree of technical mastery that commanded respect, though not legitimacy until late in his life. His economic works attracted much unfavourable comment, but they *were* noticed, provoking rebuttals from the pens of senior economists. Moreover, his serendipitous discovery by Lenin secured his reputation as an anti-imperialist among movements and theories outside the compass of British radicalism. But many scholars display to this very day, as they did in the past, an impatience with the man and his arguments. This amounts to more than challenging some of his ideas, for that is a fate no theorist can escape. They also take objection to his lack of rigour in argument, to his woolliness, to what is contemptuously referred to as a 'journalistic' style. If Hobson is to be reclaimed and justice done to his impressive and influential achievements, a strategy must be adopted that detaches the message from the medium, that rejects modes of philosophical argumentation and quasi-mathematical economic analysis as the only legitimate contenders for serious regard. For Hobson reflected the increasing importance of a major change in the formulation of influential social and political ideas. A shift had taken place away from the elitist preserve of a few 'great philosophers' and towards new social and professional groups that were entrusted with the production and dissemination of working ideologies. Those ideologies differed in style from the traditional methods of theorizing, but they nevertheless maintained a high level of sophistication, relevance and attractiveness. Eschewing the form of the dry academic treatise, they were circulated in more popular literary and journalistic media – reactive tracts for the times that nevertheless displayed a general viewpoint. As representative of a new mode of discourse, the middle range of theorizing, Hobson is one of the most important and interesting British thinkers of modern times. [1.2]

J. A. Hobson was born in Derby in 1858 into a family that bestowed upon him two valuable gifts: a strong connection with Liberal journalism through the person of his father, William, a proprietor of the *Derbyshire and North Staffordshire Advertiser*; and a prosperity that enabled him to engage in independent writing for the rest of his life. Gaunt-looking and tall, with a dry and sardonic sense of humour, a penchant for quiet but devastating argument, and an occasional stutter, he was reputedly in indifferent health, though a keen athlete in his youth. His friends and colleagues testified to the kindliness, wit and charm of his personality and to his fearless independence of mind.[1] An Oxford education in Classics and Modern Greats was followed in 1880 by seven years as a schoolmaster in Faversham and Exeter. From 1887 Hobson began lecturing in English literature for the Oxford University Extension Delegacy and for the London Society for the Extension of University Teaching, under whose aegis he later and against some resistance branched out into teaching economics.[2] This unusual range had an echo in some future writings and set the pattern for Hobson's lecturing activities throughout his life.[3] However, Hobson's growing interest in economics had, as he put it, 'momentous' consequences in the form of an unanticipated rejection by the world of academic economists, a world he dearly would have liked to join. That rejection never ceased to rankle, though the feeling was seldom observable. Hobson's first major work, *The Physiology of Industry* (1889), a collaboration with the businessman A. F. Mummery and written mainly under the latter's inspiration,[4] stated the under-consumptionist thesis which eventually established his long-term reputation as an economist but resulted in a series of highly critical reviews, especially in the leading professional organ, the *Economic Journal*. Over a number of years its editor, F. Y. Edgeworth, L. L. Price, Edwin Cannan and even J. M. Keynes, later to acknowledge generously Hobson's pioneering work, repeatedly challenged his theories and blocked his potential advance on an academic path.[5] Instead, Hobson painstakingly and assiduously turned to making his name via journalism, books and lecturing, and by the end of his life had attained a prodigious and regular output in all three. He was also lucky to be able to consort with like-minded people whose views sustained his own.

Among the many important groups Hobson was associated with, two in particular were crucial to the crystallization of his ideas from the 1890s onwards. He was a founder-member in 1894 of the Rainbow Circle, a monthly discussion group of progressives that served over the next two decades to formulate and test the liberal-collectivist theories and presaged many of the new liberal programmes that gained political ascendancy after 1905. The second forum was even more significant personally, both in terms of Hobson's own growth and as a long-standing outlet for his views. This was the South Place Ethical Society, which provided him with the intellectual ambience from which to draw and to develop. The ethical societies were organizations devoted to the construction of a humanist, rationalist ethic that would in part replace the function of religious bodies, but mainly constitute foci for personal spiritual betterment and, increasingly, for social reform. Initially, Hobson was attached to the London Ethical Society, but then joined South Place, which was not tainted by what Hobson felt was the excessive moral individualism of the former.[6] It is culturally and sociologically significant to note that the advanced liberals and progressives who populated those various coteries had overlapping circles of membership. Ramsay MacDonald and J. M. Robertson were both members of the Rainbow Circle and of ethical societies, and Hobson made many friends and acquaintances such as William Clarke, Herbert Samuel, Graham Wallas and later C. Delisle Burns from among the growing and mutually supporting structures of political and social reformers. Furthermore, Hobson's work for the *Manchester Guardian* brought him into contact not only with its illustrious liberal editor, C. P. Scott (a connection cemented by the later marriage of Hobson's daughter, Mabel, to Scott's son and successor as editor, Edward), but into a close friendship with the liberal social philosopher and journalist L. T. Hobhouse. These links also served to introduce Hobson to a most fruitful period of work on the weekly *Speaker*, transformed in 1907 into the *Nation*, edited by the redoubtable H. W. Massingham and supported among others by H. W. Nevinson, H. N. Brailsford and J. L. Hammond. Hence by the early years of this century Hobson was situated at the core of some of the most exciting intellectual, cultural and political developments of the period. In his economic explorations Hobson also relied on frequent and informed analyses of the American scene. His strong transatlantic connection was maintained through lecture tours, contributions to American periodicals and personal friendships, and his writings acquired some influence in the USA.[7]

II

Hobson was nothing if not a system-builder, a fact that alienated him in his day as it has in ours from some of his more pragmatic readers. This was not consciously and aggressively the case,[8] nor did he adopt an abstract approach; rather, the thrust of his analysis was to insist on the indissoluble empirical interconnections among the fields that examine human activity and culture, so that the inevitable end-result had to be a convergence upon *a* social science. His contribution to the new field of sociology was to recognize that all spheres of human activity, including significantly the production of ideas, were the subject of scientific study. At the same time, though, a social science and its historical setting could not be value-free but were subservient both ethically and methodologically to the postulation of certain ends. [1.3] In all those respects Hobson was influenced by a variety of scholars, American and German as well as British, whose works he diligently read.[9] In particular, he owed a considerable debt to another resident of Derby, Herbert Spencer, notwithstanding the sharply divergent political views and concepts of society to which both men subscribed. As did Spencer, Hobson regarded desirable values not merely as the personal preference of the analyst but as the outcome of a considered and rationally inspired examination of the social context of human action in evolutionary perspective. In that sense, and inasmuch as present society departed from the rational order that could be predicated on biological, psychological and ethical components of human behaviour, it was the duty of the analyst to transform himself into social reformer. At that point, sociology as a science linked up with social progress as an art.[10] Specifically, Hobson contributed importantly to the sociology of elections and to that of class,[11] but unsurprisingly his sociology, as with so many early sociologists, took on the features of a social philosophy. Hobson's theory of progress was incorporated in a view of history that rejected economic determinism, yet insisted that the rise of reason was an ineluctable consequence of industrialization and the social integration that its work-practices encouraged. Like Hobhouse, he located the essential mechanism of progress in the emergence of human consciousness, but allowed for evolutionary choice through assigning to the social reformer the function of moulding the moral and intellectual opportunities for improvement that presented themselves.[12]

Hobson's economic heresy lay not merely in his underconsumptionism, of which more later. Primarily, it was a case of placing economics in its correct context, without which it remained a truncated abstraction. Heavily influenced by the implications of Ruskin's aphorism – 'there is no wealth but life'[13] – Hobson reacted sharply against the narrow specialization, the inductive and quantitative utilitarianism, and the reductionism that were typical of Victorian political economy. [**1.1**] It had transformed the production of measurable wealth into an obsessional dogma and had replaced the study of human beings with that of a unidimensional 'economic man'. [**1.2**] Any quantitative science of society could only deal with the uniform, to which machinery might be harnessed; but it was subservient to the art of social progress. Hobson was himself a product of the general nineteenth-century identification of human utility and welfare as the criteria and ends of beneficial social activity. But he embarked on the little-trod and at the time unfashionable route of interpreting the costs of both production and consumption as expenditure of life and their utility as its enrichment, grounded on a flexible and expandable conception of human needs, and aimed at the elimination of waste in human organization.[14] [**2.6**] As a humanist in the Millite-liberal mould, he sought to maximize the opportunities for human development in all wholesome directions. It was, however, particularly as an organicist that Hobson made his mark as a radical, both in method and in substance. His organic perspective enabled him to draw attention to the interlinkages among all aspects of human behaviour. It underpinned his recognition of individuals as total, integrated human beings. It allowed him to dismantle the barriers between man as matter and man as spirit and to include the physical, biological and psychological facets of being human within the legitimate compass of the study of societies, welding them to the more traditional concentration on the moral and the intellectual. It encouraged him to stress the futility of dogmatic distinctions between the individual and the social, insisting instead that these were dual, mutually supportive aspects of the human personality. It propelled him, at his most radical, to explore the outer limits of liberal theory by postulating the separate existence of a social entity with its own life, will and consciousness. [**2.3**] Humanism and organicism were hence the two hallmarks of Hobson's approach, first formulated clearly in *The Social Problem* (1901). Combining the two, the art of life, incorporating enjoyable and expressive labour, meant for Hobson the self-development of one's productive-cum-creative faculties concomitantly with liberation from those social and physical hindrances that could be removed mainly by co-ordinated communal effort. This was complemented by a keen awareness that the quality of human life was also a function of the vital utility of *consumption* patterns – in other words, the partaking in natural and social goods that enhanced life and maximized the individual's power to enjoy its benefits.[15] As Hobson was later to put it, his was a 'New Utilitarianism in which physical, intellectual, and moral satisfactions will rank in their due places'.[16]

Hobson broke with conventional British scholarship on a number of fronts: in the role he accorded ideas, in his understanding of social structure and action, in his consequent reinterpretation of liberal thought and, of course, in his economic theory. To begin with, he took issue with the fondness of his contemporaries for piecemeal historical and social explanation, and with their belief in the *ad hoc* and accidental nature of social and political change. Hobson's assertion of the possibility, nay desirability, of intentionality, even of planning, in human affairs was further reinforced by his recognition of the role of ideas in human action. Discernible principles underlay the logic of events;[17] moreover, the practical test of a social philosophy was for Hobson its translation into measures of social reform, and this could only be accomplished through the intellectual grasping of the total, unified structure of a problem.[18] Clearly constructed ideas were the prerequisite for successful political action; in effect this was an endorsement of the importance of rational ideologies in social life. It was hence very much at odds with the dominant hostility towards identifying systematic political ideas as observable facts or as methodologically significant.

Hobson's strong attraction to the notion of a social organism isolated him on that issue from the theoretical positions of most of those near to him in outlook – certainly from liberals such as Hobhouse, even if not from the moderately socialist Ramsay MacDonald. The renewed interest of social theorists and philosophers in biological and evolutionary models was of course something Hobson shared with many contemporaries still absorbing the impact of the Darwinian revolution. But Hobson's imagination was fired by the implications for social action of a conception of society that, in his hands, supported the separate psychical (and in some of his writings even physical)[19] existence of society. He could therefore entertain the notion of independent social purposes and ends and postulate the primacy of the community over atomistic individual desires, and do so not as a socialist or Idealist. True, British Idealists would have recognized this metaphysical conception, but Hobson was not one of their disciples;[20] in contradistinction Hobhouse, though trained in Oxford Idealism, distanced himself (as did his mentor T. H. Green) from any suggestion of society as a living organism which presented claims that were accorded priority over those of its members, and frequently argued the case with Hobson.[21] In fact, Hobson obtained his ideas through both absorbing and reacting to the works of Ruskin and Spencer. In rejecting Spencer's extreme individualism, Hobson reflected the former's holistic predilections, again entirely against the grain of professional specialization in Britain. Like Spencer, Hobson placed man firmly in nature and thus echoed the revolutionary synthesis that nineteenth-century continental thinkers had brought to bear on the social sciences. [2.2] Hobson consequently wove the study of man into an intricate network that encompassed psychology as well as biology, ethics as well as sociology. Unlike Spencer, however, Hobson drew politically radical conclusions from the organic analogy through emphasizing not the self-sustaining abilities of the parts but the capacity of the whole for self-regulation.

Hobson's organicism was more subtle than his critics would concede, even if inadequately worked out. He had no intention of denying the supreme importance of the individual; he merely wished to stress the essential interdependence of people and the dangers of sectionalism. For him, the 'separate action of individuals can never attain a social end, simply because they are *ex hypothesi* not acting as members of society. Social evils require social remedies.'[22] Having, as we have seen, defined human welfare in a broad, life-enhancing sense, Hobson also attached it to a conception of the *social* good as the measure of welfare. In so doing he followed the lead of the progressive Idealist D. G. Ritchie[23] and advanced Bentham's utilitarianism a notable step forward. Individuals on their own lacked the total perspective necessary to protect them from particularistic and egoistic wants. In intimating that they might have to be protected from their own desires, Hobson was appealing not so much to the Rousseauist tradition that contemplated the imposition of a general will on recalcitrant individuals, but rather to that rationalist tradition which, as

Hobhouse had argued, maintained the possibility of harmonizing social and individual goods.[24] Hobson was abetted in that undertaking by subscribing to a notion of personality that allowed for individual action to be socially orientated. Within each human being was a personality endowed with unique elements, but encompassing a dual social tendency: in terms of a common humanity buttressed by shared needs, and in terms of a psychological, intellectual and moral predisposition towards community-sustaining behaviour.[25] Hobson never quite succeeded in reconciling the resulting tensions: problems concerning the delimitation of the private from the social and defining the limits of compulsion presented continual areas of difficulty.

In his early work, Hobson was living proof of the impact of Darwinism on British thinking. The lure of the psychological, however, eventually held Hobson's attention in his quest for further empirical proof for his social theories, though it never bestowed the certainty and intellectual stature with which evolution had been endowed. Although Graham Wallas has been credited with introducing into British political thinking a limited notion of irrationality by means of the analysis of human behaviour in society,[26] Hobson attempted all along, in passages scattered over numerous works, to transcend the liberal concern (an unduly cerebral one, critics would say) with man as a rational being. This he did not as an irrationalist, but precisely in order to integrate irrationalities of nature with rationalities of social structure. Among the few British social thinkers of his time to cast an eye in the direction of continental theories, Hobson eclectically synthesized his newly acquired knowledge with Hobhouse's empirical findings and those of the social psychologist William McDougall, to arrive in the interwar period at an appreciation of the necessity as well as the dangers of atavistic, spontaneous and disorganized behaviour. [2.5] However, reason itself, though not simplistically instinctual, was an integral component of human co-ordination. It was not superimposed on human nature but evolved as part of the process of human growth, anchored in biological and psychological processes. That Hobson still maintained his essential organicism is especially interesting in the light of his hostile reaction, in conjunction with other liberals, towards the high level of state intervention during the First World War. [5.3] Yet it was clear that Hobson was no opponent of the state as such. He was merely exercised by the state's misdirection into activities and areas that reflected its domination by particular groups, whose interest was not the communal interest. Hobson's organic society would above all be a truly democratic one, in which social ends originated from consciously held social ethics, human development was the prized object of societies, and political participation was widespread, being based on an equality that recognized the right of all groups to be heard as well as those social claims that transcended class and group. [2.7] This was bolstered by his belief that all components of society obtained coequal benefits from its development, and – as Hobson became less elitist – that the common sense of the people would prevail.[27]

III

It is first and foremost as a liberal that Hobson made his mark in social and political theory. Although his work in this sphere has long lain in the shadow of Hobhouse, whose reputation was based on his authorship of the classic and highly influential *Liberalism* (1911), Hobson's contribution to British liberal thought and practice was extensive and seminal, worthy of detached consideration from the work of his better-known friend; indeed, more original and adventurous if possibly less studiedly analytical. That contribution lies primarily in the application of Hobson's general system of ideas to the relationship between individual and society, liberty and welfare, development and control. Inasmuch as nineteenth-century liberalism was pervaded with precepts culled from Benthamism and political economy, the questioning of the latter could either destroy or resuscitate it. Hobson was instrumental in reformulating liberalism and enabling it to emerge from a period of considerable self-questioning and of competition with rival solutions to pressing social and political problems, not only unscathed but stronger, more coherent and more relevant. In his productivity, consistency and range, he was the leading theorist of the new liberalism that began to take root in the late 1880s and that, gaining intellectual ascendancy within a generation, laid the ideological foundations of the modern British welfare state. The liberalism that predominated in Hobson's youth was predicated on categories of analysis that had lost whatever utility they may have had in the past. The individual as a self-sufficient and independent entity; society as an aggregate of such individuals; the maximization of untrammelled individual liberty and development as the sole end of society; government as a necessary concentration of undesirable power to be imposed in sharply limited areas; politics as a constraining activity that assumed hard and fast boundaries between individual and society – these were some of the assumptions built into Victorian liberal theory. Obviously, they could not coexist with the new fashions of social theorizing nor function as panaceas to industrial malaise; the question, however, was how could liberalism survive as liberalism while rejecting many of its old premisses?

Hobson attempted a revival of liberalism by insisting that it was mistaken to regard it as an ideology of atomistic individualism, maximization and *laissez-faire*. He was, of course, not the first to suggest this, but he was one of the few who appreciated that liberalism could benefit from and thrive on social theories that socialists had been co-opting for their own. However, it would be wrong to suggest that Hobson plundered socialist doctrines in search of baubles with which to decorate liberalism; he proceeded on a logical path of his own, arguing from within the rationale of liberal premisses, and in *parallel* with the efforts of British socialists to devise their own solutions. Hobson recognized within liberalism the features of a rational humanism dedicated to pluralistic human development, but saw that it could proceed on that path far more successfully than hitherto by attaching itself to a new idea-environment. The perception of individuals as social entities, organically inseparable from the community, allowed him to promote the liberal ends of free and rational development by arguing that they were first and foremost in the *social* interest. That interest manifested itself in individual action as well as in directly attainable social action, for the organic analogy taught that the health of the whole depended on that of its parts. Hence, in a masterly and original inversion of the usual authoritarian undertones of organicism, Hobson posited the happiness and welfare of the individual as of supreme importance to the group. [2.4] He thus mirrored Mill in extolling the virtues of variety, now typically anchored in biological and psychological justifications for 'experiments in life', and even in recommending a reasonable leeway for egoism and irrationality as means to such creative experimentation.[28] At the same time, we must recall that within

11

the well-constituted individual was embedded a deep fellow-feeling, ensuring that optimal individual development would emphasize the social aspects of personality.

Integral to the development of a new liberalism was a more sophisticated interpretation of the nature of liberty itself. Hobson followed in the footsteps of T. H. Green in departing from the negative association of liberty with unimpeded individual activity and in linking it with the granting and seizing of opportunities for wholesome and self-enhancing development. Employing a model of continuously evolving human nature, liberty related to the working-out of that changing potential. If this also necessitated inviting outside assistance (and even obtaining it uninvited in clearly circumscribed instances), liberty would not suffer so long as the ends of human self-development and self-expression were ultimately preserved. [2.3] In practice, genuinely equal opportunities were a concomitant of this viewpoint. While Hobson never abandoned a belief in responsible 'negative' freedom of action, he occasionally trespassed upon an illiberalism that endorsed social intervention in individual lifestyles.[29] In his earlier work, he came under the spell of eugenic proposals which he regarded as a means of minimizing human wastage and maximizing social rationality, on one occasion even challenging the absolute sanctity of human life.[30] On the whole, however, this reflected the experimentation of Hobson himself, repeatedly assimilating complex concrete issues into a body of thought he held with great consistency over many years as an observer of the British scene. His ultimate aim was to encourage those liberties that were conducive to attaining desirable personal and social values (on his analysis) and to suppress those that were not.[31]

Salient among the defining features of Hobson's new liberalism was a growing reliance on the role of a benevolent and impartial state to further the ends of individual and society alike, a state that assumed the mantle of the prime ethical agent of the community. He was instrumental in directing liberalism towards a collectivist stance that nevertheless distinguished itself from socialism both in the scope of envisaged social control and in the values that organized co-operation was intended to promote. [2.3] Arguing from that premiss that the value of work was a function both of individual and social effort,[32] he sanctioned private ownership side by side with communitarian property – each form being necessary to the self-realization of the moral life of the two agents in question: man and society. [2.1][33]

The state was thus accorded not only the tasks, long accepted by most liberals, of controlling natural monopolies or of entering areas of enterprise that entailed risks too high for individuals, but the task of catering to common necessities.[34] The state was further entrusted with responsibility for the sphere of machinery – the uniform and the routine – whereas the individual needed a sphere of artistic productivity, creativity and originality. [2.4] A clear separation of functions emerged: the former was the realm of socialism; the latter of an individualism that in its conception of wholeness and creativity bore an affinity to Marxist ideals.[35] Unlike most socialists, though, Hobson extolled the virtues of competition – assuming it was for excellence rather than survival – and accepted the psychological necessity for incentives; and he recognized the importance of a private realm that allowed for individual tastes and rights. Those rights were not, however, innate as in the old natural rights tradition but a guarantee of natural physical and psychological needs, originating in social recognition of their permanent utility for individual and society alike.[36] When confronted with the excesses of the British state turned military-bureaucratic during the First World War Hobson did indeed relinquish some of his optimism, but he still hoped that the state could be 'conquered by democracy'.[37] Before the war Hobson was intrigued by the mechanics of democracy, supporting, for example, proportional representation and a limited use of the referendum.[38] After the war he became interested in various proposals to increase industrial democracy, while remaining opposed to non-statist political forms such as syndicalism or guild socialism.[39] Throughout, Hobson preached the vision of a welfare state, democratically regulating the affairs of its members, concerned equally with improving the lot of the underprivileged and promoting a sense of community, opening up the bounties of society for all while providing the wherewithal for each to develop his or her special capacities and, ultimately, dissolving the antagonism between state and society which was the bane of the systems that had failed humanity.

IV

Many of Hobson's works were aimed at a specialist audience of economists, and economics remained the only academic sphere in which he demonstrated informed expertise, albeit insufficiently to satisfy his critics. Hobson's underconsumption thesis, which initially secured his reputation, was yet another radical repudiation of nineteenth-century thought. While it could certainly stand on its own and has been treated independently of his general opus, it is more useful to regard it as an adjunct to his wider views on welfare and ethics. Underconsumption was in Hobson's hands at once an economic and an ethical explanation for the ills of capitalism and its cyclical crises. Rejecting the classical doctrine embodied in Say's Law that production created its own demand,[40] and profoundly dissatisfied with the failure of nineteenth-century economic theory either to give a convincing account of economic behaviour or to ensure the smooth running of the economic affairs of the community, Hobson sought to supply an alternative theory that would both explain capitalism's faults and recommend ways to increase its efficiency and social utility. An inability to consume capital goods seemed to him to lie at the heart of the recurrent gluts and depressions that befell industrial countries; and rather than dismiss these as unfortunate hitches in a healthy system, he saw them as endemic to the present nature of capitalism. Through his mentor Mummery, Hobson was at first primarily concerned with oversaving by the rich as the cause of such underconsumption, a phenomenon that alone could deny the rest of the population sufficient effective demand to stimulate production.[41] It also specifically gave the lie to the Victorian injunction to thrift and parsimony: a misguided form of economic activity as well as an individualism that was socially harmful. Only later did Hobson begin to develop a broader and distinctive perspective that looked for the roots of underconsumption not in the behaviour of a particular group but in the maldistribution of wealth. For economic as well as ethical reasons he condemned a system in which low income, especially low wages, created a lack of demand by depriving the many of the power and will to spend and consume while, conversely, there was a limit to what the rich both wanted to consume and could. [**3.1**]

Hobson challenged the nineteenth-century faith in the justice and impartiality of free markets, in 'perfect competition' and in the futility of human intervention in the 'natural' laws that regulated them. He came retrospectively to regard the view that 'markets are intrinsically unfair modes of distribution' as his 'most destructive heresy',[42] though its originality lay not in the assertion *per se* but in the analysis attached to it. Unlike both Marxist and conventional economists, Hobson applied the notions of marginal productivity (in the idiosyncratic sense of the least efficient unit of productive power)[43] and differential rents to land, capital *and* labour. This involved him in a much-criticized departure from accepted marginalism – the dominant explanation for prices based on the costs of production of marginal units of supply.[44] Instead, he insisted that to isolate any unit was to depart from the organic principle. Exhibiting the growing liberal concern over the perverse power of monopolies, Hobson sought the causes of price fluctuations elsewhere. He maintained that superior bargaining power enabled some suppliers of goods or services to gain an irrational and inequitable advantage over the consumer, hitherto erroneously considered to be the beneficiary of competition.[45] The concomitant of this argument was the important postulation of a surplus that identified profits unnecessary to production.[3.4] Originally Hobson associated that notion of surplus with the accepted liberal distinction between 'earned' and 'unearned' income,[46] but that classification did not correspond to the convention of interpreting earned income as work-related. Rather, the distinction Hobson made was between legitimate costs (which, for example, could also include a reasonable amount of interest to induce economic activity) and illegitimate surplus (which could also include extortionate wages). Drawing upon his organic viewpoint, Hobson then claimed the surplus for society, utilizing two main arguments: first, the community endowed the product of each individual – through education, protection and the provision of a market – with a social value that was irreducible to individual effort, and in which the community could hence demand a share (organicism as interconnection); and secondly, joint productive co-operation created more value than could each individual separately (organicism as entailing a distinct social entity).[47] [2.1] In the postwar years, reflecting his partial reaction against the power of the state, Hobson relented slightly, expressing a pluralistic willingness to consider the claims of other key social groups, such as the workers, on the surplus;[48] and in his psychological ruminations he spoke of a 'surplus of organic energy' necessary for individualization as well.[49] Nevertheless, he continued to stress the ills of surplus, now subsumed in his notion of impropery.[50]

The question then became: how could the surplus be eliminated in practice? Here Hobson attempted to tie up neatly the various components of his analysis. Society, intervening rationally through its agent the state, was to employ a policy of taxation that linked a humanitarian concern with social reform to a technical solution for the crises of capitalism. Hobson saw the surplus as a justified target of graduated taxation on incomes and, especially, on inheritance. He insisted that such taxation could not be shifted on to the consumer [**3.2**] and that it would provide the revenue for catering to social needs, while at the same time performing a redistributionary function that would establish the right ratio between spending and saving, namely the amount of new capital needed to furnish a given increase of consumption goods. [**3.3**] Parallel devices would be the discharging of state responsibilities in the fields of pensions,[51] public works (in his early writings),[52] a minimum wage[53] and social insurance.[54]

Hobson has been criticized for virtually ignoring the role that changing rates of interest (because in his view they react too slowly), or deficit finance, could play in the rate of saving.[55] He also made no distinction between saving and investment and hence did not appreciate the role investment and credit expansion could play in reducing oversaving, a fault for which Keynes took him to task.[56] But while his deficiencies as economist may be legion, his heresies, with their qualitative and humanitarian perspective, suggested novel ways of looking at utility and rationality and had a salutary influence on welfare economics as associated with the elimination of human waste and with dynamic and developmental conceptions of growth.[57] Above all, they were authoritatively appealed to in support of the ethical and ideological positions which left-liberals and moderate socialists were advancing on their road towards the welfare state.

V

When Lenin wrote *Imperialism, the Highest Stage of Capitalism*, he did as much as anyone to secure the permanency of Hobson's reputation by incorporating into it extensive comments based on the latter's *Imperialism: A Study*. Indeed, Lenin complimented Hobson on being 'more reliable' in his observations than a number of

Marxist theorists, precisely because Hobson was not intent on harnessing his analysis to Marxism. Lenin was also rare, even among later students of Hobson, in describing him accurately as a social liberal.[58] This label is the crux to understanding Hobson's theory of imperialism. His *Imperialism: A Study* has frequently and narrowly been examined as a separate work instead of, as Lenin indicated, part of the general social and political framework Hobson set out to construct. Hobson's work on imperialism, and to a large extent on internationalism as well, is not primarily a specific contribution to a theory of imperialism but a particular application of his social and economic thought.[59] To appreciate that, one has to consider the intellectual function of imperialism in Hobson's early work. He employed it as a fulcrum for his politico-economic critique, a foil against which he could construct a positive, radical theory of society. *Imperialism: A Study* intersected with many of the emerging themes in Hobson's thought: protection and free trade, poverty and social reform, power and sectionalism, human nature and social structure, responsible liberty and welfare. It was imbued with his underconsumptionist arguments and had direct bearing on the nature of the social relationships he sought to foster and on the organizational arrangements to secure them. Once again, its style and concerns reflected the mixture of broad theorizing and immediate reaction to political exigencies that so typified the new liberals and many of their contemporaries, and which endowed it both with permanent and ephemeral features. Hobson's theory of imperialism, though remarkable and influential on its own terms, is in effect comprehensible only when perceived as fashioned out of the linkages he was so adroit at forging.

For Hobson, imperialism was the product of a combination of the underconsumptionism he was deploring in the 1890s and of many of the political and social factors which his communitarian organicism purported to expose and counter. A particularly unfortunate concatenation of those elements was the catalyst that had triggered imperialism off. It was therefore not only the exercise of political control by a mother-country over its colonies; it was also the reflection of economic and financial forces that directed its form and development, and it was specifically fashioned by private, sectional and antisocial interests that exerted harmful influence over both sides of the imperial relationship. Here the superficial resemblance between Hobson and Lenin ends. For Lenin, imperialism was the apotheosis of capitalism; for Hobson, it was capitalism unreformed and rampant. Unlike Lenin, Hobson did not regard imperialism as the final, inevitable development of capitalism. Instead he sought to assail imperialism by recommending correctives to the defects of finance capitalism that gave rise to the more pernicious forms of investment, and by restraining the human behaviour that occasioned it.

When, as in the late nineteenth century, domestic social and economic arrangements were bereft of measures designed to minimize underconsumption, the accumulations of surplus capital had to seek alternative outlets. Much of Hobson's originality lay in explaining the drive for political control over external markets in those terms. It had become increasingly clear to the late Victorians that trade did not, as was fervently hoped by the advocates of imperial expansion, follow the flag. Proportionately to the general volume of trade, only a fraction went to the new colonies. What Hobson had to explain, however, was that, unlike trade, investment abroad was more attractive to capitalists. British consumption was saturated and there was little possibility of selling more home-produced goods in Britain. As long as the proportion of effective demand possessed by the working classes was so small, such goods would not find sufficient domestic markets. The great accumulations of capital in industrialized countries were in the hands of a few. [4.1] As Hobson wrote in 1898, 'it is the excessive purchasing power of the well-to-do classes which, by requiring foreign investments, forces the opening up of foreign markets, and uses the public purse for the purposes of private profit-making'.[60] Here was sounded a theme central to Hobson's later analysis. For grafted on to the economic explanation was an identification of non-economic factors that fuelled imperialism, factors such as force and greed and aggressive competitiveness, that operated to the detriment of the mother-country. Underconsumption was a necessary, but not sufficient, cause of imperialism.[61]

Hobson's exploration of imperialism was hence one of considerable complexity and refinement. The progressive debate over imperialist ventures in Africa and the Far East intensified in the 1890s and even split progressives themselves, prompting Hobson to remark in despair that 'the yielding of certain progressives to imperialism is one of the worst features of present day politics'.[62] Hobson was unquestionably sensitive to the political costs of imperialism for the colonized countries and, while accepting the terminology of the times that referred to 'backward' or 'lower' races, denied the validity of the idea that European values and institutions could advantageously be imposed on subject-peoples.[63] But he always perceived his principal concern to be the deleterious effect of imperialism upon the social, political and ethical constitution of Britain itself and his critique was a severe indictment of the internal affairs of his own society. Hobson was becoming aware not only of the emanation of imperialism from the upper and middle classes but of their geographical concentration in the south of England (a theme to which he returned in later, more sociological writings),[64] where their incomes 'were in large measure wrung from the enforced toil of vast multitudes of black, brown, or yellow natives, by arts not differing from those which supported in idleness and luxury imperial Rome'.[65] This offended some of Hobson's main sensibilities: his predilection for a communitarian ethic, his liberal fear of unrepresentative power, economic and social as well as political. The selfish pursuit by such groups of their self-interest, removed from democratic control, was both morally unacceptable and an autocratic hangover from past days that 'made reform in democratic machinery impossible and blocked the way of social reform'.[66] Moreover, the military machine was enlisted to guarantee the security of the necessary markets, thus forging a link between finance, commerce, industry and the armed forces that was to disturb Hobson increasingly in the gradual build-up to the First World War.

There were, however, further issues at stake. In late 1899 Hobson was sent by C. P. Scott to report for the *Manchester Guardian* on the Boer War in South Africa. As he later wrote, that war 'was both a turning-point in my career and an illumination to the understanding of the real relations between economics and politics which were to occupy so large a place in my future work'.[67] Over the next three years, Hobson put pen to his impressions and produced three different books: *The War in South Africa* (1900) set forth the immediate findings of his trip; *The Psychology of Jingoism* (1901) reflected on the causes of popular support for imperialism; and *Imperialism: A Study* (1902) elaborated a general theory. In all these works a new element in the analysis of imperialism emerged: the role of the financier was highlighted against a background of menacing militarism and jingoism, transforming an economic and social argument into what later commentators have labelled a 'conspiracy theory'.[68] Because the systemic weaknesses of capitalism could not alone account for imperialism, Hobson now identified the factor that conclusively linked the two. British and continental financiers were manipulating the foreign policy of their countries in order to maximize their own profits. [4.2] Again, this assertion served as linchpin for a number of Hobsonian concerns. First, the unwholesome irrationalities of human nature, as Hobson understood it, were uncovered. The financiers were an example of crude, unrestrained and unsocial behaviour, individualistically 'rational' in a narrow, privately expedient sense, but failing the crucial test of social rationality. To make matters worse, they fed upon the latent irrationalism of the unthinking and unregulated mob or crowd and stirred up atavistic passions that lent them vital support. Second, the financiers were a particular case of the general rule that any sectional interest that was not socially controlled would tend to act against the interest of the whole. Third, they were yet another manifestation of the dangers of monopolies of power in the hands of a few. Hobson adapted the first theme from continental thinkers such as Le Bon; whereas the last two were extensions of central nineteenth-century liberal tenets. Unfortunately, Hobson accompanied his analysis with a blatant anti-Semitism unworthy of a liberal standpoint. It was not, as we have seen, the only time he strayed from liberal essentials, but it was his worst lapse. His immediate reaction to his South African visit was to single out Jewish financiers of German extraction as responsible for the imperialist excesses, adding that many of them were 'the veriest scum of Europe'.[69] The astringency of this 'ignominious passion of Judenhetze'[70] (Hobson's own terms in apologizing for raising the issue) diminished in his later works on imperialism, though it did not disappear entirely. He now became interested in the interaction between political manipulators and their dupes and in so doing resorted to one of his frequent incursions into psychology. This time, it was mass psychology that came under his scrutiny. Much as Hobson extolled the social virtues and structural importance of the group, with its order, rationality and human empathy, the mob represented its obverse. It was as if every form had a true and a false manifestation: patriotism inverted into jingoism, the creative irrationality of play and instinct metamorphosed into uncontrollable and destructive passions, the harmonious integration of thinking and feeling individuals into the collective was usurped by the collapse of the submissive individual into the whole. [**5.1**]

From another perspective, Hobson's strictures on imperialism can only be understood in the context of his views on international relations, which developed in logical and chronological sequence to the former. Spurred on by his distaste for the assaults on civil liberties perpetrated by the state during the First World War, Hobson became particularly active in the Union of Democratic Control, founded in 1914 to secure popular supervision of foreign policy and, effectively, to promote a peace settlement,[71] and he also campaigned for the formation of a League of Nations. Hobson was a disciple of Cobden in his commitment to a moral and pacific foreign policy, and he could see the merit of Cobden's principle of non-intervention in the internal affairs of a state. Self-determination and self-development were ends that could be extended from individuals to communities and that demanded peace and national liberty.[72] However, Hobson departed from Cobden's national separatism by gently extending his conception of the social organism to encompass mutually responsive and co-ordinated intercourse among nations.[73] Through international government and rational co-operation he wished to pave a path, parallel to the one of increased internal democratization, towards ending the selfish, particularistic and nationalistic behaviour of existing states, ruled as they were by financial and nationalist-military cliques.[74] [**4.4**] Genuine internationalism would render an extreme non-interventionist stance obsolete for, as Hobson explained, federalism and self-determination had to qualify each other, as part of the harmony of unity and diversity.[75] An international federalism would, as with the relations between individual and society, parcel out areas of self-determination and areas of subordination to higher fraternal claims.[76] [**4.5**] He originally held out high hopes that this function could be fulfilled by the League of Nations; later, when its failure was patent, he referred instead to a hypothetical Society of Nations.[77] Although Hobson maintained a dogged, if occasionally uneasy, allegiance to the Cobdenite ideal of free trade, he came to question its excesses in the form of unrestricted freedom of contract and exchange that benefited specific groups; indeed, by the 1930s he was privately expressing signs of agnosticism towards the issue as a whole.[78] While still opposed to the offensive nationalist undertones of wholesale protectionism [**4.3**], Hobson feared that free trade

21

could no longer cure unemployment, and would simply reinforce the liberty of selfish commercialism. International co-operation, on the other hand, could increase the creative liberty both of individuals and of nations.[79] Paradoxically, only within this rationally controlled system would free trade be truly beneficial. On economic grounds, too, international co-operation would protect standards of living and secure better distribution of the world-product between labour and other factors.[80] Hobson's radical theory of property transcended boundaries when he wrote that 'the claim that the people in occupation of a country are the absolute owners of those resources, and entitled to leave them undeveloped, is a quite inadmissible assertion of national sovereignty'.[81]

VI

Hobson's reaction to the encroachments and 'Prussianization' of the state during the First World War [5.2] heralded an impending breach with the Liberal Party, though not with liberalism. Having failed to be elected as an Independent in 1918, he eventually gravitated towards the Labour Party, though he 'never felt quite at home' in it.[82] Hobson eschewed its dogmatic socialism and trade unionist sectionalism and sided with the progressive ideas formulated under liberal inspiration, as enunciated in *The Next Five Years* plan of 1935. He frequently called for a practical alliance between the Liberal and Labour parties. [5.5] Yet, though Hobson repeatedly addressed the central interwar problem of unemployment, his brand of redistributionism no longer came to grips with the dominant economic issues, increasingly revolving round structural changes, productivity and early Keynesian proposals on credit and investment manipulation.[83] Nevertheless, he assisted the formulation of Labour politics throughout the 1920s, notably as senior partner of the team that drew up the ILP manifesto *The Living Wage* [5.4], and wielded considerable influence both on Labour politicians and activists, attracted by the scientific basis Hobson gave to the demand for a minimum standard of living, and on Labour theoreticians such as G. D. H. Cole, impressed by Hobson's humanist economics.[84] Undoubtedly, Hobson was co-opted to the cause of Labour rather than seeking to support it actively. Indeed, as he grew older and more detached from party politics, his liberalism strengthened and matured. Nourished by a thorough and wise understanding of the forces that fashioned the world for good and evil, it shed its youthful impatience and elitist utopianism, acquiring instead a deeper commitment to equality and democracy along with a tolerance for human foibles. When Hobson died in 1940 a townsman wrote: 'a prophet is not without honour save in his own country . . . one of the greatest minds of the age . . . has passed on, his works remain. Our political and economical ideas may change in this age of transition, but whatever happens we shall owe to him a debt that can never be repaid.'[85]

Notes

1   See the obituaries by C. Delisle Burns, *New Statesman and Nation*, 6 April 1940, and G. D. H. Cole, *Economic Journal*, vol. 50 (1940), 359.
2   Hobson's training in economics was acquired not through school or university, but by means of the Cambridge University Extension Movement courses in Derby in 1875. See J. A. Hobson, *Confessions of an Economic Heretic* (London: 1938), pp. 23–4.
3   cf., for example, J. A. Hobson, *A Modern Outlook* (London: 1910) and various lectures to the Rainbow Circle (see Rainbow Circle minutes, British Library of Political and Economic Science), e.g. on Marx (9 April 1902); on Olive Schreiner, Ellen Key and feminism (13 March 1912).
4   See E. E. Nemmers, *Hobson and Underconsumption* (Amsterdam: 1956), p. 26; J. Allett, *New Liberalism: The Political Economy of J. A. Hobson* (Toronto: University of Toronto Press, 1981), p. 9.
5   cf., for example, *Economic Journal*, vol. 4 (1894), 673–6 (Price); vol. 7 (1897), 87–9 (Cannan); vol. 23 (1913), 393–8 (Keynes). See also Hobson, *Confessions*, pp. 30–1; Allett, *New Liberalism*, pp. 10–11.
6   I. D. MacKillop, *The British Ethical Societies* (Cambridge: 1986), pp. 21–6; Hobson, *Confessions*, pp. 55–8.
7   ibid., pp. 64–70; Allett, *New Liberalism*, p. 30.
8   Hobson, *Confessions*, pp. 91–2.
9   See, for example, Hobson's reviews of S. N. Patten, *The Theory of Dynamic Economics*, and of L. Stein, *Die Sociale Frage im Lichte der Philosophie*, in the *Economic Journal* (respectively vol. 2 (1892), 687–90 and vol. 8 (1898), 378–81); and of H. Dyer, *The Evolution of Industry*, in *International Journal of Ethics*, vol. 6 (1895–6), 127–9.
10 cf. J. A. Hobson, *John Ruskin Social Reformer* (London: 1898), pp. 74, 79, 87 and J. A. Hobson, *The Social Problem* (London: 1901), p. 65.
11 J. A. Hobson, 'The General Election: a sociological interpretation', *Sociological Review*, vol. 3 (1910), 105–17; J. A. Hobson, *Work and Wealth: A Human Valuation* (London: 1914), p. 140.
12 J. A. Hobson, 'The possibilities of popular progress', *University Review*,

vol. 1 (1905), 150–69 [reprinted in *The Crisis of Liberalism* (London: 1909) under the more topical but less accurate title 'The higher tactics of Conservatism']. cf. M. Freeden, *The New Liberalism* (Oxford: Clarendon Press, 1978), pp. 89–91.

13 See especially Hobson, *John Ruskin Social Reformer* and J. A. Hobson, 'Ruskin as political economist' in J. H. Whitehouse (ed.), *Ruskin the Prophet* (London: 1920).

14 Hobson, *The Social Problem*, pp. 7–16, 47–50; Hobson, *Work and Wealth*, pp. 33, 37, 168, 330 and *passim*. H. B. Davis, 'Hobson and human welfare', *Science and Society*, vol. 21 (1957), 304, regards Hobson's identification of the human costs of production additional to wages as his main contribution to economic literature.

15 See especially J. A. Hobson, *Wealth and Life* (London: 1929), xx–xxi; Hobson, *Work and Wealth*, pp. 106–20.

16 Hobson, *Wealth and Life*, p. 16.

17 J. A. Hobson, *Problems of Poverty* (London: 1891; 3rd edn, 1896), pp. 195–6.

18 cf. J. A. Hobson, 'The ethics of industrialism', in S. Coit (ed.), *Ethical Democracy: Essays in Social Dynamics* (London: 1900), p. 88; Hobson, *The Social Problem*, pp. 2–3, 281–2.

19 J. A. Hobson, 'The re-statement of democracy', *Contemporary Review*, vol. 81 (1902), 262–72 [reprinted in Hobson, *The Crisis of Liberalism*]. See [2.3].

20 Note, though, Hobson's favourable review of the idealist J. S. Mackenzie's *An Introduction to Social Philosophy*, in *International Journal of Ethics*, vol. 2 (1891–2), 388–91.

21 M. Freeden, *Liberalism Divided* (Oxford: Clarendon Press, 1986), p. 232; Freeden, *The New Liberalism*, pp. 105–6.

22 Hobson, *John Ruskin Social Reformer*, pp. 198–9.

23 See especially D. G. Ritchie, *Principles of State Interference* (London: 1891).

24 e.g. L. T. Hobhouse, *Liberalism* (London: 1911); L. T. Hobhouse, *The Rational Good* (London: 1921).

25 See, for example, J. A. Hobson, 'Character and society' in P. L. Parker (ed.), *Character and Life* (London: 1912), pp. 72–6, and J. A. Hobson, *Towards Social Equality* (London: 1931).

26 In his book *Human Nature in Politics* (London, 1908). See M. J. Wiener, *Between Two Worlds. The Political Thought of Graham Wallas* (Oxford: 1971); T. Qualter, *Graham Wallas and the Great Society* (London: 1980).

27 On the latter point contrast his 'The re-statement of democracy' with *Democracy and a Changing Civilization* (London: 1934).

28 Hobson, 'Character and society', pp. 95–6; Hobson, *Work and Wealth*, p. 304; J. A. Hobson, 'The Ethical Movement and the natural man', *Hibbert Journal*, vol. 20 (1922), 673. See [2.5].

29 M. Freeden, 'J. A. Hobson as a New Liberal Theorist: some aspects of his social thought until 1914', *Journal of the History of Ideas*, vol. 34 (1973), 436–7.

30 J. A. Hobson, 'The population question. II.', *Commonwealth*, vol. 2 (1897), 170–1; Hobson, *The Social Problem*, pp. 214–17. See also M. Freeden, 'Eugenics and progressive thought: a study in ideological affinity', *Historical Journal*, vol. 22 (1979), 645–71.
31 See, for example, J. A. Hobson, 'Democracy, liberty and force', *Hibbert Journal*, vol. 34 (1935), 40.
32 Hobson, *The Social Problem*, p. 148. cf. also Hobson, *Problems of Poverty*, p. 198.
33 Hobson, 'The ethics of·industrialism', p. 104.
34 Hobson, *The Social Problem*, p. 175.
35 ibid., pp. 181–3 and *passim*.
36 ibid., pp. 198–201.
37 See Freeden, *Liberalism Divided*, pp. 26–44.
38 Hobson, *The Crisis of Liberalism*, pp. 13, 17–49.
39 J. A. Hobson, *Democracy After the War* (London: 1917), p. 181; Hobson, *Democracy and a Changing Civilisation*, pp. 95–6. cf. Freeden, *Liberalism Divided*, pp. 71–3.
40 Though as Nemmers (*Hobson and Underconsumption*, pp. 97–8) and Allett (*New Liberalism*, pp. 101–2) have observed, Hobson's dismissal of Say's Law was not unequivocal. See also Davis, 'Hobson and human welfare', 296; he notes Hobson's claim that when actual savings were equal to the need for investment, there could be no unemployment.
41 A. F. Mummery and J. A. Hobson, *The Physiology of Industry* (London: 1889), *passim*; cf. Nemmers, *Hobson and Underconsumption*, pp. 26–32.
42 Hobson, *Confessions*, p. 168.
43 ibid., p. 45; cf. P. T. Homan, *Contemporary Economic Thought* (New York and London: 1928), p. 308n.
44 J. A. Hobson, *The Industrial System* (London: 1909), pp. 103, 112–20. cf. Homan, *Contemporary Economic Thought*, pp. 318, 328–9; Nemmers, *Hobson and Underconsumption*, pp. 95–7.
45 cf. J. A. Hobson, 'The law of the three rents', *Quarterly Journal of Economics*, vol. 5 (1891), 263–88; Hobson, *Confessions*, pp. 44–8.
46 See Allett, *New Liberalism*, p. 106. P. Clarke, *Liberals and Social Democrats* (Cambridge: 1978), p. 52, questions Hobson's assumption that unearned income was functionless.
47 Hobson, *Problems of Poverty*, p. 198; Hobson, *The Social Problem*, pp. 146–7. cf. Freeden, *The New Liberalism*, pp. 44, 137; Allett, *New Liberalism*, p. 75.
48 J. A. Hobson, *Incentives in the New Industrial Order* (London: 1922), pp. 107–8. cf. Freeden, *Liberalism Divided*, pp. 64–5.
49 Hobson, *Wealth and Life*, p. 15. cf. Freeden, *Liberalism Divided*, pp. 238–9.
50 J. A. Hobson, *Property and Improperty* (London: 1937).
51 J. A. Hobson, 'Old age pensions. II. The responsibility of the state to the aged poor', *Sociological Review*, vol. 1 (1908), 295–9.
52 J. A. Hobson, 'The right to labour', *Nation*, 8 February 1908.
53 Hobson, *The Social Problem*, pp. 198–201.
54 Hobson, *Work and Wealth*, p. 200.

55 Nemmers, *Hobson and Underconsumption*, pp. 68, 128; Allett, *New Liberalism*, pp. 114–15.
56 J. M. Keynes, *Collected Writings*, Vol. xxix (London: 1971–83), pp. 208–11. cf. Clarke, *Liberals and Social Democrats*, pp. 227–30.
57 Homan, *Contemporary Economic Thought*, pp. 305, 333, 360; D. J. Coppock, 'A reconsideration of Hobson's theory of unemployment', *Manchester School of Economic and Social Studies*, vol. 21 (1953), 11.
58 V. I. Lenin, *Imperialism, the Highest Stage of Capitalism* (1917), in V. I. Lenin, *Selected Works* (Moscow: 1977) esp. chapters 7–9.
59 On the latter see Nemmers, *Hobson and Underconsumption*, pp. 33–59.
60 J. A. Hobson, 'Free trade and foreign policy', *Contemporary Review*, vol. 74 (1898), 178. N. Etherington, in *Theories of Imperialism: War, Conquest and Capital* (London, 1984), chapters 3, 4, contends that Hobson was heavily influenced by American analyses of investment imperialism, in particular Gaylord Wilshire's, but this is qualified by P. Cain, 'J. A. Hobson, financial capitalism and imperialism in late Victorian and Edwardian England', *Journal of Imperial and Commonwealth History*, vol. 13 (May, 1985), 5–6. For a more sanguine, but atypical, view of foreign investments held by Hobson see his *An Economic Interpretation of Investment* (London: 1911).
61 B. Porter, *Critics of Empire* (London: 1968) was one of the first contemporary studies to stress this important point.
62 J. A. Hobson, 'The Progressive Party. II', Rainbow Circle minutes, 7 June 1899.
63 J. A. Hobson, *Imperialism: A Study* (London: 1902; 3rd edn, 1938), pp. 237ff. See also P. J. Cain, 'International trade and economic development in the work of J. A. Hobson before 1914', *History of Political Economy*, vol. 11 (1979), 416–18.
64 cf. Hobson, 'The General Election: a sociological interpretation'. See P. J. Cain, 'J. A. Hobson, financial capitalism and imperialism in late Victorian and Edwardian England', 8–20.
65 Hobson, *Imperialism: A Study*, p. 151.
66 Rainbow Circle minutes, 7 June, 1899.
67 Hobson, *Confessions*, p. 59.
68 See, for example, Porter, *Critics of Empire*, pp. 200–6; Clarke, *Liberals and Social Democrats*, pp. 92–3. See also the dispute over the relevance of a conspiracy theory between P. F. Clarke ('Hobson, free trade and imperialism', *Economic History Review*, vol. 34 (1981), 308–12) and P. J. Cain ('Hobson's developing theory of imperialism', ibid., 313–16).
69 Letter from Hobson to C. P. Scott, Hobson–Scott correspondence, John Rylands University Library of Manchester (quoted in Porter, op. cit., p. 201). cf. also H. Mitchell, 'Hobson revisited', *Journal of the History of Ideas*, vol. 26 (1965), esp. 389–404, who argues that Hobson was mistaken in the centrality he accorded to Jewish financiers.
70 J. A. Hobson, *The War in South Africa* (London: 1900), p. 189.
71 cf. M. Swartz, *The Union of Democratic Control in British Politics During the First World War* (Oxford: 1971).
72 J. A. Hobson, *Problems of a New World* (London: 1921), p. 251.

73 J. A. Hobson, *Richard Cobden: The International Man* (London: 1919), pp. 390–1, 396–400.
74 See also Hobson, *Democracy After the War*, p. 197; Hobson, *Problems of a New World* (London: 1921), p. 227.
75 See also Hobson, *Problems of a New World*, p.251.
76 Hobson, *Democracy and a Changing Civilisation* (London; 1934), pp. 135–6, 138.
77 ibid., pp. 140–2.
78 *Guardian* Papers, A/H69/17, Hobson to Scott, 9 February 1930 (John Rylands University Library of Manchester).
79 Hobson, *Richard Cobden*, p. 406.
80 See Nemmers, *Hobson and Underconsumption*, pp. 140–1.
81 Hobson, *Democracy and a Changing Civilisation*, pp. 141–2.
82 Hobson, *Confessions*, pp. 29, 124–6; Freeden, *Liberalism Divided*, pp. 356–63.
83 See D. Winch, *Economics and Policy: A Historical Survey* (London: 1972), pp. 129–30; Freeden, *Liberalism Divided*, chapter 5.
84 See Cole's knowledgeable survey of Hobson's work in *Economic Journal*, vol. 50 (1940), 351–60. H. N. Brailsford observed that 'round about that time Hobson was the most respected intellectual influence in the Labour Movement' (*The Life-Work of J. A. Hobson* (London: 1948), p. 13).
85 A. Goodhead in the *Derbyshire Advertiser*, 5 April 1940.

— 1 —

General Methodology

Hobson's autobiography, *Confessions of an Economic Heretic*, published in 1938 when he was eighty, sheds little light on the man, but much on his thinking and intellectual development. Surveyed from the end of his life, that development displayed remarkable substantive and methodological consistency. The excerpts relate to Ruskin's influence in directing Hobson towards a qualitative conception of wealth and dwell on the difficulties Hobson encountered on his way towards formulating a theory of human welfare when attempting to define the relationships between economics as a science and other interconnected branches of human studies.

The Social Problem (1901), a compilation of essays Hobson wrote in the late 1890s for the weekly *Ethical World*, is one of the most thoughtful and wide-ranging of his works. The selections show his desire to occupy the middle ground of social philosophy by proffering an analysis that ensured a larger readership while protecting him against the charges of dilettantism. His revised utilitarianism was superimposed upon a critique of economists old and new and a bold, even reckless, challenging of the theoretical underpinnings of political economy. Central to his broader perspective was the rejection of an inductive approach in favour of a rational, purposive articulation of human ends. Consequently, empiricism had to be subservient to the realization of human values and social progress. In *Free-Thought in the Social Sciences* (1926) Hobson expounded further on the specific features of the social studies that rendered an empirical, disinterested science of society unlikely. He opposed the positivist tendencies that had had such impact on nineteenth- and twentieth-century conceptions of social research, cautioning the student of society against unavoidable biases and the looseness of the subject-matter.

1.1 Confessions of an Economic Heretic (1938) [pp. 38–43, 164–71]

The two main lines of this departure [from economic orthodoxy] lie in the development of a 'humanist' interpretation of the processes of production and consumption, and in the revolt against the accepted theory of *laisser-faire* as a security for the welfare of the community regarded as a productive and consumptive whole.

The need for the humanization of economic science and art was intensified by the study which I gave to Ruskin in the mid-nineties. Here again the initiative was not mine but came from Sir Charles Mallet, who asked me to write the book which I published in 1898 under the title *John Ruskin; Social Reformer*. I had read and admired *Unto this Last* [London: George Allen & Unwin Ltd], some years before, but had regarded it rather as a passionate rebellion than as a critical and constructive work. The violence of its assault upon modern processes and the demand for 'captains of industry' to dominate economic life repelled me. But when I took it up again and read it in conjunction with *Munera Pulveris* [London: George Allen & Unwin Ltd], which sets forth in logical order Ruskin's claim to be a scientific thinker, I recognized that his insistence upon interpreting the terms 'wealth' and 'value' in their proper meanings 'welfare' and 'vitality' was not the mere freak of a literary verbalist but a genuinely scientific demand. 'There is no wealth but life. Life including all its powers of love, of joy, and of admiration. That country is the richest which nourishes the greatest number of noble and happy human beings; that man is richest who, having perfected the functions of his own life to the utmost, has also the widest influence, both personal and by means of his possessions, over the lives of others' [*Unto this Last*, p. 156]. Here, as elsewhere, the rich and impassioned eloquence of Ruskin was, and still is, an obstacle to his acceptance as a scientific teacher in a country where every form of eloquence is still apt to be regarded with suspicion as an attempt to cloud our reason. But Ruskin's main charge against the current political economy was that it had deliberately and systematically degraded the true and formerly accepted meaning of such terms as 'wealth', 'value', and 'profit' by putting them to the narrow service of business mentality.

Though Ruskin often protested that his indictment was 'scientific', it can hardly be questioned that it derived its force and validity from his appreciation of life as the finest of the fine arts. This required him to introduce the ethical standard of an 'ought' into the valuation of every economic process or result. I expressed this important need in the following passage of my book. 'The true "value" of a thing is neither the price paid for it, nor the amount of present satisfaction it yields to the consumer, but the intrinsic service it is capable of yielding by its right use. Of commercial goods, or any other class of goods, those which have a capacity for satisfying wholesome human wants are "wealth", those which pander to some base or injurious desire of man are not wealth, but "illth", availing as they do, not for life but for death. Thus he (Ruskin) posits as the starting-point of Political Economy a standard of life not based upon present subjective valuations of "consumers", but upon eternal and immutable principles of health and disease, justice and injustice' (p. 79).

From him I drew the basic thought for my subsequent economic writings, viz. the necessity of going behind the current monetary estimates of wealth, cost, and utility, to reach the body of human benefits and satisfactions which gave them a real meaning. But it is one thing to judge that all costs of production and utilization of consumption should be expressed in terms of human satisfaction and quite another thing to formulate such a judgment. Several sorts of difficulty at once become apparent. In this 'human' economics it is almost impossible to differentiate the satisfaction and dissatisfaction one calls 'economic' from other vital goods and ills which lie outside this economic ambit. That is to say, there is the tendency to fuse economic with other vital processes so as to disable them for separate study. Next there is the question how far one can take as criteria of human value the actual satisfactions and dissatisfactions currently attributed to various acts of production and consumption or should insist upon reference to what Ruskin terms their ' "intrinsic" values'. Lastly, there remains the question how far the pleasures and pains of one man can be compared with those of another.

I cite these difficulties here, not with a view of presenting ready solutions, but because they affect the substance of nearly all my later thought and writing. I did not even grasp them in their full significance at the time, and they proved to be sources of some confusion when I came to formulate my economics in terms of 'human value'. In the nineties my mind was fumbling after the conception and expression of an economics which was more art than science, and, therefore, more qualitative than quantitative in its estimate of value, wealth, cost, and utility. But the full significance of this revolt against a distinctively quantitative science did not emerge until a good deal later.

If one gets away from the economics of the market in which money is the measure of work and wealth into the economics of human values, one is inevitably drawn into what may appear to be 'the jumble' of politics, ethics, art, religion, which constitutes the setting of my thought. My main endeavour, however, has been to show that though the human treatment of economic activities links up with all these other activities, they do not form a 'jumble' but a moving harmony of relations, in which the several values, though capable of separate study, must finally be seen as contributory factors in the art of living. I cannot pretend that my development of this thesis has been an orderly continuous intellectual journey. Far from it. My earliest statement of the over-saving heresy was a quarrel with orthodoxy within the range of quantitative economic science. It was only later on that it led me to a closer analysis of the bargaining processes in the markets for goods and productive services which disclosed the inequalities of income that gave rise to 'over-saving' and the waste it brought about in periods of depression. An almost chance excursion into the field of imperialist enterprise in South Africa brought me to perceive and trace the intimate causal relations between a rate of saving excessive for home purposes and the drive for the exploitation of backward countries which is the economic core of imperialism. Thus I was launched upon two different yet not unrelated theses, a distinctively moral criticism of that bargaining process which is the core of distribution, and an equally distinctive political activity in which the profiteering motive played a determinant part . . .

It would be foolish for me to pretend that my human interpretation of cost and utility, and economic value has not led me into serious intellectual difficulties. With these difficulties I have sought to cope in several of my later books. So long as economics concerned itself exclusively with saleable goods and services, it

31

could be kept separate from non-economic activities and values. But my interpretation in human terms brings economic values into close organic relations with other human values. Man is seen as an organism all activities of which are interdependent. The good or bad results of economic activities must react upon the values of other activities. The simplest instance, of course, is the effect of the nature and duration of the working day upon the uses of leisure. But, when we regard man as an organic unity, we perceive that each of his non-economic activities, his play, his politics, his home life, his reading, etc., must react both upon his economic activities and upon the specific costs and utilities that appertain to them. Such intricate interactions evidently preclude much of the specialism and separatism which economic, political, and other social theorists have been prone to claim for the study to which they devote themselves. The organic nature of man, as person and member of a society, requires that each result of a special social study in a particular field shall continually be submitted for its appraisal to the wider survey of all human values. It is perhaps unlikely that this statement will be denied. But the whole trend of orthodox economics has been to safeguard economic practices from submission to such a general survey of human values. This is the real meaning of the attempt to keep economics within the limits of the quantitative measurements of markets, and to prevent the intrusion of ethical considerations into its field. The failure of this strictly quantitative science is due, as we have seen, not so much to its intellectual weakness, as to the recent political and humanist invasions into large fields of business arising from the failure of planless industry, commerce, and finance to 'deliver the goods'. The 'planning' under which capitalists seek to establish or retain their economic control involves a multifarious co-operation between politics and economics, with 'ethics' for the protection of the weak producer and the weak consumer and for the furtherance of 'social services'. The current struggle in the surviving 'democratic' countries is between this reformed capitalism, figuring as disinterested expertism, and a governmental control representing the popular interests and will. Reformed capitalism will make strictly necessary concessions in the way of limitations upon profits, collective bargaining with labour, minimum wages and maximum hours, representation of workers and consumers upon joint boards, provided that the substance of the financial and business management is left in their hands with the opportunities of profit which it affords.

Economic Democracy demands something more and something different. It demands that the whole of economic life shall be brought under a planning based on a conception of a desirable human life as interpreted and administered by the popular will through the instrument of Government. This view, however, as I take it, does not imply a rigorous control by the State over the whole body of economic processes. The main purport of my latest reasoning has been to apply to State socialism certain limitations derived from the view that men are both alike and different in their organic make-up of body and mind, and that this likeness and difference should be reflected properly in the organization of industry.

1.2   The Social Problem (1901) [pp. 4–5, 33–8, 281–3]

The first requisite of a really profitable setting of the Social Question under its new conditions is that such setting shall be intelligible to all persons possessed of a moderate literary education and average capacities of thought. Such a setting must probably, in the nature of words and things, fail fully to conform to the metaphysical niceties. But the latter cannot, and will not, be apprehended by any considerable section of a society, and will not, either directly or indirectly, wield any great influence on social conduct. The inherent deceitfulness of philosophy leads such a man as Tolstoy to maintain that in the unlettered peasant's ideas and language we must seek the most satisfactory statement of problems of life. But this is merely one implication of the ultimately false logic of 'no compromise'. There is nothing absolute in language, or even in ideas; if we wish to secure an end, we must select those which are most convenient to our purpose. In the present case, seeking to formulate the Social Question in a practically serviceable form, it is essential to adopt a middle course, shunning alike the refinement of philosophic specialism and the equally defective simplicity of common speech: the one sterilizes action, the other understanding.

The best apprehension of the greatest number being taken for our intellectual focus, it follows that our setting must be in the full

sense of the word, 'utilitarian'. The premature abandonment of the
utilitarian setting by many thinkers, through pique arising from the
narrow and degrading interpretation given to the term, has not been
justified. English people are habituated to conceive and express the
'desired' and the 'desirable' in terms of utility; and even
philosophers, like the late Professor Green, who are stoutest in
repudiating Utilitarianism, invariably return to that terminology to
express their final judgment on a concrete moral issue. The revolt
of a few superior minds against the general conceptions and
expressions of a nation embodied in a language is always futile and
commonly mischievous. The particular vices of some special form
of utilitarianism, the insistence that desirability was entirely to be
measured by quantity and never by quality, the stress upon physical
enjoyment, and the short range of measurement, which were
somewhat incorrectly attributed to Bentham's system, are not
inherent in utilitarianism, and need not deter us from using its
convenient language. Thus much in preface; the real justification of
this form of stating the Social Question is its success.

The New Political Economy

The 'old political economy' is often supposed to have passed away.
More modern teachers – J. S. Mill, Cairnes, Jevons, Marshall – are
believed to have 'humanized' the study, and made it no longer a
vulgar tradesman's science, but a many-sided, cultured,
gentlemanly science, which conjoins accuracy of thought and
expression with the most generous sentiments, which has ever a
good word for education, patronizes trade unionism and co-
operation, and even admits that the clergy are producers.

So liberal a study might even be competent to confront the Social
Question! But is it? I think that a closer scrutiny of the modern
writers will show that, in its essential character, the old structure
is still retained, the old dogmas still dominant. There is not what
religious people call 'a change of heart'. Some considerable changes
are, indeed, perceptible.The simplicity and rigour of the old fabric
have gone; pieces have been built on to hide the bareness; it has
been painted and decorated to recommend it to more modern tastes.

But the scope and method of political economy still render it quite
inadequate to our task. It is not really 'humanized'. It is no easy
thing to reform an individual thoroughly. To reform a science is still

more difficult. Half conscious of the insufficiencies of the older study, our 'moderns' have not yet ventured upon 'structural repairs', but have rather tinkered at the gaps and crevices. Some portions they have enlarged and elaborated − e.g. laws of supply and demand, theory of rent; other portions they have so altered and built over that it is hard to say whether the old part stands or not. For instance, you may ask the modern economist whether wages are advanced out of capital, whether rent ever enters into price, or whether demand for commodities is demand for labour. He will wriggle and shuffle with complicated verbiage, but will give no straight, intelligible answer.

The 'Manchester' character of the science still survives in the following essential features.

1. It is still a commercial science, with material, marketable wealth as its main and dominant consideration. But, whereas the older economists had commonly confined themselves to material wealth, the moderns usually admit some non-material forms, floundering about hopelessly to get a logical footing for them. The general idea is to extend 'wealth' so as to include all 'marketable' goods. Yet, curiously enough, none of the representative writers takes the complete step. J. S. Mill, after defining wealth as 'all useful or agreeable things which possess exchangeable value', and including human skill, persisted in excluding non-material services which are bought and sold − e.g. a musical performance, or professional advice − on the ground that political economy concerns itself only with 'permanent utilities' [*Political Economy* (People's edition), Introduction, p. 6].

Professor Marshall includes certain kinds of non-material goods in the wealth of a person − 'those immaterial goods which belong to him, are external to him, and serve directly as the means of enabling him to acquire material goods' [*Principles of Political Economy*, bk ii, ch. ii]. This last proviso curiously illustrates the survival of the material standpoint. Marshall, moreover, definitely excludes certain classes of saleable articles. Skill he excludes on the ground that it is not 'external', though he admits it may be included in a 'broader definition of wealth, which has indeed to be taken for certain purposes', though what purposes he does not here or anywhere explain. Marshall also excludes 'services and other goods which pass out of existence in the same moment that they come into it'. Thus, while the materials of a dinner are wealth, the cooking and the attendance are not, though the price paid for a dinner lumps them together inseparably.

The notion of 'permanency' as a condition of economic wealth is a peculiarly weak survival of the narrower materialistic basis, lending itself to the most illogical distinctions. There is clearly no such thing as permanency of economic values, and any attempt to force definitions by laying stress upon duration fails utterly to serve even the narrowest purpose of commercial science. Is a cheese wealth, and an omelette, which perishes as soon as it is made, not wealth? Sidgwick is open to discover the illogic of excluding all personal services: 'There would seem to be a certain absurdity in saying that people are poorer because they cure their diseases by medical advice, instead of drugs; improve their minds by hearing lectures, instead of reading books; guard their property by policemen, instead of man-traps and spring-guns; or amuse themselves by hearing songs, instead of looking at pictures' [*Principles of Political Economy*, bk ii, ch. iii, sect. iv]. But Sidgwick, on grounds of usage, excludes 'culture' from wealth, even when regarded as a saleable commodity to be bought from teachers, thus cutting out the whole of intellectual wealth. And so, having quitted the narrow standpoint of material, marketable goods, economists fail to obtain a sound logical foothold by making wealth cover all kinds of saleable goods.

Their only agreement is in the definite exclusion of non-marketable goods. As Sidgwick expressly excludes 'culture', so Marshall excludes 'moral wealth', remarking that 'the affection of friends, for instance, is a good, but it is not ever reckoned as wealth, except by a poetic licence' [*Principles of Political Economy*, bk ii, ch. ii]. As comment upon this, let me recall Matthew Arnold's words: 'Now, poetry is nothing else than the most perfect speech of man – that in which he comes nearest to being able to utter the truth.'

It must suffice to say that, even in the new and more humane political economy, leisure, health, friendship, freedom, love, knowledge, intellect, and virtue are excluded from wealth, and are only taken account of as far as they are means to the production of certain sorts of marketable wares.

2. Other motives besides the purely self-seeking ones of the old 'economic man' are generally admitted into the modern scheme. Man is no longer regarded merely as a 'covetous machine' driven by greed and idleness.

But how is he treated? Professor Cairnes shall tell us: 'Moral and religious considerations are to be taken into account by the economist precisely in so far as they are found, in fact, to affect the conduct of men in the pursuit of wealth' [*Logical Method of Political Economy*, p. 44]. In other words, 'allowance' is demanded for the friction of non-economic forces in working out an economic problem. With the logic of this method of 'allowances' I shall deal presently. Here it is enough to reflect that moral and religious considerations are not to be treated as having any meaning or worth in themselves, but only as affecting 'the pursuit of wealth'. Does this place economics on a human basis?

3. Production or accumulation of marketable wealth still remains the backbone of 'economics'. This statement will probably be disputed, and reference made to the formal emphasis laid upon and the space assigned to distribution in the current text-books. But this is quite illusory. No consistent, no intelligible organic theory of distribution of wealth is to be found in the modern English text-books. Taking Marshall and Nicholson as types of the ablest and most advanced modern work, one may yet defy any reader to find a unified theory of distribution which shall relate the laws which are given to explain the several forces regulating wages, rent, interest, and remuneration of management. No general theory of the determination of the proportion of produce falling to the several claimants is there set forth. Nor is there any definite attempt to ascertain the bearing of consumption upon production and distribution, either in a quantitative or a qualitative way. We are sometimes told – as, for instance, by Jevons and his followers – that 'consumption is the keystone of economic thinking'; but beyond a few platitudinous *obiter dicta* in favour of 'plain living' and in condemnation of luxury, or some quite general discussion about the influence of a good standard of comfort upon efficiency, there is no attempt to go behind the market value of desires to the organic results of different sorts and quantities of consumption.

The theory of production is still the only strongly and closely wrought portion of economic science. The attainment of a large quantity of commercial goods is still the real standpoint of what remains a distinctively industrial science.

If the modern text-books give some attention, as they often do, to the human claims of workers, to the character of labour, and the influence of industrial facts upon human happiness or worth, this treatment is purely parenthetic, and is not built into the body of the science. Taking economic science as it stands in current English thought, the changes of the last generation have not made it capable of human service in the solution of the Social Question.

Regarded even as commercial science, it is very defective. Consisting of a number of separate little theories – some deductively, some inductively derived – it furnishes a singularly ill-fitted and disjointed whole. The intellectual man, or the reflecting business man, gets little satisfaction from it, for he cannot find the organic unity he seeks, and the 'laws' which are given do not show him commercial society as a 'going concern'. There is neither logical consistency nor actuality. Its very efforts to humanize itself have been injurious. The old system was far more convincing. It had a well-jointed system and a specious intellectuality, which charmed so keen a mind as De Quincey's.

The Manchester framework still survives, but in a rickety condition. The standard of wealth and value is still commercial. Man still poses, along with capital and land, simply as a factor of production – a means and not an end.

In face of these facts, there is something half-humorous, half-pathetic in the efforts made by modern political economy to assume a refined and cultivated aspect, like the successful retired trader who buys pictures, grows orchids, subscribes to the hunt, and does other polite and public-spirited things to make himself agreeable. It has been a dismal failure. Political economy has not succeeded in convincing and winning the attention either of the cultured class or of the practical reformer, because it has not really changed its nature.

Half-civilized, like the inhabitants of some remote island just known to foreign ships, it has stuck on bits of refinement and humanity, and wears them like 'foreign ornaments' – a mortal offence to true aesthetic taste. A science which still takes money as its standard of value, and regards man as a means of making money, is, in the nature of the case, incapable of facing the deep and complex human problems which compose the Social Question.

The Range and Area of 'Social Utility'

All the larger abstract terms which it is necessary to employ in getting any wide conception of social conduct, 'greatest happiness of the greatest number', 'realization of the cosmic purpose', etc., are necessarily lacking in substance, unless and until history fills in the concrete facts. So with 'social utility'. For a statesman or any common citizen in England to-day its worth and meaning as a vital principle will evidently depend in large measure upon the grasp of present and past fact which history discloses. The contents of social utility to him will become 'real' and valid for conduct, just in proportion as knowledge of facts and of the laws of facts enables him to construct a feasible future in accordance with true principles of continuity. He will know what is possible, what is probable, in the future, from his knowledge of the past. If he has made history into an organic science, the full form and contents of social utility, at any given range and area, may even be deemed a direct product of historical study. But two considerations of great importance enter here. The history by means of which a social ideal of utility shall receive substance transcends the common acceptance of the term 'history'. It is no longer the accurate presentation of fact, but something which is really different – namely, facts ordered and interpreted. This process of ordering and interpretation is, in the last resort, the work not of the specialist historian or the statistician (who is a quantitative historian), but of the 'philosopher'. The notion that a social science capable of yielding an art of social progress can be formed upon inductive lines by setting a number of persons to study facts, and then by ordering these facts and extracting their common measures in laws and tendencies, is the futile product of an incapacity to think clearly upon the conditions of science. The laws or principles needed for the selection, the ordering, and the interpretation of concrete facts of history cannot be got out of these facts themselves, but must be imposed by a process which, at any rate relatively to these facts, is *a priori*.

The failure to recognize this adequately, and the consequent disparagement of 'philosophy' by many students of 'history' and many practical reformers, is a grievous source of intellectual waste which is visible in defective correlation of intellectual forces. Whether the principles of order and interpretation required to utilize historic study are themselves reached inductively by prior study of historic facts is a question which would lead us back into one of the great intellectual 'impasses' – viz. the statement of the true relations between the 'forms' and the 'contents' of thought, which need not concern us here. It is sufficient that, for the purpose of the statesman or the common citizen, conceptions which in relation to his facts are *a priori* are essential. To him there must be a 'telos'

39

which cannot be extracted directly and wholly from the concrete experience at his command, but which yet must be moulded into general consistency with that experience. Social principles can never be 'ground out' of history in the almost mechanical way which the pure inductionist requires. If history really did 'repeat itself', this might in some sense be done. But it is only to the superficial view that 'history', in the objective meaning of the term, repeats itself; a closer view always discloses differences beneath apparent 'repetition', and the more minute the investigation the greater the variety and number of these differences. This study of facts always discloses 'the many', never 'the one'; yet, if there is to be a 'science of history', it will consist in this very discovery of the 'one', the 'unity', the 'laws' of action, which induction alone is impotent to disclose. Indeed, one must go further, and insist that the mere historical researcher and the mere statistician are everywhere incapable of the processes of induction on which they rely. Induction implies and uses conceptions of uniformity in nature which are imposed *a priori*. It is not too much to say that, without some large principles which are *a priori*, and may for convenience be called philosophic (since they must ultimately depend upon a conception of 'order in the universe', with which philosophy is primarily concerned), history becomes a mere chaotic accumulation of unordered and, therefore, unintelligible facts, while statistics is really what some of its enemies have described it – *le mensonge en chiffres*.

1.3 Free-Thought in the Social Sciences (1926) [pp. 11–21]

The Disinterested Pursuit of Knowledge

How far and in what sense the pursuit of knowledge can be 'disinterested' are questions to which no easy and certain answer can be given. Each primary instinct of man, nutrition, reproduction, motor-activity, combativeness, defence, etc., proceeds by exploring and experimenting with some part of man's environment and so acquires a cunning and technique for its special purpose. Even when instincts appear to operate with automatic accuracy, it is difficult to suppose that this natural skill has not been bought by 'trial and error' or some rude process of experimentation. If, ignoring lower forms of vegetable and animal life, we confine our attention to man, his elaborate tactics, or behaviour, in hunting and other search for food, in courtship, combat, and other primary activities, seem to imply observation, memory, and reasoning directed to secure the means of a specific satisfaction [i.e. they are not wholly instinctive in the strictly biological sense]. It seems reasonable to hold that the beginnings of some at least of the physical and mental sciences are to be traced to these early fumblings after special bits of useful knowledge, useful in the sense of aiding some instinct or group of instincts to do its particular job more easily or more successfully. This specific search after knowledge cannot of course be described as 'disinterested', though the special interest it serves need not impair but rather assumes the soundness of the observation, memory, and reasoning upon evidence, which it employs.

But when the operation of these instinctive urges is thus raised to the level of consciousness and employs 'reasonable methods', we can no longer regard the tactics as those of the specific instincts, each acting on its own, and using in its separate interest some purely private fund of energy. At some stage in organic evolution a general intelligence (or biological cunning) must come in, to co-ordinate and to control the operations of the various specific urges in the general interest of the whole organism and of the species. A highly centralised nervous system takes over in large measure the work formerly done by specialised local centres. This physiological centralisation is accompanied by a similar centralisation of intelligent control. The direction of a large part of the fund of organic energy is thus placed at the disposal of the control-board in the brain. As in the case of the separate instincts, so in the case of this general intelligence, a growing knowledge and skill arise from the employment of the surplus energy which remains after the 'costs of maintenance' are defrayed. This surplus, absorbed, in the case of lower organisms, in the 'play' or tactical cunning, or perhaps the decorative display of the special organs, passes through the more developed central control of the human brain, into the play, art, or 'science' of the organism as a co-ordinated whole. The question how far science is 'disinterested' thus emerges in a new form. So far as the intelligence of man and the fund of energy available for its operation are released from the control of the separate instinctive interests, and are put to the account of the central control, they

41

may be said to have become 'disinterested'. But if the change only consists in the interest of the whole being substituted for the several interests of the parts, have we yet got what is meant by a disinterested pursuit of knowledge? If science is consciously directed to secure the general good of the human personality or of mankind, conceived in biological terms of survival and development, or in any other terms descriptive of human welfare, have we a fully disinterested science? Or must that term be reserved exclusively for a pursuit of knowledge which, though indirectly and incidentally conducive to human welfare, takes for its direct and conscious aim knowledge as an end in itself, as the satisfaction of an intellectual curiosity which is in no sense the servant of the other special instincts. Or, perhaps, it is unnecessary to assume that this general curiosity, or drive for knowledge, belongs to the original outfit of man. It might be that, at first a separate and subservient part of the primitive instincts of nutrition, sex, defence, etc., it came, with the developing brain, to assert its independence of these particular controls and to set up as a purely intellectual interest on its own account. In either case it will rightly rank as 'disinterested' in the double sense of being devoted directly and exclusively to the attainment of knowledge, and of operating free from the mandates of the special instincts that are its indirect and strictly unintended beneficiaries . . .

How far it can be true of any branch of intellectual inquiry that it can ever proceed wholly unaffected by the influence of the special instincts and interests may remain an unsettled question, though certain conditions of the intellectual life, to which later reference will be made, seem to indicate that no study is so abstract or remote from the passions of humanity as to boast complete 'disinterestedness'.

But in whatever way we interpret the disinterested pursuit of knowledge, its activity and the satisfaction that attaches to it must be taken as elements in the welfare of individuals and of mankind. Equally certain is it that this disinterested activity of the mind will be continually exposed to the violent assaults or the insidious machinations of particular instincts and interests, seeking to secure the authority and fruits of science for the promotion of their several ends, and to prevent the discovery and spread of truths or speculations likely to disturb any beliefs or institutions advantageous to their cause.

It is with the limits of 'disinterested' culture, or conversely, with the biases to which it is liable by the operation of special instinctive urges, that we are concerned.

Now the measure and modes of such interferences will be dependent partly on the nature of the material in the sciences and arts and its relative adaptability to purposes of immediate utility by dominant interests . . .

When we enter directly the sciences of man, body and mind, it becomes self-evident that what we would like to believe is liable to interfere at every point in the selection of inquiries and areas of attention, the formation of hypotheses, the observation and assessment of evidence, the reasoning upon the evidence. Human physiology and psychology, anthropology and history, even if they purport to concern themselves purely with facts of registered behaviour, cannot escape the constant play of passionate interests. The important judgments which these sciences yield to the arts of moral and social conduct cannot be regarded as evoked by rigorously objective inquiry in a dry light. The desire to sustain certain pre-conceived opinions and lines of conduct helps to direct the course of the scientific investigations, and so to form the conclusions which are then taken as 'disinterested' supports for these opinions and lines of conduct.

When we come to that study of the social sciences and arts which is our special theme, we shall find these disturbing influences at their maximum. This is because the material of these studies is softer, more plastic, and more complex, while the interests involved in the attainment of certain judgments and certain rules of conduct are more intense.

As we approach the interest-affected areas of knowledge, we encounter a middle sphere of semi-intellectualism, a mass of loosely related concepts and passion-laden opinions couched in language of popular appeal, which constitutes a public opinion, or a variety of conflicting public opinions. Politics, economics, ethics, sociology, philosophy, differ from the physical sciences in that they are surrounded by these popular opinions which they are compelled to use as part-material for their scientific treatment, and which, as we shall see, use them. Popular notions and interested opinions, couched in emotional rhetoric, have little influence on the sciences of physics and chemistry: while botany and biology have had

43

difficulty in pursuing a disinterested course and keeping their light dry, their terminology and methods have lain too far from the path of popular thinking to be great sufferers. For, though certain specific needs of man and not a merely 'idle curiosity' prompted those early questions and discoveries about man's environment that formed the rudiments of astronomy and physics, botany and biology, and have always kept a selective hand upon the sciences that sprang from those loose empirical studies, they have not much infected with interest and emotion the methods of these sciences.

But when we enter the sphere of the mental sciences, the case is very different. Rigorous ratiocination here seems impossible. This insusceptibility to exact measurement and to stability is particularly applicable to the most important classes of social facts. To certain elementary dispositions of men, the senses, the reflexes, memory, for example, it has been possible to apply laboratory tests which can yield exactly measured records. Not so with the prime facts in social psychology. 'The facts of human nature which are of the greatest importance to the social psychologist are just those to which laboratory methods are least applicable. It is almost impossible to arrange a series of identical experiments to illustrate the working of patriotism or ambition or the property instinct or artistic and intellectual creativeness' [G. Wallas, *The Great Society*, p. 32]. The material of a social science is soft, variable, and mixed with observer's feeling.

Under such conditions hard objective fact is non-existent, and sound generalisation impossible. We believe what we wish to believe. 'We may thus consider the first stage in human thought to be one of which the process of organising experience into common categories is incomplete, and the evidence for the truth of an idea is not yet separate from the quality which renders it pleasant. This is the stage characteristic of the most primitive peoples' [L. T. Hobhouse, *Development and Purpose*, p. 96]. More of this primitive mind survives to-day in the beginnings of our social thinking than we care to admit. The notion of applying a strictly inductive reasoning to a primitive mass of objective facts, or phenomena, which by classification and a series of abstractions, shall discover truths or laws in an ascending scale of generality, building them up into the unified structure of a science rendered ever more exact by quantitative analysis, will not bear close consideration.

A purely 'idle curiosity' fumbling about in a primitive deposit of human phenomena would get nowhere. A moral or social science cannot start with an inductive process. A social student, set to work at the face of some human deposit, must bring with him certain specific questions and hypotheses, if his study is to be fruitful. He must put some order into his mass of raw material, if he is to get more order out of it. A single illustration will suffice. A researcher set down in a slum district, confronted by an immensely intricate mass of human and environmental phenomena, would flounder hopelessly unless he came provided with a number of speculative questions, deduced from prior knowledge acquired elsewhere, bearing upon such issues as the measurement of overcrowding and its relations to infant mortality, family budgets and the relation of their composition to the different grades of family income, the part played by charity in supplementing real incomes, the contribution of the woman towards the family wage, the regularity of school attendance, and the percentage of children getting secondary education, with a score or more of other questions derived by some preconceived social interest.

Thus we recognise that the very foundations of social science are laid in a pre-existing deposit of social interests, themselves infused with certain ideas of social betterment. In other words, social art precedes social science, and is in its turn nourished and informed by that science.

But it may well be said that, though these social interests underlie all processes of social science, they need not impair the disinterested conduct of the science. The selection of certain issues, as a basis for classification of phenomena and for inquiry, does not imply any bias in the rigour of the observation and the reasoning. The 'interests' which lay down the basis of inquiries are selective, but not injurious to the attainment of truth, nor need they blunt, distort, or otherwise impair, the scientific instruments employed.

This brings us to the need for a brief consideration of Reason, regarded as a scientific instrument, in its application to the social sciences. It is first desirable to distinguish Reason as regards the nature of the work it does, its reasoning. By whatever name we describe the reasoning processes, including attention, observation, classification, and the interrelated induction and deduction, much of it is evidently applied to furnish means to the satisfaction of the particular instincts, interests, and desires of man, the technique

45

of the various arts of life. But, as we have seen, reason must be assigned another or perhaps two other distinguishable functions. It must exercise a central control over the whole fund of activities in the interest of the personality and of mankind (i.e. of a social personality); and, if a special instinct of curiosity be held to exist, directed to the pursuit of knowledge 'for its own sake', that special interest must have its due provision in the general economy of the personality.

Now it is important to realise that in each of these functions, error is possible from two sources. (1) There may be false reasoning, due to the imperfect working of the instrument, or the refractory or obscure nature of the material. Or (2) there may be a falsification of the weights and measures, a faking of evidence, a cooking of results, due to the intrusion of motives alien to reason. The peculiar difficulty of the social sciences is their susceptibility to injury from both sources of error.

The social sciences, inclusive of psychology and philosophy (regarded as *Scientia Scientiarum*) differ, as we see, from the more exact sciences in that they find their prime material in the feelings, thoughts, judgments, and conduct of man. Now, in endeavouring to grip this material, in its nature mobile and incommensurable, so as to apply to it reasoning processes, they are confronted with a loose popular terminology, grown up for immediate practical uses, and with a large unordered body of popular feeling and opinion, loose generalizations from experience and tradition, often incorporated in the language of proverbial philosophy. Much sifted wisdom and shrewd common sense are doubtless contained in this popular conceptualism, but it hampers, heavily, the beginnings of the sciences. Consider, for example, how unfitted are such terms as 'politics', 'economy', 'soul', 'society', for exact instruments in the sciences whose 'title' they prescribe. Everywhere the beginnings of these sciences are cumbered by a litter of these 'idols of the market', popular concepts laden with diverse emotional contents, and couched in terms that have no fixed meaning even for the same user. Yet they cannot be shed. Attempts are made to define them, and to get the definitions accepted for scientific purposes. But largely in vain. Words like 'profit', 'will', 'Nature', 'nationality', 'instinct', make it very difficult to get dry light or accurate thinking into the problems where they figure. Most even of the phraseology in which early abstract thinkers couch their thoughts, such as 'the natural rights of man', 'equality of opportunity', 'the product of labour', 'Liberty, Fraternity, Equality', has been a terrible impediment to disinterested science, not only by reason of its slipperiness, but because of the interested and often impassioned burdens it carries.

— 2 —

Political and Social Theory

The chapter reproduced from *The Social Problem* includes an impassioned, concise and vigorously argued case for social, in addition to individual, property. Dismissing atomistic individualistic theories of property, Hobson analyses *all* property as naturally containing a social component, and he furthermore makes out a radical-liberal case for direct social ownership of *some* property as necessary to the self-realization of a society. A demarcation between the claims of individual and society is possible, though only on the assumption that enough useful goods exist to cater to the life, needs and progress of both.

Despite his attack on Herbert Spencer's individualism, Hobson appreciated Spencer's contribution to the moulding of modern thought. When Spencer died, Hobson commemorated him in a lecture at South Place Ethical Society. From Spencer, Hobson learnt the fundamental role of biology and evolution in understanding social behaviour and in placing man in nature and, even more crucially, the synthetic holism of knowledge itself, which Hobson tried to emulate.

In the years leading up to the First World War, Hobson developed his organic theory of society to an extent uncommon in British political thought. *The Crisis of Liberalism* (1909), another collection of essays ranging back for over a decade, included his strongest statement on the subject — 'The re-statement of democracy' (first published in 1902), demonstrating the extent to which he was prepared to overwork the analogy and consider society as a physical as well as a psychical entity. Marked elitist overtones disappeared in later works such as *Work and Wealth* (1914), where Hobson considerd the federal implications of organicism as enhancing the welfare of the units as much as that of the whole. *The Crisis of Liberalism* also contains lucid expositions of the new liberalism, projecting it even beyond the policies of the Liberal Administration of 1906, insisting on a large role for the state compatible with liberty, and allowing now for a greater equality of opportunity than previously envisaged. A short excerpt from *Towards Social Equality* (1931) shows that Hobson travelled further on the road to participatory equality as he grew older.

Work and Wealth was the major prewar summary of Hobson's social philosophy, elaborating his conception of organic welfare and offering a highly optimistic view of incentives that related to the satisfaction of the social will, at odds with his more usual recognition of the role of personal financial reward in eliciting effort. It also contains his distinction between the creative artistic aspect of work and routine labour that can be socialized. This creativity was further scrutinized in 'The Ethical Movement and the natural man', which gives vent to Hobson's ambivalent attitude to developments in psychology – on the one hand affording empirical observations about human nature that an ethical position had to build on; on the other, spreading the illusion that 'animalistic' instincts could be sublimated, rather than integrating them into a total conception of human behaviour. In the passages reproduced from *Wealth and Life* (1929) Hobson returned to explore the process in which considerations of human welfare replaced the narrower ones of monetary wealth. He expounded the arts of consumption as well as production and re-emphasized the broad utilitarian issue of human costs, waste and satisfactions as progressing on a rational evolutionary pattern.

2.1 The Social Problem (1901) [pp. 141–54]

Society as Maker of 'Values'

The greatest single source of error in dealing with the Social Question is the failure to understand the claim of society to property based upon the ground that society is a worker and a consumer. Outside a narrow class of economic students, an almost universal belief prevails that property and the value in it are attributable to individual agency alone. Though Mr Herbert Spencer, for instance, claims to have given closer attention than others to the structure and functions of society, we find him, in one of his latest books, broaching a theory of value which is nothing else than a sheer denial of society as a working unity. The rights of property of the 'community' are denied in the following instructive passage: 'We must admit that all which can be claimed for the community is the surface of the country in its original unsubdued state. To all that value given to it by clearing, breaking up, prolonged culture, fencing, draining, making roads, farm buildings, etc., constituting nearly all its value, the community has no claim. This value has been given either by personal labour, or by labour paid for, or by ancestral labour; or else the value given to it in such ways has been purchased by legitimately-earned money. All this value, artificially given, vests in existing owners, and cannot, without a gigantic robbery, be taken from them' [*Justice*, p. 92].

Since it will be generally admitted that, if society contributes nothing to the creation of value in land, and has no rightful claim to such form of property, her claim to create other values and own other property must *a fortiori* collapse, this passage may be considered to offer a test case.

In order to clear the way, we may dismiss all consideration of the legitimacy of inheritance or purchase of land raised in the awkward and redundant language of the last sentence. The interest to us consists in the assertion that land values are the product of personal, in the sense of individual, labour; who gives forth this personal labour is a matter of indifference, so far as this theory of origin of value is concerned. Moreover, the slight qualification of the opening sentence, which seems to give some property to the community, may be cancelled. To assign to the community the value of 'the surface of the country in its original unsubdued state' is to assign nothing. Prairie value, to use the ordinary term, is *nil*. The 'original and indestructible properties' of the earth, in Ricardo's well-worn phrase, have no value until the labour of man makes them available, and the wants of man give them human utility. Spencer's *real* proposition, therefore, is that all land value is the product of individual activity.

In order to test this proposition, let us briefly trace the growth of value of a piece of prairie land as it passes under cultivation. A settler crosses the frontier of civilization, and takes up virgin soil. He brings with him strength, knowledge, skill, and tools – all of them, to some extent, admittedly the products of the slow growth of social institutions and social knowledge in the community which bore and educated him. But let us make him a gift of these social qualities, and suppose him to start operations upon his new land as a fully-equipped and independent individual. Whatever concrete improvement of the land takes place is obviously attributable to his personal labour; every increase of product is due to him. Let us present him with a family, which helps him to work the land. Though the co-operation of the members of this family renders it no longer strictly possible to attribute the improvement of the land to the personal labour of any particular individual – introducing, in fact, in miniature, the whole question of social productivity – we may waive it at this stage, and treat the personal labour of the family as a unit, assigning to it all increase of 'value' of the land. So long as the family keeps to itself, using the produce of the land for its own consumption, and providing by its own labour for all its wants, the claim of society is *nil*; no social influence enters. If other families settle in the same country, and pursue a similar policy, entering into no directly economic relations with one another, the position is unaltered. The industry of a family may constantly raise the productivity of the soil. The so-called 'value' of the land under these circumstances is 'value in use', and not what the ordinary language of commerce or of economics means by 'value'. As families grow upon the newly-settled land, we may take it that they will enter into business relations with one another, will devote themselves more particularly to growing and raising articles for which their particular land has some natural advantage, and will establish, first, informal exchange, and, afterwards, regular markets for disposing of their surplus produce. The value of the first farm is now no longer identified with its productivity, but also has reference to what can be got in exchange by disposing of some surplus produce. Now the 'how much' of this 'what can be got' – in other words, the exchange value – will depend partly upon the needs of the other farmers for this kind of produce, partly upon the number of other persons from whom they can get it if our original farmer is unable or refuses to supply it, and partly upon the number of other things useful to the first farmer which they are able to offer in exchange.

51

Now, just in proportion as exchange or market value enters and displaces use-value, so does social determination of value displace individual determination. While value in use is strictly personal, value in exchange is distinctively social. A market, however crudely formed, is a social institution; the value of our farmer's produce is now partly determined by the personal labour he has put into them, but partly by the needs and capacities of others; and not even by the needs and capacities of any definite individual, but by a great variety of needs and capacities expressed socially through the instrument of a market price, which is a highly elaborate result of bargaining, and does not represent the needs or the capacity of any single purchaser. So, when our farmer is enabled by the creation of this social institution of a market to give special attention to growing certain crops, and exchanging part of them for other commodities which he no longer raises, the productivity of his farm business has increased. But part of this increment is not due to his 'personal labour', but to the labours and the needs of others expressed through the market. This social influence not merely increases the annual productivity of his farm, but gives it an increased capital value, in the sense that, whereas he could have got nothing for it at the beginning, since there was no possible buyer, and but little for it when the market was first established, every year the enlargement and improvement of the market increases the price he could get for his land if he chose to sell it.

Now, when we speak of 'land values' in a civilized community, for purposes of sale or taxation, we mean not that early use-value which seemed to be entirely the product of 'personal labour', but the exchange value which we have seen cannot be produced at all by personal labour, but requires the assistance of society. But the social needs expressed through a market are only one of the ways in which land values are made by society. Our farmer, finding neighbours close around him, may suffer injury as well as receive service from their presence; in order to enjoy security for his property, and to prevent risks and waste of energy in defending the product of his labour, he will co-operate with his neighbours for mutual defence, thus laying the basis of the social instrument, the State. This co-operation, both on its industrial and its political side, will constantly grow; as population increases, not only the defensive functions will become more important, but various directly productive uses of co-operation will arise; social instincts will combine with economic gain to organize large enterprises which a single farmer could not undertake at all; large irrigation or drainage schemes, improvements of the market by roads, establishment of schools, churches, and other co-operative schemes, will be adopted, improving the skill, knowledge and character of the individuals, and reflected in improved working of the land and raised land values. Co-operative industry gives birth to towns. Our farmer's land lies just outside one of these towns; he finds it pays to use some of this land for market gardens. This gives a great increment of value attribut-able *ex hypothesi* not to his personal labour, which is no greater than it was before, but to the social pressure of the needs of a congested industrial population; in a word, it is a product of the social institution called a 'town'. Other land he rents or sells for suburban buildings at an enormously enhanced value, which not merely represents the present value set by 'society' upon the land, but the future value which society will hereafter set upon it.

Thus we perceive that economic value cannot attach to land at all, except by the operation of social forces, and that the influences which normally cause increase of land values are distinctively social. It is, of course, possible that increased industry or skill of an individual landowner may co-operate with these social forces to raise the value of his land, but this is not normally the case; most instances that are adduced mean merely that the landowner has had the skill or cunning to foresee some change of the social forces of demand which will give an increased value to his land for some special use, as where land is acquired and adapted for speculative building purposes.

We now see that since land values are not chiefly due to personal labour, but to the operation of social forces, society has some right of property in these values, and may assert this right without the 'gigantic robbery' of which Mr Spencer speaks.

The real underlying error of Mr Spencer and his legion of followers is that they persist in regarding society as an aggregate of individuals. It seems to them 'a mere superstition to look upon society as anything other than the members who compose it'. This declaration sounds final, and yet its very language carries its refutation. 'Compose it.' Composition implies an orderly relation of parts. This relation is not found adhering to the individuals, as such. Is a 'composition' in music the mere addition of the notes employed? Can we break up the composition of a poem into its component words or letters, and, shuffling them, still maintain that we have the poem?

If society is a composition, it must have a unity consisting in the relations of its members. The maintenance and activity of these relations can be shown to be a source of value.

Let us leave land and turn to some other industry. Brown, Smith, and Jones, working together by agreement, build a boat. Does the value of this boat, when made, represent the value made by Brown, *and* that made by Smith, *and* that made by Jones? No such thing. Why, Brown, by himself, could not have lifted the log to make the keel. Or suppose he could have made a boat, could he, in a given time, have made a boat worth one-third as much as the joint product of all three during the same time? Obviously not. Supposing all three to be equally efficient workmen, it is evident that their joint product, in a given time, will be worth much more than three times the product of Brown alone. Organized co-operation is a productive power. The associated or 'social' productivity of Brown, Smith, and Jones is not the mere addition of their productivity as individuals, even supposing they can, as individuals, produce something. In a certain sense, this social productivity is even capable of measure. If we set Brown, Smith, and Jones to work, first separately and then together, the difference in value between their added and their joint product might rank as the quantity of social value. This supposed case is not, of course, really accurate, for it supposes Brown by himself could produce something of value. We have already seen that, even supposing an individual could produce something of use to himself, he could not produce something of 'value' in an economic sense. In a thousand different subtle ways society works in and with Brown. Let him be no longer boat-maker, but solitary shoemaker. The value of the pair of shoes which he 'produces', working by himself, is just as much determined by society as the land-values of our farmer, as soon as they begin to emerge. The skill and knowledge of his craft is an elaborate social product, and is taught him by society; the same society protects him while he works, assists him by an elaborate organization of markets to get leather, tools, thread, and a workplace, provides him with a market in the form of persons who have evolved the need of wearing boots, and the industrial arts whereby to pay for them, and so forth. The value of the boots when made will obviously depend, to an indefinite extent, upon the innumerable factors which affect the supply and demand of all other products, along with which boots figure in processes of exchange. It is needless to labour further the proof that society co-operates with individuals in producing the value which attaches to material goods. The same conditions hold of non-material goods, which can be said to have either a use-value or an economic value. The maker of a poem or play, or other non-material work of art, is in no sense an absolute creator. He works upon words and other intellectual forms, which are the plastic embodiments of thoughts and feelings that are not his private property, but are the slowly-grown, elaborate products of his nation, his age, and humanity at large. Society helps him in the very effort of that 'inspiration' which seems so peculiarly his own, through the public understanding and appreciation which lighten, stimulate, and direct the creative effort. So the intellectual maker has no full and absolute right of property in his product, but only a right limited by the relative importance assigned to his individuality of effort. The exact measure of such right of private property it is not easy, perhaps not possible, to ascertain. Who shall say how far the *Œdipus Tyrannus* was the product of Sophocles, how much of Athens, how much of the Hellenic genius, or how much belongs to humanity? Indeed, the boundary of such property seems an ever-shifting one. Humanity – society in its widest significance – is ever claiming, and making good, its larger property in the great masterpieces of human achievement; they become less and less the property of the man, more and more of the race and of mankind.

Society has, then, a natural claim upon property, on the ground that it is a maker of values of property.

We have seen how an individual suffers in the efficiency of his work and life, and in his capacity of progress, if he is deprived of that property in the result of his labour which is necessary to support and educate his powers. The same is manifestly true of an organized society. We have seen that such a society is rightly regarded as a maker of wealth. If society does not receive an adequate share of the wealth she makes, for direct expenditure on social objects, she suffers in vigour and progress of life and character as does the individual.

The results of the social activities which we have investigated form a 'property' which belongs to society, and which coalesces with each piece of individual property. In the language of political

55

economy, this social property consists of increments which, not being in their origin assignable to individual activities, are called 'unearned', but which, in sober fact, are the earnings of society, arising from public work and public wants. Bad social administration, unjust stewardship of society, enables certain individuals or classes to take and enjoy some of this social property which is needed to support the full healthy progressive life of the community.

This view of the rights and needs of society differs very widely from the commonly accepted view, which grudges society the small fraction of her rightful property that she takes by taxation, regarding such taxation as an encroachment upon individual rights of property, justifiable only upon specific grounds of the particular public use to which the taxes will be put. This false, narrow view of the claim to social property has resulted in an equally false and narrow conception of the meaning and the possibilities of social life. It is true that society will perform certain bare necessary functions, even if most of the 'property' which is her due is taken from her, and administered by individuals for their own purposes. The stable order of society, a certain necessary change and growth of institutions, the increase of population and of external structure can proceed within certain limits without the direct design of creating property, and without the full enjoyment of the property it does create. Hence, the fact that individuals take away and consume this property, as though it were their own, does not prevent the reproduction of fresh forms of social property. Society, like individuals, may do her work though she is 'sweated' of the major part of her product. But the natural penalty is not escaped. This misappropriation drains the strength and impairs the productivity of society. A society, where the just rights of individual and social property were observed, would yield a social life far stronger, far richer, far more cohesive than we have any conception of. If individuals got for their own private use all the product of their labour that is rightly theirs – *i.e.* such portion as is needed to support the best individual life of which each is capable, and only that – leaving society to administer the whole of her property for public uses, such an economy would be attended by an incalculably great enrichment of the political and industrial life of the community. A starved society or a parasitic society is injured just as the individual starveling or parasite is injured. This is apparent directly we grasp the organic conception of society: whether society be defined as an 'organism' or as an 'organization', the character of organic progress which is conferred upon her implies conformity to the same natural laws of property that apply to individuals. If an individual producer has no security of his property, he not merely suffers in lack of enjoyment, but the loss of incentive weakens his functional activities and impairs his vitality. The same is true of society.

Every defence of the principle of individual property is likewise a plea for social property.

Individual property, we are told, is required for self-realization. Man needs to have a 'permanent nucleus in the material world' (as Dr Bosanquet excellently phrases it) [*Aspects of the Social Problem*, p. 314], such security of material property that he can look ahead, plan, and regulate his life as a whole, not living from day to day, from hand to mouth. Not only do we admit this claim, but we have found the 'natural' justification of it. But, with the abuse of this doctrine of self-realization, used – as it often is – to suggest that a rich man, drawing rents and profits of monopoly, can justify his property by the good rational use he makes of it, we must join issue. We have seen that, in so far as at any given time material productivity of wealth is limited, a limit is imposed upon the right of any individual to 'realize' himself in material forms of property – i.e. the limit of his single contribution to material wealth. No one has a right to realize himself in the property of others – as sweater, in the property of other individuals, as taker of 'economic rents', in the property of society. For society also needs to realize herself by means of her property. It is strange that a logician like Dr Bosanquet, who so strongly builds his philosophic support of private property, should ignore the corresponding need of social property. 'The point of private property,' he tells us, 'is that things should not come miraculously, and be unaffected by your dealings with them; but that you should be in contact with something which, in the external world, is the definite material representation of yourself' [*Aspects of the Social Problem*, p. 313]. This is urged as a defence of private property; but no word is added to explain the limit it imposes upon individual property, or to extend its application to the property of society. Yet, taken rightly, this judgment is strikingly conclusive on both issues. It presents a clear condemnation of 'economic rents' and monopoly profits as individual property, on the ground that 'they come miraculously', and are 'unaffected by your dealings with them'; that they are not 'the definite material representation of yourself', seeing that none of your vitality has gone into their making. Turning the matter round, we find that these 'economic rents' and 'unearned increments' are 'definite material representations' of social activities, and the property they constitute is required for the self-realization of society. It is the denial of this full property which starves our social life today. Look, for example, at the civic life of an average municipality in England, the richest country that the world has ever known. Is this civic life as strong, as rich, as beautiful, as noble as it might be? Is even its provision for sanitation and the common conventional civic services adequate? Are its streets, its public buildings, worthy expressions of a rich and civilized community? Is it not a commonplace that these external embodiments of our civic life are, in every quality of excellence, inferior beyond all comparison to the attainments of most of the great cities of antiquity, the private wealth of whose citizens was not a hundredth part as great as ours?

Or, turning to that larger instrument of social life − the State − do we not find its services everywhere crippled by lack of property? The miserably penurious provision for the vast expansive needs of that public education which the State professes as a public duty is one crucial instance of the poverty of our State. Or take another instance. At the present time the State of England is so starved that, while recognizing that public utility demands the provision of some monetary aid for the aged poor, she is utterly unable to lay hands upon the few millions needed to defray such an expense. Yet these instances refer to the prime necessities of a healthy stable society. No social property is accumulated to work out the progressive character of a society which should seek constantly to develop and to satisfy higher and more complex needs of social life, building up a growing commonalty which shall correspond with, and react upon, the rising individuality of its constituent members.

This public progress is impossible until the State, as representative of society, shall claim for its use and administration the property which it makes and needs.

It is no policy of confiscation that is here advocated, but a just, rational demarcation between private and public property. Let the individual and society each own, out of the property they jointly create, that portion which is necessary to support the life and sustain the progress of each. We thus refute a false individualism by setting property upon a sound, natural, and rational basis. Mr Spencer imagines that 'A is taxed in order that B's children may read books'. No such thing! The tax imposed on A is simply the most convenient way of taking the results of social work which commingle with the work done by A: the joint product is not in itself directly divisible, so that society takes her share in a tax. This tax it uses to educate B's children, not as a favour to B, nor even as an 'abstract right' on the part of B's children, but because it is socially important to society, of which A and B are members, that all children shall be educated.

This view of social property summarily disposes of the objection that society should not be allowed to administer much property, because its administration will be incompetent and wasteful. We do not take away a piece of property which A rightly owns, and give it to B, on the ground that the latter can make a better use of it. We say: 'It is A's property; he alone made it; he has a right to it; even if he makes a bad use of it now you must not take it from him; he will learn to make a better use; having made it by his hard work, he *will* presumably make a better use of it than one who obtained it without effort.' So with social property. Wherever the State or Municipality can make good its claim to a piece of property, it is no answer to urge that the public cannot well administer such property. If a community can show that the values of certain land, tramways, gasworks, or other forms of wealth are wholly, or in large measure, the products of social activity, are a social property, it is a right and a duty to administer such property. If it refuses, it thereby weakens the social life; if it consents, it strengthens it, and learns by experience how to administer properly the property which belongs to it. The objection on the score of bad administration is peculiarly impertinent. You deprive a man or a race of liberty; keep him or it in forcible subjection; then, when it is proposed to confer freedom, you raise the cry that your victim is unable to make a good use of freedom. So it is with property. A wrong injures the doer and the sufferer, and on both sides the evil lives even after its cause is redressed. Is that a conclusive reason against redress? Society is precisely in this position. She has been starved so long, her rightful property has been meted out to individuals, and she has not fully learned to use her own. But it is her duty and her right to learn to care for the commonwealth by an economical administration of common property.

This view of a progressive socialism turns the edge of the stock arguments of the individualist school by basing the claims for social property upon the same reasoning which defends individual rights of property.

2.2 'Herbert Spencer' (1904) [*South Place Magazine,* pp. 49–52]

It is fitting that we should turn our thoughts to the great thinker who has passed away, the last of the great figures of the nineteenth century – the most representative English thinker of that century. It would be alike presumptuous and unprofitable for me here to attempt an estimate of the enduring place he will occupy in the world of thought or to enter a critical examination of his doctrines. He lies too near – his loss is too heavy on the intellectual life of England. All I can do is to trace a few outlines of his large services and to accord some recognition to the great personality behind.

In what sense was he representative? He has not succeeded in making us a nation of scientific philosophers. It cannot even be claimed that he has a large, widespread school or cult. Fame – even a moderate degree of recognition – did not come to him until late in middle life. Though he had been writing closely and continuously since 1842 (many of his most germinal thoughts are to be found in his early scattered writings) it would be safe to say that in 1870 not one in a hundred 'educated' Englishmen knew of him more than his bare name. In our Universities and in orthodox scientific circles the claims of a Synthetic Philosophy were regarded with chilly disparagement, or with unintelligent contempt, as the sensational folly of a self-educated outsider. And yet he is 'representative'. We are all Spencerians today, whether we like it or not. It is true that he had important intellectual allies, such as Lewes, Huxley, Tyndall, Darwin. But while one of these, Darwin, exercised a more direct, immediate, and distinct impression on his age, Spencer must be regarded as the most important, because the largest interpretation and application of the new scientific principles came from him. He was born, 1820, into an England of strong formative intellectual influences and a growing belief in Science. The dominating mind of Bentham was a most significant sign of the new unifying and ordering force in human life. The Utilitarianism of Bentham was only another name for science in the service of man. Law, Politics, History, Ethics, Sociology, were just becoming possible as Sciences. This force of utilitarianism coalesced with another impulse. The New biology was transforming the statical conception of life into the dynamic. Haggling about precedence in the co-operative commonwealth of thought is an idle occupation. Malthus, Spencer, Darwin, Wallace, all contributed to formulate the revolutionary meaning of the new knowledge as applied to Man. Spencer's paper entitled 'The Development Hypothesis' (1852), was admitted by Darwin to have been the first clear anticipation of the leading doctrines of Evolution. Biology – the seed-bed of the new thought – furnished formulæ and analogies, sometimes perilous, but necessary tools in scientific progress.

The general pressure of the time was towards specialism – division of labour – as the most fruitful method. It required a mighty fund of moral courage to resist this tendency and to pursue the more hazardous path – the broader one which leads often to destruction, but in a few rare cases marks the pioneer in the supreme work of broadening the common high-road of knowledge for mankind.

Spencer chose to risk the imputation of being a sciolist and an intellectual adventurer. He chose to take his stand among that scanty band that 'have taken all knowledge for their province'. In his own day Comte alone showed this same splendid audacity and the relation of these two forms one of the most interesting passages in modern intellectual life. With the same monumental courage, the same confident persistence, they set themselves to the same great general task – though with a somewhat different purpose. That task consisted in a restatement of the known Universe, its positive facts or phenomena, in an ordered synthesis, furnishing at once an explanation of the history of the world and a classification of the sciences. The positive spirit pervaded the work of both. Theological and metaphysical conceptions were rejected by both. Yet each may be said to have generated a metaphysics of his own.

The endeavour to work by pure Induction is always doomed to futility, and a reversion to the Deductive always brings Metaphysics in its train. Spencer's is packed into his *First Principles* – which most of his followers and admirers find the least convincing of his works and the most open to the onslaughts of destructive logic.

Some critics have even claimed that by showing flaws in his doctrines of the Unknowable and the Infinite they have destroyed the work of Spencer. A practical answer may, however, be made to such: 'Put up your own metaphysical substitute and see if it fares better in the hands of the logical house-breaker.' I venture to affirm three propositions. (1) You cannot get rid of metaphysics if you are a searcher after God, i.e., after Unity in Nature. (2) Every Metaphysic can be crushed by logic. (3) It does not matter so much as it seems. The foundation may be unsound, but the house does not fall. The ordinary Law of Gravitation does not hold in intellectual architecture – a house built on something hardly more substantial than sand can yet hold together and afford really serviceable shelter – for a time. For all such systems are essentially hypothetical and temporal; they are provisional attempts to read unity or harmony into an everchanging body of human experience. No philosopher can build an 'eternal habitation' for the Truth. That is why you do not destroy his house by sapping his metaphysical foundations. The Synthetic Philosophy, first clearly conceived in 1860, and brought to slow conclusion in 1898, will remain – in spite of Green and Ward – a monumental contribution to human knowledge.

What has it achieved? It has helped to bring order into the kaleidoscope of life and has achieved a vast expansion of the Reign of Law. Chance, caprice, spontaneous activity, blind catastrophe, were not even expelled from the operations of inanimate Nature as seen in the crude sciences of the early nineteenth century. As for human conduct and history, these were still great provinces of the Kingdom of Unreason: Miracle, Fate, Accident, Free Will, were the forces governing events – anything but Law. The Synthetic Philosophy achieved a huge process of annexation – sweeping in, by an invincible logic and an assimilative march of formulæ, the whole body of refractory outlaws, and establishing for the first time something which could be called a Science of History, of Politics, of Ethics. His most revolutionary work was the extension of evolutionary thought to this newly-conquered realm. Man is henceforth part of Nature. For the educated world Spencer killed all the brood of superstitious formulæ which exempted Man from Nature. The achievement doubtless is yet incomplete – even in the philosophic world; there are mystical revivals to which scientific men give countenance. How hard a thing it is to break down human pride and exclusiveness – and to set man firmly in the common course of Nature.

Many a halt is still made at Dualism – a retention of some mysterious, isolated dignity of Man. But the idea of all-pervading Law and of the necessity of Unity is gaining the day, and through many channels permeates the ordinary vein of life. It is not the least of Spencer's victories that he has forced evolution on the idealists – those who approach Unity from the other side. Hegel's presentation of world-history as a progressive development of Reason, itself fertilised by scientific evolution, yields in the hands of men such as Green and Bradley a mature concession of the Universe as an orderly procession and expression of experience. We now have little conception of the bitterness of the early fight. Not only orthodox theology, but orthodox science and academic philosophy strove against Spencer, riddling with their shafts his abstract formulæ. Spencer's great formula of evolution as a 'process from an indefinite, incoherent homogeneity to a definite coherent heterogeneity' is not invulnerable, sharing the final futility of philosophic formulæ – the suicidal endeavour to say something about the final abstraction, the highest Unity.

The Spencerian bridges over the chasms and crevasses of nature and of thought in tracing the doctrines of Evolution are often condemned, e.g. the bridge from the Inorganic to the Organic found in crystallisation, the Emergence of the Conscious from the Unconscious, the arrival of Justice in the mind of Man. But if Spencer has not given a final answer to the critical question, 'Why *ought* I to serve my fellows?' he has come nearest to showing how that sense of *ought* does actually germinate and grow in the mind of man. Which of his critics can give a better answer?

Man, Society, Human Conduct in all its branches, are set in the common current of Nature: their finest arts, their noblest activities, are but the most complex products of 'an infinite and eternal energy from which all things proceed' (1884).

Spencer's great services to Sociology and Ethics demand fuller recognition than can here be given. He was the first English thinker clearly to apply the organic conception of growth to the structure of Society. This he combined with a strangely perverse refusal to apply this same principle as a formative progressive force in the perfection of the organic nature of Society in politics and industry. He finds Society a low-grade organism, without a sensorium, and thinks it must remain so. After straining the organic analogy in the analysis of modern industrial structure, in politics he fell back on the

Atomism of the so-called Liberty of a wrongly-conceived individual and of a Society composed of a mechanical balance of individual rights. This failure in Consistency I impute to the fact that he was less *free* in his political than in his scientific thinking. The early radical *laissez-faire* was the dominant atmosphere of his youth. Instead of evolving his Politics from his Science – the former preceded. He committed himself too thoroughly in his earliest writings: 'The Proper Sphere of Government' in *The Nonconformist* in 1842 and *Social Statics* in 1850. No false sense of Consistency stayed the growth of his politics, but a subtler binding force of habit growing firmer with age, made him the implacable, even the fanatical foe, of any policy which seemed akin to Socialism. The foundations of his political and economic thought were laid too early and were not adjusted to conform with later facts of industrial evolution. He did not learn, as J. S. Mill lived to learn, (1) the plain lesson of economic inequality impairing that very 'selection' which is the instrument of progress in social evolution; (2) the disappearance of individual liberty and free competition over large areas of industrial Society.

2.3 The Crisis of Liberalism (1909) [pp. xii, 71–82, 91–5, 133–8]

From the Preface

Liberalism is now formally committed to a task which certainly involves a new conception of the State in its relation to the individual life and to private enterprise. That conception is not Socialism, in any accredited meaning of that term, though implying a considerable amount of increased public ownership and control of industry. From the standpoint which best presents its continuity with earlier Liberalism, it appears as a fuller appreciation and realisation of individual liberty contained in the provision of equal opportunities for self-development. But to this individual standpoint must be joined a just apprehension of the social, viz., the insistence that these claims or rights of self-development be adjusted to the sovereignty of social welfare.

The Re-Statement of Democracy

The question whether we shall speak of a human Society as an organism, is, of course, largely one of convenience in language. If society is an organism it is not quite the same sort of organism as the individual body of an animal, and for some reasons, therefore, it might be best not to adopt the same word in describing them. But those who jump from this to the conclusion that it is a barren, unprofitable, academic question to discuss whether Society is essentially organic, are quite unjustified. The question is one of supreme practical importance, involving, among persons capable of practical politics, the complete re-adjustment of their conception of democracy and of the means of attaining it.

It is not here necessary to follow out in detail the biological analogy between the animal organism and Society regarded as an organism. It is sufficient to observe that recent biological researches strengthen the tendency to regard Society as an organism even on its physical side. The two gravest objections, put by Spencer and others, against the organic view were, first, that the separateness in space of the individual members of Society, their mobility and their power over their own actions, had no analogy in the cellular life of the units of an organism; and, secondly, that there was nothing corresponding to the sensorium, no central seat of conscious life, in a Society. Now modern biology tends to impair both of these objections, and so to make the conception of Society nearer to that of an animal organism. In the first place it shows that a cell is a more distinct, a more individual vital unit than was supposed, that it is itself of an organic structure, that it is not physically continuous with other cells, that it performs what may be termed free acts, giving out effort and even exercising choice in movement and in the selection of its food from its environment. Though most cells are tolerably closely fixed in local relation to other cells (i.e. have status), others, connected with the work of digestion and protection against disease, are endowed with great freedom of movement. Modern psychophysics further tends to hold that this separate cellular life is accompanied by some degree of consciousness, in other words, that the specialisation of consciousness to the grey matter of the brain is not complete, but that some degree of cellular consciousness pervades the body.

The great German scientist, Virchow, recently summarised this view in the striking assertion that 'the organism is not an individual but a social mechanism'.

Nor can the other objection that there is nothing corresponding to the sensorium in Society be considered fatal. There are in fact two answers. Turning to lower forms of animal life we find composite beings, such as the myxomycetes and the sponges, which though consisting of almost undifferentiated units with no signs of a sensorium, can hardly be denied to be organisms. Indeed, the whole evolution of organic life is from forms in which there is no discernible sensorium towards forms which are more distinctly specialised in this regard. If, then, we could find no sensorium in Society, we are not therefore entitled to deny its organic nature, but only to conclude that it is as yet a low order of organism. This, indeed, is the conclusion at which some sociologists (e.g. Professor Lester Ward) arrive.

But, regarding Society merely on its physical side, it is by no means clear that there is nothing corresponding to a sensorium in the highly-developed and differentiated life of the educated and actively-governing classes. The great mass of the people do no more real thinking, exercise perhaps no more real initiative, than the separate cells of the individual human body.

It is not, however, essential to my purpose to insist that Society is a highly-evolved organism in a physical sense, or even to insist that it is to be called a physical organism at all, though I think this view is justified and will obtain more and more acceptance.

The problem of Government with which I am concerned is primarily not a physical but a psychical one, and its solution depends upon the psychical relations between the members of a society. Now, whatever view we hold about Society on the physical plane as a collection of individual bodies living in some sort of union, it can, I think, be made quite clear that Society is rightly regarded as a moral rational organism in the sense that it has a common psychic life, character, and purpose, which are not to be resolved into the life, character, and purpose of its individual members.

It is easy to see why the organic life of Society is more easily admitted on the psychic than on the physical plane. Every man stands in his own skin, with an indefinitely big and expansible belt of inorganic atmosphere between him and any other man who is a member of his Society. Common sense is therefore disposed to insist that physically Society is nothing but a number of separate individuals. At first, no doubt, the same common sense is disposed also to insist that all the thinking and the feeling of these individuals is done separately by minds which are inside these bodies, and never get into any nearer contact with one another. But reflection and experiment oblige us to admit that the contact between minds is far more intimate and constant than between bodies, and that the inter-relations set up are far closer.

Turn to such a work as Maeterlinck's fascinating study, *The Life of the Bee*. It is possible to deny the organic unity of the hive, or of the swarm, considered as a physical fact, or to regard it as a mere physical arrangement or organisation. But what the author terms 'The Spirit of the Hive', the mysterious unity of instinct or conscious life, which minutely dominates the hive and the will and separate interests of the individual bees, is an example of organic psychic unity which cannot be denied. All through the animal kingdom we find examples of this common purpose of the herd, the drove or other social group, imposing itself upon the mind and conscious conduct of the individual animal, directing him to actions often opposed to his own interest or pleasure, not seldom demanding the sacrifice of life itself for the gain of the group or the continuance of the species.

This Spirit of the Hive or of the Herd is a true spirit of Society, a single unity of purpose in the community. Those who would cut the Gordian knot of this problem by saying that individuals alone are ends, and that Society is nothing but a means to these ends, will find it difficult to make their theory square with the facts of natural history in which the individual always appears as a means to the collective end of the maintenance of the race.

Those who would distinguish in kind this social or gregarious instinct of the lower animals from the individual reasonable consciousness in man have no warrant for their distinction. For there is ample testimony that the mind of man, in its feeling, its thinking, its will, is not the separate thing it seems at first to be.

Setting aside all the dubious and difficult evidence of direct international impact of one mind upon another by telepathy, and other similar methods, the growth and operations of a common mind or purpose formed by the direct interaction of many individual minds cannot seriously be questioned.

Even the fortuitous concourse of a crowd shows this: a mob in the streets of Paris or of London exhibits a character and a behaviour which is uniform, is dominated for the time being by a single feeling or idea, and differs widely from the known character and behaviour of its component members. Look at the effect of an orator upon a crowd, the power of a sudden panic, the contagion of some quick impulse to action; it is quite evident that the barriers which commonly encase the individual mind have given way, that the private judgment is inhibited, and that for a time a mob-mind has been set up in its stead, in which the reasoning faculties are almost suspended, and in which the passions of animal ferocity, generosity, credulity, self-sacrifice, malignity, and courage express themselves unrestrained.

A great personality, a great religious or political idea, a mere mis-statement invented by a lying Press, may weld into a common desire, a common will, the minds of a whole nation: the result is not intelligible as the added action of the same idea acting on so many separate minds: it is the inter-action of these minds growing by stronger social sympathy into fusion that is the real phenomenon. The mere fact of human beings living in proximity to one another produces a force of neighbourhood which for good or evil is a restraint upon all its members. There is not a school, a church, a club, even for the lightest and most recreative object, embodying some purpose or idea and the common pursuit of it, which does not impress a common character upon its members. The public opinion of any of these bodies is produced by some direct assimilation of the separate minds, and implies the formation of a common consciousness.

For political and social purposes in ancient and mediæval times, the City has been the largest and most convincing example of this real moral unity. The civic spirit was no mere phrase to describe the views of the average citizen: the City State of the Greeks is only intelligible as a moral unity, or as Mr Bradley puts it, 'The armed conscience of the community'.

In modern times the wider social area of the nation has for many purposes displaced the City State. As a psychical organism it seldom presents so close a unity, but that the habit of common thought and action among the members of a nation can take place without creating and establishing a common consciousness, a common will and common obligations, cannot for a moment be admitted. Now, if the habits of thinking, feeling, and acting together among members of a nation thus bring their minds into a single mind which is dominated by thoughts and feelings directed to the ends of the whole body politic, then we have the clear admission of a social organism on the psychical or moral side.

This is the doctrine of the general will, as I understand it, which Rousseau, among moderns, was the first clearly to enunciate, which has been developed on its political side by Hegel and his followers, and which in English finds its most masterly expression in Mr Bosanquet's work, *The Philosophic Theory of the State*. I have approached the matter from the psychological rather than from the philosophical standpoint, and in applying the term organism I go beyond the judgment of some of these thinkers. But what I seek to establish is the admission that a political society must be regarded as 'organic' in the only sense which gives a really valid meaning to such terms as 'the will of the people', 'national duty', and 'public conscience'. The individual's feeling, his will, his ends, and interests, are not entirely merged in or sacrificed to the public feeling, will and ends, but over a certain area they are fused and identified, and the common social life thus formed has conscious interests and ends of its own which are not merely instruments in forwarding the progress of the separate individual lives, but are directed primarily to secure the survival and psychical progress of the community regarded as a spiritual whole.

To the common-sense objector who says, 'A nation does not think, a nation does not feel, it is individuals who do these things', I would reply that if you could talk with a 'cell' of the human body it would tell you it is not *we* who think and feel, but the separate cells, each of which is conscious in itself of such processes, but from the nature of the case is not and cannot be conscious of the feeling and thinking which goes on in the organism as a whole.

A nation does feel, and think, not so fully, so wholesomely, so happily as it should and will, when the process of forming a social organism has gone further, but within the limits of such conscious unity as it has attained.

The practical value of this thought consists in the material it yields for restating the doctrine of Democracy. It is quite evident that the conception of Society as a moral organism negates the old democratic idea of political equality based on the notion that every member of a political society had an inherent right to the same power as every other in determinating the action of Society. The

69

idea of natural individual rights as the basis of Democracy disappears. Take, for instance, the formula of 'No taxation without representation.' From the standpoint of individualist Democracy this is understood to imply that, when the State takes away some of my property by taxing me, I have some right to earmark the tax I pay and to say what shall be done with it, or with a corresponding portion of the public funds afterwards. Now a clear grasp of Society as an economic organism completely explodes the notion of property as an inherent individual right, for it shows that no individual can make or appropriate anything of value without the direct continuous assistance of Society. So the idea of Society as a political organism insists that the general will and wisdom of the Society, as embodied in the State, shall determine the best social use of all the social property taken by taxation, without admitting any inherent right of interference on the part of the taxpayer. This does not, indeed, imply that 'No taxation without representation' is an unsound maxim of government: on the contrary, it may be, and I think is, strongly advisable that those from whom taxes are levied shall watch and check the use which Government may make of them: but the worth of this practice is defensible not on grounds of individual right but of general expediency, because persons who have paid a tax will be found to be better guardians of the public purse than those who have not paid it.

So with the other individualist notion that political power belongs as a right to those who have 'a stake in the country'. When 'a stake in the country' meant property or rank it brought class government. Democracy, taking over the phrase, insisted that a man's life was his stake, and that since every man's life was worth as much as every other man's life, political power should be equally divided amongst all. The popular doctrine, 'One man one vote' is as a theoretical principle pure undiluted individualism. It rests upon a curious twist in the logic of Equality. Every man's life is worth as much to him as every other man's life. Society consists of all men, therefore every man's life is worth as much to Society as every other man's, and every man ought to have the same voice in directing social conduct as every other man.

Now there is very little meaning in the first proposition that all men's lives are of equal value to them; and there is no possibility of proving its validity. That every man's life is of equal value to Society, in the sense that it can yield equal social service, is not only false but absurd: and, if political power rightly varies with the capacity for public service, the case for equality of franchise utterly collapses. There is, of course, a sense in which the equal value of life for all is admitted, and is embodied in the equality of all men before the law. But this equality of all men as objects of social conduct does not imply a corresponding equality as agents in social conduct. The old individualist Democracy did not indeed often go so far as to maintain that every man was as competent as every other man to exercise a power of government, though the American theory and practice, so far as white men are concerned, have gone marvellously near to this position. It rested partly on the notion of an equal right in virtue of common humanity, and partly upon an obscure notion that since each man presumably knew best his own interest, or at any rate what he wanted, the aggregate, which was what they understood by 'Society', knew best the general interest. And this would be so, if society were a mere aggregate, an accumulation of human atoms, incapable of any really organic action.

The organic view of Society entirely repudiates any such equality as a theoretic principle. Even J. S. Mill, when he came to apply his utilitarianism to politics, left a good deal of his individualism behind. 'In all human affairs,' he writes, 'every person directly interested, and not under positive tutelage, has an admitted claim to a voice, and when his exercise of it is not inconsistent with the safety of the whole, cannot justly be excluded from it. But though everyone ought to have a voice – that everyone ought to have an equal voice is a totally different proposition. When two persons, who have a joint interest in any business, differ in opinion, does justice require that both opinions should be held in equal value?' Though few persons, on mature reflection, are likely to admit the examination test of political competence which Mill suggests, and may not be prepared with any alternative measure of such competence, they cannot deny the validity and importance of his general admission that political power ought to be distributed in proportion to ability to use it for the public good. The suggestion of individualist Democracy, that the public good is simply a bundle of private goods, and that every man ought to have a vote in order that he may keep an eye on his particular contribution to the public good, was felt by Mill to be untenable when government was regarded as a joint stock business.

Mill, in fact, was feeling his way to the true formula of political as of economic justice, 'From each according to his powers'. Once grasp the idea of the public as a Social Organism, or even as a Corporation administering a property corporately made, it becomes clear that no *right* appertains to any individual to administer any portion of this property, because as an individual he has made no part of it.

But while he has no *right* as an individual, he has a *duty* as a member of Society to contribute as best he can to the administration of the common property for the common good. His vote thus comes to him primarily as a duty, and the question of equality takes this form, 'Is the duty equal in all cases?' Clearly not, for all have not equally the power to fulfil it. Knowledge, intelligence, strength, good-will, vary, and with them varies the ability to perform public duty. It is as absurd to demand the same contribution to the collective wisdom of the nation from all alike as to demand the same contribution to the collective purse. 'From each according to his powers.' Tom, Dick, and Harry have very little powers. Why should the State require of them what they have not got?

Does this imply that in a properly ordered State the more ignorant masses are to have no vote, no voice in the Government of the country? Are we to entrust all power to a Government of experts?

Let us see how far the fact or the analogy of organism carries us. From each member in a biological organism are demanded certain functional activities for the support of the life of the organism, the kind and quantity of this work being determined by the neural apparatus and regulated in accordance with the nature and strength of the several organs. So when a functional demand is made upon a particular organ, the work is delegated to its several parts, and is ultimately divided up among the countless cells which are regarded as the primary units of the organ. In a body which is in health and functions economically, every cell contributes to the life of the organism according to its powers. The direction, the demand for labour, at any rate so far as conscious actions are concerned, comes from a specialised governing centre. But this is only half the truth. 'From each according to his powers, to each according to his needs,' is the full organic formula. In a healthy organism the demand of functional energy from each member, from each cell, is accompanied by a continual replacement of tissue and energy conveyed by a just circulation of the blood. I use the ethical term 'just' advisedly. Ruskin, in an eloquent passage of *Unto this Last*, points out that the circulation of the blood is the true type of equitable economic distribution. It also gives the true significance to political rights. Each limb, each cell, has a 'right' to its due supply of blood. It has a 'right' to complain if it does not get it, and it does complain. It is to this right and habit of complaint that we must look for what in social politics corresponds to the franchise. So far as the conscious polity of the animal organism is concerned, the direct work of Government is highly centralised: a highly specialised portion of the nervous system issues the commands, it is the normal function of the several organs to obey, and in the ordinary course of nature they do so. They have had no separate voice in determining the organic policy, or in issuing the order which they help to execute.

Are the separate organs, the separate cells, then, politically powerless and destitute of rights? It is doubtless to the real interest of the organism as a whole to distribute blood in accordance with the needs of the individual members and their cells. But, even in the most highly-developed organisms, such absolute and unchecked power is not entrusted to the expert government of the cerebral cells. The entire afferent nervous system attests the contrary: the individual organs and their cells are continuously engaged in transmitting information to the cerebral centre and in offering suggestions. This information and these suggestions are chiefly if not wholly self-protective in their purport. The ability of the local centres to transmit stimuli to the cerebral centres is of course essential to the politics of the organism. It is equally important to recognise that not merely is information thus given to the cerebral centres for their guidance, but by the same channels protest is conveyed against orders which injure or oppress the organ; the right to petition against grievance on the part of the organs and their cells is accompanied by an ultimate 'veto', or the right of rebellion, which is the basis of popular government.

Nor are these the only 'rights' exercised by the 'cells'. When a certain demand for functional activity is transmitted to the local centres, its distribution is determined by an elaborate system of local self-government, in which each cell participates, striving to throw off upon its neighbours any disproportionate strain, and they doing the same, until in a healthy organ the total strain is divided economically in accordance with the powers of the several parts. Understand that these rights of the members and their cells are not in any sense a qualification or denial of the truth that the good of the organism as a whole is the absolute criterion of conduct, and may in extreme cases require the complete sacrifice of an organ and its cells. But it is advantageous to the organism that these rights of suggestion, protest, veto, and revolt should be accorded to its members. Accept the view of Society as an organism, corresponding rights remain to its individual members, and a political machinery for enforcing them must exist.

The Vision of Liberalism

Bacon's saying that 'adversity does best discover virtues' is of doubtful application to a political party. Twenty years of almost unceasing struggle against reaction have left their traces upon Liberal Parliamentarians in a strain of timidity and even of conservatism, which is evidently a source of moral and of intellectual weakness. There have always been voices ready to proclaim that the active mission of Liberalism was well nigh fulfilled, and that, for the present, at any rate, it was all-important to preserve what had been won, to regain what had been lost, and to do just as much or as little tinkering as was needed to maintain the fabric of our liberties. We do not for one moment suggest that this has been the conscious prevailing sentiment of the majority in the House, or in the country, and the strenuous warfare waged by the Liberal Government in many fields will appear to many a sufficient answer to such criticism. But without arguing the matter here, we cannot refrain from pointing out that almost all the important measures of domestic policy before this Parliament are, in substance, endeavours to recover, for the people and the State, liberties or properties or privileges which had within recent generations been lost or encroached upon by some class, trade, or other vested interest.

In this sense, the Trade Union Act, the Education and Licensing measures, and even the Government's land policy, in its essential features, are conservative. This admission by no means derogates from their importance, but it helps to make us comprehend why Liberalism appears in some quarters lacking in organic purpose and in free enthusiasm. While to Protectionists and Socialists politics are real, positive, and fervent gospels, stirring the imagination and evoking a fanatical energy, the zeal of Liberalism is everywhere chilled by doubts and difficulties. No sooner are we approaching such large issues of social policy as are involved in taxation of land values, pensions, unemployed relief, the House of Lords, than everywhere the atmosphere is kept abuzz with whispers about 'sanctity of contract', confiscation, pauperisation, and those hints of popular indifference which take the heart out of reformers.

Does this mean that coldness and placidity of purpose belong essentially to Liberalism as a middle course, and is Liberalism committed to an embarrassing and disheartening opportunism? No such thing. But we have evidently reached a period when a more conscious organisation of Liberal energy is demanded. It is a time to follow Matthew Arnold's advice and 'Let our thought play freely upon our stock notions and ideas.' The first result of such an operation will be to illuminate our commonplaces regarding the nature of that liberty to the service of which the party is devoted. The negative conception of Liberalism, as a definite mission for the removal of certain political and economic shackles upon personal liberty, is not merely philosophically defective, but historically false. The Liberals of this country as a party never committed themselves either to the theory or the policy of this narrow *laissez-faire* individualism; they never conceived liberty as something limited in quantity, or purely negative in character. But it is true that they tended to lay an excessive emphasis upon the aspect of liberty which consists in absence of restraint, as compared with the other aspect which consists in presence of opportunity; and it is this tendency, still lingering in the mind of the Liberal Party, that to-day checks its energy and blurs its vision. A more constructive and a more evolutionary idea of liberty is needed to give the requisite *élan de vie* to the movement; and every cause of liberation, individual, class, sex, and national, must be recharged with the fresh enthusiasm of this fuller faith.

Liberalism will probably retain its distinction from Socialism, in taking for its chief test of policy the freedom of the individual citizen rather than the strength of the State, though the antagonism of the two standpoints may tend to disappear in the light of progressive experience. But it will justify itself by two great enlargements of its liberative functions. In seeking to realise liberty for the individual citizen as 'equality of opportunity', it will recognise that, as the area and nature of opportunities are continually shifting, so the old limited conception of the task of Liberalism must always advance.

Each generation of Liberals will be required to translate a new set of needs and aspirations into facts. It is because we have fallen so far short of due performance of this task that our Liberalism shows signs of enfeeblement. We must fearlessly face as our first, though not our only question, 'What is a free Englishman today?' If we answer this question faithfully, we shall recognise that it comprises many elements of real liberty and opportunity which have not been won for the people as a whole. Is a man free who has not equal opportunity with his fellows of such access to all material and moral means of personal development and work as shall contribute to his own welfare and that of his society? Such equal opportunity at least implies an equal access to the use of his native land as a workplace and a home, such mobility as will enable him to dispose of his personal energies to the best advantage, easy access to that factor of capital or credit which modern industry recognises as essential to economic independence, and to whatever new form of industrial power, electric or other, may be needed to co-operate with human efforts. A man is not really free for purposes of self-development in life and work who is not adequately provided in all these respects, and no small part of constructive Liberalism must be devoted to the attainment of these equal opportunities.

But all such distinctively economic liberties are evidently barren unless accompanied by a far more adequate realisation of spiritual and intellectual opportunity than is contained in our miserably meagre conception of popular education. For education in the large meaning of the term is the opportunity of opportunities, and the virtual denial to the majority of the people of any real share of the spiritual kingdom which is rightly theirs must remain for all true Liberals an incessant challenge to their elementary sense of justice, as well as the most obvious impediment both to the achievement and the utilisation of every other element of personal liberty. It is this truth that also underlies the great struggle against militarism and Imperialism which assumes so many shapes upon the stage of politics, and which, driven to its last resort, will always be disclosed as the antagonism between physical and moral force, as the guardian and promoter of civilisation. The practical interpretation and realisation of moral and intellectual liberty for the people as the most urgent and fruitful of all tasks of Liberalism, though standing first in order of importance, cannot, however, be detached in political endeavour from the other more material liberties. It is the peril, as it is the glory, of Liberalism that it is required to drive several teams abreast along the road of progress.

Finally, though Liberals must ever insist that each enlargement of the authority and functions of the State must justify itself as an enlargement of personal liberty, interfering with individuals only in order to set free new and larger opportunities, there need remain in Liberalism no relics of that positive hostility to public methods of co-operation which crippled the old Radicalism. When society is confronted, as it sometimes will be, by a breakdown of competition and a choice between private monopoly and public enterprise, no theoretic objections to the State can be permitted to militate against public safety. Just in proportion as education guides, enriches, and enlightens the will of the people, and gives spiritual substance and intellectual power to democracy, the presumption which still holds against the adequacy of public as compared with private co-operation will be weakened, and Liberalism will come more definitely to concern itself with the liberation and utilisation of the faculties and potencies of a nation and a municipality, as well as with those of individuals and voluntary groups of citizens. It surely belongs to Liberalism to think thus liberally about its mission and its modes of progressive achievement. Not, however, of fulfilment. For it is this illimitable character of Liberalism, based on the infinitude of the possibilities of human life, in its individual and social aspects, which affords that vision without which not only a people but a party perishes, the vision of

> That untravelled world, whose margin fades
> For ever and for ever when I move.

Socialism in Liberalism

The charge of Socialism brought against the Liberal and Progressive Party by their Conservative opponents is commonly resented as a merely tactical device to shift the strain of political controversy from the Tariff issue and to blacken an enemy with a vituperative epithet. An effective technical answer is afforded by an appeal to the party of avowed Socialism which still continues to designate Liberals here, as upon the Continent, a party of capitalists. But motives and technicalities apart, there is enough substance in the charge, as applied to the section of Liberals committed to advanced social reforms, to demand a fair examination. For the first time in the history of English Liberalism, leaders with a powerful support of the rank and file have committed themselves with zeal and even passionate conviction to promote a series of practical measures which, though not closely welded in their immediate purport, have the common result of increasing the powers and resources of the State for the improvement of the material and moral condition of the people. These measures, aiming to secure the use and the value of the land for the people, to obtain for municipalities and other public bodies increased ownership or control of local services, to strengthen governmental supervision of private industries, to enlarge the public machinery of education, to afford increased public assistance to the young, the sick, the aged – such measures and the policy of public finance which they involve are correctly designated as 'socialistic' in their character.

It is true that each measure is urged upon its separate merits, that the pace of its advancement and the spirit of compromise which dogs its footsteps hide the logic of the revolutionary process even from many of its active agents. For revolutionary in one sense it is. Not that it involves any violent breach of continuity with Liberal traditions, still less any such sudden dangerous disturbance of public order or of property as is commonly associated with the term. But the general underlying meaning and motive of the social policy, struggling now for the first time into clear consciousness, is the intention to use the popular power of self-government to extirpate the roots of poverty and of the diseases, physical and moral, associated with it. This process of practical reform, if it is to be effective, assuredly demands an interference by Government with existing rights of private property and private business enterprise, and an assertion through taxation of public rights of property, so novel in character and so considerable in size as rightly to be considered revolutionary. The real revolution is in the minds of men. The recent Parliament contained some scores of men passionately moved by a sense of social wrong, of undeserved poverty and riches, of baneful waste in the resources of the commonwealth, and eager to apply large organic remedies. It is the strength of these men's faith and the size of the remedies they are willing to apply that distinguish their social policy from the tinkering devices of the earlier programmes of the Liberal Party. Experience has taught them the profound truth of John Mill's

saying: 'Small remedies for great diseases do not produce small
results: they produce no results.'

Will this policy of social reconstruction go forward? The last
century has shown several epochs of ebullience of the reform spirit
in our nation. The 'thirties and 'forties were seething with
constructive Socialism of a swift, idealist order. The Christian
Socialism of a generation later was the sentimental utterance of
popular protest against the new miseries of city poverty. The Radical
Party of the late 'seventies and early 'eighties gave in their
programmes a dim fragmentary reflection of demands in which the
new teaching of Henry George and of Continental Socialism found
vigorous expression. But these movements achieved almost
nothing; their fervour was soon spent, their forces dissipated. Will
it be the same with our Parliamentary party of social reform and the
popular enthusiasm which swept them to the fore? Have they the
principles, the strength of conviction, and the grit of character
demanded for the task of constructive Liberalism assigned to them?
The answer to this question we think depends upon how clearly the
larger body of the party can be led to realise the grave historic nature
of their task. Let them plainly recognise the truth that this is the
last chance for English Liberalism. Unless it is prepared for the
efforts, risks, and even sacrifices of expressing the older Liberal
principles in the new positive forms of economic liberty and
equality along the lines indicated in the programme of its advanced
guard, it is doomed to the same sort of impotence as has already
befallen Liberalism in most of the Continental countries.

We believe that what we term the advanced guard is well aware
of the historical crisis which confronts them, that they are willing
to make the necessary effort and to undergo the necessary risks. But
can they succeed in rallying round them the genuine support of the
Liberal 'centre' in Parliament and in the nation? This 'centre' is,
alike in sympathy and in formal policy, more advanced than it has
ever been before. But upon the critical issues of social reform it lacks
passion and principle, and is continually disposed to enervating
compromise. In Parliament it consists largely of well-to-do men
whose social policy is weakened by fears of high taxation and of
encroachments upon private profitable enterprise; in the country
this same large class, well but not vigorously disposed towards
social reforms, stands halting in opinion, fearful of the Socialistic
movement, not because of any definite individualism or abstract

theory of the limits of the State, but because certain spectres and phrases have got upon their nerves. Holding, as most do, a difficult and slippery footing in some business or profession, they are nervous about attacks on property, disturbance of business, bureaucracy, corruption, mob domination. Though not opposed to social experiments, they are not prepared for efforts or for risks, and their genuine desire to see improved conditions for the people is invalidated by an excessive belief in the possibilities of narrow forms of self-help, a survival of the *laissez-faire* Radicalism of the Victorian age.

Unless a sufficient proportion of these men can be won over, their objections met, their fears dissolved, their sense of justice stimulated, the Liberal Party as the historic instrument of social reform is doomed to failure. For a small band of 'righteous men' will not save a party; they must carry with them the majority of solid Liberals in the centre if the reform policy is to be substantial. Let it be clearly understood that this policy cannot consist in mere economy, in good administration at home, peace abroad, in minor legislation for education, temperance, or even land reform. The volume, the direction, the pace, and the substance of the positive measures for improving the economic condition of the people must be adequate, and these conditions involve a larger provision of public income than is yet recognised by most politicians, a larger development of interference with existing landed and other economic interests than is yet admitted.

Whether a sufficient Liberal Party can be brought to face this task, with its risks and difficulties, depends upon the education of this 'middle' section in the principles of social reconstruction. For their real difficulties are mainly of principle. Any Radical social policy must, of course, involve a shedding of Whigs, even of a few honest Radical individualists, and of some Liberals whose business interests too closely based on privilege will dominate their policy. It is with the large remainder, probably a majority of the Liberal Party, that we are concerned. The situation, as we understand it, is this: their mind is at present impeded for effective co-operation in the great work of social reconstruction by certain doubts and fears and difficulties, which are real in the sense that they are honestly held, and are important in that they rest not on points of practical detail but on deep-seated notions respecting the meaning and effects of social reconstruction.

These doubts and fears relate, some to Socialism, some to democracy, and are due in large degree to the spirit and the forms which social democracy have taken in the programmes of the Socialist parties, on the Continent and here. Though Marx and the philosophers of Socialism have been little read in this country, certain characteristics of their criticism, its materialistic interpretation of history, its crude assertion of the rights and functions of 'labour', its wholesale repudiation of the legitimacy of rent, interest and profit, and its doctrine of the absorption of all industry by the State, have become accepted formulae and have naturally been adopted as the authoritative exposition of the movement. While this hard-cast revolutionary Socialism has softened even on the Continent and never had much vogue in this country, the milder and more opportunist brands suffer from excessive vagueness. If the Radical policy of social reconstruction is to be effective in this country this lack of intelligible formulation of principles must be remedied. The real difficulties must be met; the right limits of State and municipal collectivism must be laid down; the questions, how far brains, how far 'labour', are makers of wealth, how far freedom of private profitable enterprise is essential to secure the work of 'brains'; whether efficiency of labour can be got out of public enterprise; whether the tyranny of bureaucracy would become unendurable; whether the tendency of such Socialism will be to dwarf individuality and to make for a dead level of humanity; whether the general result of impaired productive motives will lead to so great a diminution of wealth as no improvement in distribution can compensate – these and other not less radical questions which beset the wavering mind of our 'centre' Liberals demand thorough and impartial consideration. Then there is the group of not less serious questions relating to taxation, condensed in the charge that 'Socialism' consists in taking away the property of the rich and giving it to the poor, a policy alleged to be unjust in itself and disastrous both to the receivers and the taxpayers. The timidity of the Liberal centre is based primarily upon fears engendered by these questions which imperatively demand intelligible answers, if the Liberal Party hopes to press forward with energy and confidence along the path of social reconstruction to which it is formally committed, and upon which its future existence as a party depends.

81

2.4   Work and Wealth: A Human Valuation (1914)
[pp. 301–9]

The Social Will as an Economic Force

(1)   To secure by education and reflection such a revaluation of human activities, aims and achievements, as will set economic processes and products in a definitely lower place than that which they occupy at present, is, I think, essential to safe and rapid progress. For the early steps towards a better industrial order will very likely involve some economic sacrifice, in the sense of a reduced output of personal energy and of wealth-production on the part of the average member of society. Although this loss may be more than compensated by the elimination of large wastes of competition and by improved organisation, we are not warranted in assuming that this will at once take place.

We need not assume it. For even if we do not, our analysis has shown that an economic system, thus working at a lower rate of human costs, and turning out a smaller quantity of goods, may nevertheless yield a larger quantity of human welfare, by a better distribution of work and product. But the great gain, of course, will consist in the increased amount of time, interest and energy, available for the cultivation of other human arts outside the economic field. Upon the capacity to utilise these enlarged opportunities the actual pace of human progress in the art of living will depend. At present this capacity may seem small. The increased opportunities of leisure, travel, recreation, culture, and comradeship, which have come in widely different degrees to all classes, have often been put to disappointing uses. But a great deal of such waste is evidently attributable to that prevailing vice of thought and feeling which the domination of industrialism has stamped upon our minds, the crude desires for physical sensations and external display. Not until a far larger measure of release from our economic bonds has been acquired, shall we enjoy the detachment of mind requisite for the larger processes of revaluation and realisation.

(2)   One word remains, however, to be said upon the all-important subject of motives and incentives. We have seen that, in

so far as it is possible to displace the competitive system of industry, with its stimulation of individual greed and combativeness, by a more consciously coöperative system, the will of the individual engaged upon industrial processes will be affected in some measure by the social meaning of the work he is doing, and will desire to forward it. The efficacy of this social will is not, however, adequately realised so long as it is regarded merely as a feeling for the public good originating from a number of separate centres of enlightened personality. The growing recognition on the part of individual workers, that the structure of society establishes a strong community of interests, will no doubt supply some incentive to each to do his fair share to the necessary work. But this personal incentive may not go very far towards overcoming the selfishness or sluggishness of feebler personalities. If, then, the social will be taken merely to mean the aggregate of feeling for the public good thus generated in the separate wills, it may not suffice to support the commonweal. But if our organic conception of society has any validity, the social will means more than this addition of separately stimulated individual wills. The individual soldier may have a patriotic feeling expressing his individual love of his country, which has a certain fighting value. But, as his attachment to his profession grows, another feeling of wider origin and more enduring force fuses with the narrower feeling, enhancing greatly its effectiveness. That feeling is *esprit de corps*, a corporate spirit of the service, capable of overcoming personal defects, the cowardice, apathy or greed of the individual, and of evoking an enormous volume of united effort. I have no intention of suggesting that the routine of ordinary industry can yield scope for displays of this *esprit de corps* comparable in intensity with the dramatic examples of great military achievements. But I do affirm that every conscious corporate life is accompanied and nourished by some common consciousness of will and purpose which feeds and fortifies the personal centres, stimulating those that are weaker and raising them to a decent level of effort, reducing dissension, and imparting conscious unity of action into complex processes of coöperation.

The power of this social will as an economic motive-force ought not to be ignored. As the processes of industrial coöperation grow closer, more numerous, more regular in their operation, this coöperation and coördination, representing a unity of will and purpose far transcending the vision and the purpose even of the most enlightened and altruistic member, will form a powerful current of industrial consciousness, influencing and moulding the will and purposes of individuals.

Such a force, emanating from the social whole, will of necessity not be clearly comprehensible to the individuals who feel its influence and respond to it. They are the many, while it flows from their union, which must always be imperfectly mirrored in the mind of each. Yet this direct social will only works through its power to stimulate and direct the will of each, so as to produce a more effective harmony. Vague theory this will seem to some, utterly remote from the hard facts of life! The problem is how to induce public or other salaried employees to do a fair day's work, when they might shirk it without loss of pay. Well, we suggest that when that fair day's work is not unduly long or onerous, when it is fairly paid, and when each sees that all the others are called upon to do their proper share, the general sense of fairness in the arrangement will come to exercise a compelling influence on each man to keep his output up to a decent level. This power of the social will has never yet been tested. For a society with arrangements based on manifest principles of justice and reason has never yet been set in operation. But though our organic law of distribution may never attain a perfect application, so far as it is applied it may surely be expected to act in the way here described, appealing to the springs of honour, equity, comradeship and respect for public opinion, with a force immeasurably greater than is possible in a system of industry and property where reason and fair play in the apportionment of work and its rewards are so imperfectly apparent.

(3) These conditions of organic welfare in the apportionment of work and wealth do not imply a conception of industrial society in which the individual and his personal desires and ends are impaired or sacrificed to the interests of the community. They do imply a growth of the social-economic structure in which the impulses of mutual aid, which from the earliest times have been civilising mankind, shall work with a clearer consciousness of their human value. As the individual perceives more clearly how intimately his personal efforts and effects are, in process and in product, linked with those of all the other members of society, that perception must powerfully influence his feelings. He will come consciously to realise his personal freedom in actions that are a willing contribution to the common good. This consciousness will make it

more difficult for him to defend in himself or others economic conduct or institutions in which individual, class or national conflicts are involved. Thus a better social consciousness and a better economic environment will react on one another for further mutual betterment. The unity of this social-industrial life is not a unity of mere fusion in which the individual virtually disappears, but a federal unity in which the rights and interests of the individual shall be conserved for him by the federation. The federal government, however, conserves these individual rights, not, as the individualist maintains, because it exists for no other purpose than to do so. It conserves them because it also recognises that an area of individual liberty is conducive to the health of the collective life. Its federal nature rests on a recognition alike of individual and social ends, or, speaking more accurately, of social ends that are directly attained by social action and of those that are realised in individuals. I regard such a federation as an organic union because none of the individual rights or interests is absolute in its sanction. Society in its economic as in its other relations is a federal state not a federation of states. The rights and interests of society are paramount: they override all claims of individuals to liberties that contravene them.

(4) So far as industry is concerned, we perceive how this harmony between individual and social rights and interests is realised in the primary division of productive activities into Art and Routine. The impulses and desires which initiate, sustain and direct what we term art, including all the creative activities in industry, flow freely from the individual nature. We recognise that productive activities in which these elements are of paramount importance form an economic field which society, guided by its intelligent self-interest, will safely and profitably leave to individuals and private enterprise. Industries which are essentially of a routine character, affording little scope for creative activities of individuals, must pass under direct social administration. For free individual initiative and desires will not support them. They can only be worked under private enterprise on condition that great gains are procurable for the *entrepreneurs* and an unfree body of proletarian labour is available for compulsory service. The routine services of society cannot properly be secured by appeals to the separate self-interests of individuals. So administered, they involve the waste of vast unearned gains accruing to a private caste of masters, the injury and

degradation of economic servitude in the workers, and a growing insecurity and irregularity of service to the consumers. The only volume of free-will and voluntary enterprise that can support those routine industries is the free-will and enterprise of Society. If we can bring ourselves to regard the great normal currents of routine industry, engaged in supplying the common daily needs, from the standpoint of a real live Society, we shall recognise that to that Society this industrial activity and its achievements are full of interest and variety. What to the individual is dull routine is to Society creative art, the natural employment of social productive energies for the progressive satisfaction of social needs. Though the individual will soon flags before demands for work so irksome and repellent to its nature, the social will gladly responds to work in which that will finds its free natural expression.

This is the ultimate argument in favour in the socialisation of the routine industries, viz., the release of the individual will from work that is costly, repellent and ill-done, in order to enable the social will to find in that work its healthy, interesting, educative self-realisation. For once conceive Society as a being capable of thought and feeling, these processes have an interest for it. They are social art, part of the collective life in which Society realises itself, just as the individual realises himself in individual art. Once accept the view of Society not as a mere set of social institutions, or a network of relations, but as a collective personality, the great routine industrial processes become the vital functions of this collective being, interesting to that being alike in their performance and their product. That subdivision of labour and that apparent contradiction of interests between producer and consumer which seem designed to feed personal antagonisms and to thwart individuality, now acquire rational justification as the complex adaptive play of healthy vital functions in society.

(5) Labour, thus interpreted, becomes a truly social function, the orderly half-instinctive half-rational activity by which society helps itself and satisfies its wants, a common tide of productive energy which pulses through the veins of humanity, impelling the individual members of society to perform their part as contributors to the general life. Whether those individual actions are strictly voluntary, pleasurable and interesting in themselves to those who perform them, as in the finer arts, or are compulsory in their main incidence upon the individual, and accompanied by little interest or

social feeling on his part, is a matter of quite secondary importance as viewed from the social standpoint. As labour is social, so is capital. The other apparent discrepancy, that between the interests of present and future, spending and saving, also disappears when we consider the social significance of saving. For society secretes capital by the same half-instinctive half-rational process by which it generates, directs and distributes, its supply of labour. Only by a hypothesis which thus assigns a central industrial purpose to society can we possibly understand the life of industry and the complex coöperation it displays.

Take for a single instance the wheat supply of the world – or the cotton industry of Lancashire. We see large rhythmic actions, elaborate in their complicated flows, responsive to innumerable stimuli of world-markets – a nervous system of affluent and effluent currents, directed by the desires and beliefs of innumerable producers and consumers, each consciously actuated by his own particular motives and yet coöperating towards large social ends.

We can neither grasp intellectually or emotionally, the human or social significance of these processes, if we persist in resolving them into the ideas, feelings and actions of individual persons. The harmony becomes either fortuitous or purely mystical. But, if we regard Society as having a large life of its own, the coöperative harmony of individual aims and activities becomes a corporate organic process. The social life does not suffer from division of labour and specialisation of function, but gains, as in the animal organism. The social life is not oppressed, degraded or injured by the routine of the smaller working lives, any more than the animal organism by the regularity and repetition of the respiratory, circulating and other routine operations of its organs and their cells.

(6) 'But,' it will be objected, 'even if we are justified in pushing the organic analogy so far as to claim the existence of a real social life with a meaning and end of its own, superior to that of the individual, as the life of every organism is superior to that of its organs and cells, that larger social being can only remain a shadowy or hypothetical being to actual men and women. And it is the aims, ideas, feelings and activities of these little units that, after all, will always absorb our attention and occupy our hearts and minds.'

Here is the final quintessence of individualism surviving in many professing socialists, the denial of the existence of a rational moral society. Yet such a society exists. The earliest beginnings of animal gregariousness, sexual feelings, and other primary instincts of association, with the mutual aid they give rise to, are a first testimony to the existence, even at the opening of the human era, of a real though rudimentary society, physical and psychical in its nature. Civilisation has its chief meaning in the extension and growing realisation of this unity of society, by utilising these secret threads of social feeling for the weaving of the fabric of social institutions. Thus, through these instruments of common social life, language, art, science, industry, politics, religion, society gathers a larger, more solid and various life. Race, Nationality, Church, the bond of some common interest in a science, an art, a philanthropic purpose, often present intense examples of genuinely common life and purpose. These are not mere social contracts of free individuals, seeking by coöperation to forward their individual ends. Such a conception of mutual aid is as false for religion, science, art or industry, as for politics. The statement that 'man is a social animal' cannot merely signify that among man's equipment of feelings and ideas there exists a feeling and idea of sympathy with other men. That is only how it looks *from the standpoint of the cell.* It means that humanity in all its various aggregations is a social stuff, and that whatever forms of coalescence it assumes, i.e. a nation, caste, church, party, etc., there will exist a genuinely organic unity, a central or general life, strong or weak, but, so far as it goes, to be considered as distinct from and dominant over the life and aim of its members.

This central life, though distinguishable from the lives of its members, as an object of thought and will, is yet only lived in and through the life of the organs and cells. This is the subtle nature of the organic bond.

We are told indeed that 'Society only exists in individuals'. This, however, is only true in the same restricted sense in which it is true that an animal organism only exists in the life of its cells. There is nothing but the cells *plus* their organic coöperation. But I should rather say that the organism exists in the coöperation of the cells. So I should say that Society exists in the coöperation of individuals.

This is not a matter of theoretic accuracy of statement, but of immense practical significance. For the future progress of the arts of social conduct, especially of industry and politics, must largely depend upon the measure and manner of acceptance of this view of the nature of Society. It must, indeed, to the individual mind always remain as a hypothesis, incapable of full and exact verification. For such verification would imply an absolute merging of individual personality in the social unity. Such a public spirit can never absorb and displace private spirits. But the hypothesis may, for all that, possess both intellectual and emotional validity. Its clear provisional acceptance will not only explain many of the difficulties and reconcile many of the discrepancies in those tendencies, industrial and political, which are generally accepted as making for human progress, but will afford increased economy of direction and of motive. For once let us realise Society as possessing a unity and a life of its own, to the furtherance of which each of us contributes in the pursuance of the particular life we call 'our own', the so-called sacrifices we are called upon to make for that larger life will be considered no longer encroachments on but enlargements of our personality. We shall come in larger measure to identify our aims and ends willingly with the aims and ends we impute to society, and every step in that public conduct will enrich or strengthen that social sympathy which we shall recognise to be the very life of society flowing in our veins. This is the spirit of social reform, as distinguished from the concrete measures of reform. Upon the creation and recognition of this spirit the possibility, the usefulness, the durability of every one of the institutions and policies, which are evolved by modern civilisation, depend. It is, therefore, of supreme and critical importance to obtain the widest possible acceptance of the conception of Society as a living being to which each of us 'belongs', a being capable of thinking and feeling through us for itself, and of desiring, pursuing and attaining ends which are its ends, and which we are capable of helping to realise. So long as Society is spoken of and thought of as an abstraction, no social conduct can be sound or safe. For an abstraction is incapable of calling forth our reverence, regard or love. And until we attribute to Society such a form and degree of 'personality' as can evoke in us those interests and emotions which personality alone can win, the social will will not be able to perform great works.

The final claim we make for the human valuation of industry presented here is that it helps to bring into clear relief a set of human problems which, from the conception of society as a mere arrangement for securing individual ends, are perceived to be insoluble, but for which reason and emotion alike demand a satisfactory solution. Only by substituting for the attainment of individual welfare the ideal and the standard of social welfare, are we able to obtain a method of analysis and valuation which furnishes satisfactory solutions to the problems that industry presents.

2.5 'The Ethical Movement and the Natural Man' (1922) [*Hibbert Journal*, pp. 667–78]

Good character and conduct derive their value and authority not from any supernatural or external source, but from their inherent virtue and appeal. The human reason is the proper instrument for the discovery and application of the principles and rules of a good life. The social nature of man makes it serviceable for seekers after this rational good to help one another by organised co-operation, and to win from this communion a clearer inspiration and a firmer purpose. These statements I think would be accepted generally as fundamental to the Ethical Movement. Now the age in which we live might appear particularly favourable to the growth of such a Movement. For the hold of the orthodox Churches upon the educated – or shall I better say the wealthier? – classes has long been weakening. Belief in a divine personality, another world of bliss or torment, the scheme of redemption and the entire metaphysics of Christianity has worn into an extremely attenuated acceptance. A more rationalistic attitude towards human character and conduct, the slow product of the evolutionary teaching, especially of the applied physical sciences, has broken the spell which chance, miracle, and special Providence formerly exercised upon the credulity of Man. The utter impotence of organised Christendom to prevent the crimes of War and Peace, or sensibly to moderate their physical and moral injuries, ought to have discredited finally the claim of supernatural religion to be the guardian either of public or of personal morals. It might have been expected that the moral devastation wrought by this catastrophe upon every human institution, from the family to the embryonic international order, would have compelled myriads of minds in this, as in other countries, to look with favour on a Movement which claimed to present a rational morality as the alternative to spiritual anarchy. Allowing for the host of hastily improvised new superstitions which seek to displace the old, there must, it would appear, be large numbers of intelligent men and women who should find in these societies just the sort of moral support and intercourse which they require. Why, then, does so small a fraction of this multitude enrol themselves in our ranks? What is lacking in our appeal? It may be that most of those who have broken with orthodox religion and have given up church-going feel no need of any substitute. Some possibly are suspicious of the constructive radicalism in politics and economics with which some or all of our groups are more or less associated. For free-thinking on matters of religion among the well-to-do educated classes carries little implication of political, still less of economic, liberalism. Many, again, who are keen social reformers, prefer to give their time and thought to movements of a more directly practical order. Even the occasional experiments in Labour Churches have depended for their brief success upon the personal appeal of some enthusiastic leader rather than on any widespread recognition of the need for spiritualising the Labour Movement.

But in seeking to understand why so many of those who ought to be working with us, and whose co-operation we need, are not attracted or are repelled by our Movement, I think it is profitable to make a closer inquiry into certain evident defects in our appeal. I have posed the problem by confronting the Ethical Movement with a being called the 'natural man'. I have taken this course because the body of ethical conceptions and values in general acceptance by our Societies is not likely to be widely divergent from that current among the more serious-minded adherents of our Protestant Churches. The abandonment of supernatural sanctions does not itself involve any considerable alterations in the rules and valuations of a good life. If, therefore, there is any narrowness or other inadequacy in our ethical conceptions, it may best be discovered in the processes by which our Churches moulded morals in the light of their theology and imposed them on successive generations of the faithful. Now the whole theological system, held with minor variations by the Churches, stood upon a single fundamental moral assumption, that of the natural depravity of man. Man is born bad, and the whole scheme of salvation is devoted to his rescue. That rescue consists in a transformation or conversion of his natal make-up. This is as much the root assumption of the Catholic Churches as of the Nonconformist, though standing on a very flimsy Biblical

91

foundation. The article of our Church of England puts the matter quite uncompromisingly. 'Original sin standeth not in the following of Adam – but is the fault and corruption of each man's nature' . . .

Sobriety, industry, forethought and thrift, orderliness, per-severance, honesty were the staple ingredients of positive Puritan ethics, and they admirably accommodated themselves to the conditions of the struggle for personal wealth and power in the new era. Even that rigid Sabbatarianism which counted so much for righteousness had its business value. Stamped on many generations of commercial townsmen by the united discipline of Church and family, this became the accepted ethics of respectability, not only for the dominant middle class, but, by imitation, of large sections of the working classes, thus kept docile and useful in this life and looking for an inexpensive reward in another. Older members of our Societies, brought up in middle-class Mid-Victorian families, will be well aware how strong was the hold this typically Puritan ethics then retained. Handed down, virtually intact in substance and direction, though doubtless weakened in intensity, from the seventeenth century, the attitude not only towards sexual irregularities, drinking and gambling, but towards the innocent amusements of music, the theatre, and the fine arts, nay even towards poetry and the whole literature of imagination, and indeed towards any scientific study likely to engender scepticism or intellectual pride – this attitude hung like a subtle atmosphere over the whole conduct of life.

Much of this has passed away from our more liberal Churches, but what remains – and this I hold to be most significant – is the retention of the older and in large measure Puritan conception of the sphere of ethics. Sport, the fine arts, recreation, literature, science are accepted by serious-minded people not only as innocent, but as desirable activities, but moral or ethical values are not ascribed to them, they are not real contributions towards a good life. Now I am very well aware that some of the most active workers and thinkers in our Ethical Societies have broken down for themselves this distinction between the ethical and the non-ethical activities of life, and recognise that any strong grasp of the organic unity of a good life must incorporate in that goodness every accepted form of the desirable – health, the enjoyment of physical beauty, every kind of knowledge and aptitude contributory to human well-being. What keeps many people from joining us is sheer misapprehension of our aims and objects, due perhaps in part to the abstract terms in which those aims and objects are set forth, terms like 'the good life' and the 'supreme purpose of humanity', which they associate with a cold and vague formalism. Even when they penetrate far enough to recognise something of our wider purpose, they are still apt to think that we are pinning on the recreative and cultural arts of life as mere appendages to the good life instead of treating them as integral parts of that life . . .

Safety, order, calculability are the foundation-stones of all civilised existence. But we are now told we must not try to live too safely, too orderly, and too certain in our plans. There is no fear of that, some will say, the infinite variety of environment and of events will always outrun calculation and provide a world of hazard for adventurous souls. Indeed, they go further and insist that the very end and object of each repression of personal liberty involved in social order, each reduction of an area of danger and caprice to orderly routine, each provision of security against the primary risks of life, is the opening up of larger and loftier areas of freedom, adventure, and personal achievement. This is the reply which defenders of mechanical industry sometimes make to the upholders of primitive handicrafts. It is the reply which the socialist makes against those who charge him with attacks on personal liberty. It is the reply of the philanthropist and moralist against the cruder charge of scientists that their social protection promotes the survival of the unfit and reduces the average value of human life. As in the individual life, so in the social, the reduction of certain primary activities to routine subconscious processes liberates more energy for conscious and creative work in higher spheres. It is clearly a case for compromising or harmonising contrary interests, so as to reach some ultimate economy of life. But this general principle does not carry us very far. It sometimes threatens to seek too hastily to stamp out or reduce the lower instincts, evolved for biological survival in early times, in favour of a more refined and spiritual life. Here again the protest of the natural man comes in, to claim consideration for what are called the animal needs and creature comforts. He accuses the uplifters, the organisers of a higher life, of disparaging the claims of the world and the flesh. Nay, more, he requires that his conception of 'good living', even in its ordinary sense, should find some place in the ethical conception of the good life. Does it? For it is relevant to my task to take account of these popular conceptions of good living. Nor need we confine ourselves to the luxurious conception of a gourmet. The insurance company

93

knows what it means by 'a good life', and, still more significant, the English clergyman, the proved representative of Christian ethics, has a plain and not too elevated conception of 'a good living' as one affording a handsome income to its holder.

Now all these are true though very incomplete revelations of the requirements of the natural man from life. Does our ethical conception make adequate provision for them?

I am not sure that we can truthfully say it does. Are the reasonable satisfactions of our animal wants, and the tastes and arts which appertain thereto, actually incorporated in our ideals? If they are not, then we have one plain explanation of the failure of the Ethical Movement in its appeal to the natural man.

Now, though our natural man does not himself philosophise, his objection stands on a philosophic basis, viz. a denial of any ultimate or real opposition between body and spirit, the material and spiritual universe. This opposition, with its degradation of the body, has always lain at the root of the popular dislike, distrust, and fear of priests, scholars, philosophers, and moralists, all of whom they suspect of disparaging the body for purposes of spiritual and intellectual self-esteem.

A novel danger has been recently imported into this situation by the new psychology. There the naked origins of human nature are found to reside in animal instincts and impulses. The play of these original instincts has been modified and complicated in the progress from animalism to barbarism and barbarism to civilisation, but they have never been got under sufficient control and are always liable to revert to type, or otherwise to find violent primitive expressions which play havoc with the securities and delicacies of modern life. Psychologists now urge that a more scientific economy should be applied to these more troublesome instinctive forces. They should be 'sublimated'; that is, drawn away from their original channels, and put to operate in ways in which their energy can be made not merely innocent but humanly serviceable. These new paths must have sufficient resemblance to the original paths to evoke enough of the vital satisfaction attached to the performance of the primal activities. We know this can be done. The fighting instinct can find a useful and pleasurable scope in football. The zest of hunting may pass into scientific research. Sex feeling may be canalised into art or even religion. Curiosity, the instinct of leadership or of submission, the sense of awe, can all be transformed into powerful feeders of a constructive social order.

I want, however, to ask a question here and interject a caution. How far and fast can we get rid of the awkward factors of animal instinct by sublimating them? It is accounted a gain that force sometimes gives place to public opinion as a mode of settling disputes. Men count heads instead of cracking them. I do not wish to disparage this advance. But we should remember that the practice of counting heads, i.e. of electioneering, may be almost as dangerous, as literally deadly, in its consequences as the earlier and cruder practice. The general election of 1918 has been directly responsible for the death of millions of human beings. Is the fighting instinct safely sublimated by making it turn the wheels of a party machine? Again, the hunting instinct, set to track out heretical opinions in religion, politics, or even science, may be more destructive in its persecuting zeal than in any of its primitively useful origins. Or take the instinct of property, and the sentiment of personal power which it engenders and expresses. It is sometimes suggested that, if we could, by socialisation or communalisation of material wealth, remove the play of this instinct from the economic into the intellectual field, we should be immune from the selfish power it implies. But there is some ground for holding that vested interests and the power of property in intellectual wealth and its machinery of production are more devasting than any other enemy in their attacks on intellectual liberty and progress. Or finally, take that most insistent of all instincts, the sexual, vitally creative and conservative. By some subtle alchemy this force may be transmuted on its creative side into artistic impulse or mystical religion, on its conservative side into philanthropy or social mothering. But can we feel quite sure that these rushes of creative instinct, repressed in their simple and direct outlet, into these artistic, religious, and social channels may not be responsible for dangerous neurotic excesses? I do not desire to overstress the perils of a too hasty and easy acceptance of the theory of sublimation of the instincts. But the economy of such a process must be extremely delicate, and I would commend to its over-confident supporters the wisdom of the ancient saw, '*Naturam expellas furca, tamen usque recurret.*'

What I am afraid of is the tendency of some moralists to accept too readily devices for subjugating, repressing, or rendering innocuous those elements in man's animal outfit which they find it awkward to fit in with their preconception of a good life. I suggest that it may be safer and more profitable in the long run to

95

consider how far the set of valuations and institutions which express the good life should not itself be revised, so as to include and make adequate provision for the simpler satisfactions of the natural instincts. You cannot get rid of these instincts, even if you ought to desire to do so. There is no ground for holding that any adequate satisfaction of them is attainable by methods of sublimation, therefore you are bound to find a proper place for them in your conception of a good society. The adoption of this view may, no doubt, seriously cramp us in some of our aims at reforming society. It may oblige us to concede the impossibility of the total extinction of physical conflict between individuals and groups. It may lead us to dismiss for ever the notion of expelling profiteering completely from the whole economic system. It may compel us to furnish much enlarged facilities both to marriage and divorce, perhaps even to modify that institution of monogamy which has now received general acceptance and enforcement.

Do we want to claim the title Humanist, indicating that the whole of Humanity is our concern? Now the natural man is a little suspicious of these large unfamiliar terms, and is apt to direct against them a quality which humanists could do well to take into account because its name should recommend it to them, the quality of Humour. For the natural man is certainly a bit of a humorist, and claims for Humour a definite and considerable place in life. Now this humour is particularly directed against persons whose language or bearing indicate that they take themselves too seriously. In the sharper thrusts of this humour there is, as Freud, and Hobbes long before him, have recognised, a considerable spice of malice and self-glory. But there is much more than this. Socrates did not invent, though perhaps he was the first to apply systematically, an ironic humour to the deeper work of criticism. The disconcerting judgments, the sudden contradictions, thus revealed in lofty principles or well-seeming professions, were essentially strokes of humour. Now the work of Socrates needs constantly to be done over again, for there exists a perpetual tendency for thinkers who handle the larger and the higher concepts to become dupes of specious formulas and attractive theories. The natural man has always scoffed at these products of high intellectualism. But the intellectualists easily ignored his shallow gibes. Modern psychology, however, is forcing the intellectualist and the high moralist alike to confront the duty of a self-analysis that is exceedingly disconcerting in the light it sheds upon the methods by which history, philosophy, economics, and all the moral sciences are moulded so as to satisfy the secret demands of man's instincts and the interests derived from them. To display theology as man making Gods in his own image, Morality as man pumping the pressure of his animal cravings into sacred obligations to be enforced by States and Laws, Philosophies as man's affectation at escaping his natural bonds and heritage and soaring into a realm of high abstractions, Economics designed to help defend his property or to break institutions which deny him his proper share in the good things of life – the whole of this process of 'rationalisation' of institutions, rules, theories, motives, which derive their real force and origin from primitive demands of human nature is an immense new field for the operations of what Meredith termed 'the comic spirit'.

It will not hurt us. It will do us good, if it destroys many of the sham sanctities we have set up by forcing us to see their origins. If it compels us to see that we have no right to take ourselves so seriously, to realise the foolishness of pretending to escape long ages of heredity, and to scrutinise more closely the intrinsic value of our valuations, it will be a purifying humour.

How far the criticism implied in some of the considerations I have set before you is rightly applicable to our ethical teaching I will not pretend to decide. But I think I have shown reason to hold that some of the inheritance of the Puritan Nonconformist conscience and morals is inherently likely to have embedded itself in our ethical creed, and that in any case the natural man, resentful of interference with his cruder desires, is likely to suspect its presence. It is not quite enough to make the formal reply that the ethical creed claims 'to see life steadily and see it whole'. It is much more difficult in practice to expel the long traditional suggestion of the cleavage of animal and spiritual life, and firmly to accept the view that all, even of the most sublimated and refined of our sentiments and processes of thinking, are in origin and nature products of this animal humanity of ours. The notion that we are shedding animalism, letting ape and tiger die, in the evolution of civilisation is erroneous. We are only evolving and elaborating the potentialities of animal life. If we resent the materialistic degradation of such a view, we had best proceed, not by constructing some new turn of fallacious dualism, but by lifting the whole process of evolution into some neutral zone where neither the grossness of materialism nor the vagueness of idealism is chargeable. The close, constant, and intricate interactions between the separately conceived worlds of matter and mind, the physical and spiritual processes, are reinforced continually by new discoveries on both sides, in physics and psychology, and the bridge across the secular gulf, hitherto so rickety a structure, is becoming solid and substantial to most modern thinkers. This philosophical position should have strong ethical reactions, and our Movement, released from the shackles of a cramping theology with its legacy of original sin, should be able to work out with great advantage the practical implications of this clearer conception of Unity in various fields of conduct. The intricate interrelations of body and mind thus established should have profound reactions on methods of education, medicine, penology, and indeed every department of personal and social reform.

2.6   Wealth and Life (1929)   [pp. vii–xxiv]

To perform with scientific precision the task of translating economic values into ethical or human values is manifestly impossible. For economic values in their first intent are quantities of money, while ethical or human values are qualities of life. Yet money and the economic operations for which money stands, and which money controls, play so important a part in human life as to compel students of humanity to attempt some orderly adjustment between the two sorts of value, some appreciation of economic valuations in terms of the humanly desirable. In any such attempt it is well at the outset to realise the nature of the difficulties to be overcome, and the limits within which we must work in any humanist evaluation of economic processes. To pass from monetary to vital values involves several distinguishable movements. Money values must first be translated into the concrete saleable things, the goods and services, which prices, or any sort of payment or income, express. These goods must then be resolved into their net costs of production and their net utilities of consumption. By costs we signify, of course, not money costs, for that would be retracing our steps, but the wear and tear and disagreeable exertions incurred in the productive processes. Some of this costly wear and tear is that of human beings, some falls directly upon nature and non-human instruments. But, since the task of replacing the non-human wear and tear falls mainly upon man, we may speak of 'costs' as human costs. I use the term 'net' costs, because in many human productive processes there are elements of enjoyment, or utility, as well as of cost, which should be taken into due account. So likewise with the 'utility' or enjoyment of consumption, there is often a debit account from the pains or injuries of 'illth', misuse, and excess.

This expression of economic values in 'subjective' costs and utilities does not, however, carry them on to the plane of ethical or human evaluation. For these costs or utilities register actual gains or losses as they operate in the economic system on a valuation based on current desires and estimates, which may not be reliable indices of the desirable. Thus some further adjustment is needed to assess the desired in terms of the desirable. Nor is the process yet complete. Even when we have got so far as thus to resolve monetary wealth into its equivalent in human value, we have not finished our task. For in following our economic path we have ignored the interactions that everywhere and always take place between economic and non-economic functions and activities in the human organism.

Ultimately the goods which are the concrete expression of money values must be evaluated by the total effects which by the terms of their production and consumption they exert upon human personalities and communities regarded as organic wholes.

All these steps are necessary to pass from economic wealth, as rendered by money, to human welfare – the ethical test and goal. And all these early steps, as we shall see, are slippery. Magnificent plungers like Ruskin may impose arbitrary meanings upon 'wealth' and 'illth' and bring whole civilisations to a grand assize. But those who rely upon calmer reasoning will have to test each step and make good the footing. It may, indeed, turn out that some of our difficulties are in a strict sense insuperable. One or more of these steps may be impassable. The strictly subjective element in personality may baffle all computation of concrete wealth in human welfare. The relations between economic and non-economic factors of welfare may evade observation and record . . .

The spirit of moral revolt, the appeal to justice and humanity, which took such various forms in the activities of this era [the 1880s], was by no means without its influence upon the academic economics of the time. The breakaway of Jevons from the cost theory of value, in favour of an analysis of demand which made the utility or satisfaction of the consumer the standard and determinant of economic values, was a marked advance towards the humanisation of economic science. But though Jevons's claim 'to treat Economy as a Calculus of Pleasure and Pain' (imperfectly applied in the actual development of his theory), digs below the harder concrete wealth of the classical economists, its too separatist treatment of human motives and desires, and its failure to give an equal recognition to 'costs' in his utilitarian calculus, were serious limitations in his work, regarded from the standpoint of ethics. More significant was the claim of Marshall, the great Cambridge economist of this period, in the preface to his *Principles of Economics* [first published 1891] which was to be the leading text-book of English economic teaching for a generation, that 'ethical forces are among those of which the economist has to take account' [*Principles*, p. x]. And throughout his work and those of most of his associates and followers, there is found a recognition, sometimes even a parade, of ethical considerations. They enter in two ways. First, as motives in modification of the crude greed and selfishness imputed to 'the economic man'. Altruistic motives, so far as they are operative in economic conduct, must evidently be taken into due account, as economic factors. But another ethical consideration is a wavering recognition that the operations of the economic system, as expounded by its science, do not conform adequately to the dictates of reason, justice, and humanity in the apportionment of labour and the fruits of labour. I speak of it as 'wavering', in that such recognition of unfairness appears to have been held consistent with the view that the laws of economic distribution are inevitable in their working, and are in their normal operation sound as tending to reward every producer according to 'his worth'. In other words, what condemnations of the hardships and injustices of current industrialism appear in the authoritative economics of this period were not incorporated in the structure of the economic theory, but were of the nature of *obiter dicta* or qualifying reflections . . .

The term 'Organic welfare' should, I think, readily win acceptance as the criterion of economic values even among those disposed to distinguish ethical from biological values. For, in the first place, most economic activities are definitely directed to the survival and development of the physical organism of man. In the second place, the adjective 'organic' has a wider acceptance than the substantive 'organism'. For most of those who jib at a 'social organism' will admit that a society is 'organic', by virtue of its 'organisation'. What is essential is the recognition that the elements in human welfare are organic in their relationship. The failure of most economists to give proper recognition to this truth explains the curious aloofness of the place occupied by economics among the social sciences, as well as the mistrust which ordinary men and women feel for the policies and practical advice that issue from the authoritative economists. The utilitarianism is too crude, the logic too absolute.

The organic treatment of economic values finds its field of operations in the arts of production and consumption. From the organic standpoint the subdivision of labour, by which each man in a society devotes the whole of his economic activity to some single process, appears to stand self-condemned. For man as an organism was manifestly evolved for and by the integrated use of all his organs in a large variety of activities conducive to personal and specific survival and growth. An exclusively economic analysis of production shows us 'shredded man'. The heaviest human indictment of our current system rests upon this charge. That man is not utterly destroyed by this economic assault upon his human nature is due to certain resistances, alleviations, and compensations, that lie outside the strict sphere of economic production. Larger leisure with its opportunities for gardening, carpentering, and other 'relief works', for the organic satisfactions of games and sport (pleasurable imitations or adaptations of primitive activities no longer needed) and for the inclusion of other active operations upon what is deemed the spending or consuming side of life, are more or less effective offsets to the dehumanising effect of specialised production. So far as our valuation finds it convenient to retain the distinction between production and consumption, its human computation of production must evidently include many organic activities that lie outside the income-earning class and are in a sense self-chosen to satisfy thwarted or neglected organic needs.

But if human welfare on its productive side thus requires the importation of strictly non-economic activities for its organic interpretation, so likewise with the art or activities of consumption. The organic view of consumption puts its emphasis upon standards or harmonies. The crude analysis of separate articles of diet,

101

clothing, etc., with separate utilities that diminish with each added unit of supply, loses its significance in view of the interaction of the diverse ingredients of welfare involved in the organic composition. Moreover, as on the productive, so on the consumptive side, distinctively economic consumption is merged with, and affected by, other non-economic factors, the conception of a standard of living being replaced by that of a standard of life. Again, the interactions between the productive and consumptive activities will become more intricate in proportion as life is realised as a fine art. For a fine art differs from other activities in fusing the processes of production and consumption, effort and enjoyment. Thus a human or organic valuation of economic processes will be continually traversing the distinction of production and consumption, substituting more and more the distinction between the negative value of human 'costs' and the positive value of human utilities or satisfactions. It will thus approach closer to a biological conception of human economy, without necessarily admitting the supremacy or sufficiency of the biological standpoint. For all serviceable organic activities consume tissue and expend energy, the biological costs of the services they render. Though this economy may not correspond in close quantitative fashion to a pleasure and pain economy or to any other conscious valuation, it must be taken as a groundwork for that conscious valuation. For most economic purposes we are well advised to prefer the organic test to any other test of welfare, bearing in mind that many organic costs do not register themselves easily or adequately in terms of conscious pain or disutility, while organic gains also are not always interpretable in conscious enjoyment. Even, therefore, for those who insist that all human values must ultimately be expressed in terms of individual consciousness, it is better to accept the organic criterion as provisionally serviceable. For there is this supreme advantage in this acceptance that, so far as the organic welfare is adopted, it minimises, though it cannot eliminate, the personal bias in the valuer. For the longer we can put off trying to value states of consciousness, confining ourselves to behaviour, so much the better. If, as I hold, it is impossible to rest on a purely behaviourist basis of interpretation, it is none the less good to proceed along that basis as far as it is practicable. This course enables us to enter and explore without final committal another of the great social problems that have a peculiar interest for economics, the structure and function of the community. For, postponing for the time being the heated question whether there exists a group-mind, and if so, in what sense, we may consider the community, not as a mere aggregate of individuals, but as an organic structure with a life 'of its own' both on the producing and consuming side, and a harmony of practical activities supplementary to the individual economic harmony. The relation between this communal and this individual economy will be one of our most fruitful fields of exploration, involving, as it does, the critical issue, how far community and its institutions exist for, and are to be valued exclusively by, their contributions to the human welfare of the individual, or how far they have a life strictly communal with costs and utilities not thus resolvable. From the economic standpoint the importance of this issue lies in the consideration how far distinctively social activities are productive of wealth, either indirectly in sustaining the economic order and heritage, or directly, in organised public services, and how far these public services can undertake to supply certain human needs which cannot safely or properly be entrusted to private profitable enterprise.

In our provisional acceptance of an organic test or standard of value there may, however, lurk some misunderstandings due to the too closely materialistic and biological associations of the term. For example, in estimating economic costs and utilities by their contribution to the organic welfare of individuals and communities, we are confronted by the question how far the actual economic conduct, with its accompanying desires and gratifications, can be taken as a safe index of the desirable or organic welfare in its true sense. In dealing with the life of ants and bees, we seem able to eliminate the fact or possibility of error by the completeness of the organic integration that appears in all their actions. But when conscious choice and the beginnings of reason take direction of behaviour, as in the higher primates, the correspondence between the desired and the desirable is no longer accurately assured. Error is possible. It may, indeed, be claimed that error is not really eliminated by the specific instincts of automata; that, on the contrary, this lack of adaptability to environmental changes exposes them to perils of extinction, with which the conscious central guidance of the brain enables the higher animals to cope. But this diffusion of error in the conduct of the higher animals, man in particular, does not relieve us of our difficulty. On the contrary it

103

increases it. For, whereas errors in the life of instinct are few and fatal, in the life of the reasonable animal, man, they are many and often not evident. Applying this general truth to our special theme, the human valuation of economic processes, we cannot assume a full identity of the income of an individual or a community, expressed in terms of current satisfactions, with that income expressed in terms of human welfare. Nor is the difference to be accounted for only by consideration of the distribution of the toil of production on the one hand, of the satisfaction of consumption on the other. The total process of consumption-production may contain large elements of human waste or error, in that the tastes, desires, and satisfactions which actively stimulate this wealth-creation may not conform to the standard of the desirable. Here lies the supreme problem of humanity, at once ethical, intellectual, aesthetic, how to integrate the capacities of man, as a social animal, so as to enable him to make the most of a life that consists in the progressively complex control of an environment which, by the very expression of this control, is calling forth and educating new cooperations of inborn capacities. This actively changing human nature, with its changing activities, cannot be regarded as completely expressing in its actual desires and conduct the human welfare that may be accounted as the pattern to which it would conform, if it were more moral, more intellectual, more aesthetic than it is. Nor are we warranted in taking a static view of the desirable, or of the hierarchy of values that expresses it. Regarding evolution alike in its material and spiritual aspects as motived by directive urges that constitute a general purpose, and unable to accept T. H. Huxley's divergence between biological and ethical process, I am bound to regard the actual normal conduct and desires of man, whether he be considered as animal or as *homo sapiens*, to be in general conformity with the ethical or humanly desirable. His 'sapience' thus will be directed, partly, to correcting the errors due to his incompletely integrated 'nature', partly, to those changes in the standard of the humanly desirable welfare, due to a clearer vision of a wider, longer, and more complex life for man.

2.7 Towards Social Equality (1931)   [p. 5]

. . . social equality may be taken to imply three things: first, that so far as individuals share a common experience in life, they shall enjoy an equal opportunity for the formation and expression of public opinion, whether in the political or any other field; secondly, that the occupations, sects, parties, or other social divisions into which they fall shall have equal opportunities for making an effective expression of their interests, knowledge, and valuations; thirdly, that the unique personal needs, knowledge, and abilities of every citizen shall be able to transcend the barriers of 'class', and make their distinctive contribution through personality to public policy. In other words, we have in each individual a unique personality, a member of a class or group, and a member of the wider community, of which the classes or other groups are sections.

CHAPTER

— 3 —

Economics

Hobson's economic theories are scattered across a multitude of writings. The selections below are samples of some of his recurring themes. In *The Problem of the Unemployed* Hobson first enunciated a clear version of his underconsumptionist argument independently of A. F. Mummery's influence, a version that also took non-economic factors into account. Physical constraints on possible consumption by the wealthy – the beneficiaries from unearned income – reinforced by their declining psychological need to consume, could account for oversaving. The rudiments of social property were identified in that unearned income, which Hobson demonstrated to be the result of direct exertions of the community, as well as of monopolies that owed their existence to public protection. The cure to the crises of capitalism and to unemployment lay in taxing unearned income and in social reform measures such as higher wages, which would simultaneously improve the lot of the workers and increase consumption. Hobson's *The Economics of Distribution*, based on lectures he gave at the London School of Economics, appeared in the USA in 1900. It was a serious effort to construct a more rigorous economic theory, but, as he wrote, 'this publication was unfortunate, in so much as it reached few English readers and was scarcely noticed in English reviews' (*Confessions of an Economic Heretic*, p. 48). In it, Hobson examined the role of economic 'forced gains' and contended controversially that taxes on commodities did not fall on consumers.

Whereas Hobson always maintained that the main defects of the economic system were to be found in distribution, he also wished increasingly to show, as in *The Industrial System*, how the underlying behaviour of the system depended on consumer demand.

This book, one of his major economic works, contained most of the special features of Hobson's analysis. The identification of saving and investment, and the dismissal of hoarding as abnormal, were attached to the thesis that a correct ratio of saving to spending existed with respect to all industrial communities and that in order to maintain progress and satisfy considerations of social utility, adjustments to preserve that ratio were necessary. *The Industrial System* was followed two years later by *The Science of Wealth*, a more popular, and frequently reprinted, version which succinctly set out Hobson's distinction between costs and surplus, and within the latter between productive and unproductive surplus. His discussion of productive surpluses departed from socialist positions by recognizing within that category the need for interest payments as reward for desirable economic activity (in other works, in particular in *Incentives in the New Industrial Order* [1922], this was argued more forcefully on the 'natural' grounds of eliciting psychological motivation). The role of the state as a factor in production and as responsible for public services could be legitimately sustained by drawing upon the unproductive surplus.

Hobson frequently applied the economic apparatus he had constructed in such laborious isolation to current concerns. This is illustrated through one such instance, the debate over rationalization that began in the late 1920s. The reorganization and unification urged upon industry were argued in terms of efficiency and economy, yet Hobson joined other doubters in querying whether the interests of labour as well as capital would be preserved, whether the end result would not be the resurrection of new and dangerous monopolies, and – most importantly – in insisting that economic planning had to take place within the framework of organic perspectives pertaining to the interrelated issues of industrial and human welfare.

3.1   The Problem of the Unemployed (1896)   [pp. 88–92, 98–111]

The Motives of Underconsumption. A Natural Law of Consumption

What are the motive forces which act upon individuals impelling them to a line of action which, from the wider standpoint of the community, is uneconomical? Why does the free play of individual interests fail to secure the interest of the whole community?

The answer to this vital question is found in the region of Distribution. The reason why attempts are made by individuals to establish more forms of capital than are socially required, is that they possess certain elements of income which are not earned by effort, and which are therefore not required to satisfy any present legitimate wants. In spite of all attempts to make an artificial severance between a 'producing' and a 'consuming' class, the natural relation between production and consumption, between effort and satisfaction, exercises a strong influence in the social economy. It is possible for individuals and for classes who draw large incomes *alieni vultus sudore,* or without any considerable contribution of effort, to be large and profuse consumers. But, after all, the law which relates effort to satisfaction is a 'natural' law, which, finding its simplest expression in the physical fact that a man cannot eat and digest a good dinner unless he has made some output of physical energy in exercise, penetrates in some unseen way the whole region of consumption, denying satisfaction that is not compensated by some corresponding personal effort. This 'natural' law finds an economical expression in the fact that an attempt to be a very large consumer and a very small producer in the long run defeats itself, and, when it cannot by force of social circumstances stimulate production, it limits consumption.

This, interpreted into simple language, means that a man who draws a large income without working for it cannot and does not spend it. This will seem to some a strange assertion, at variance with the lavish luxury imputed to and practised by many members of the upper unemployed class, but it is literally true. Though the bulk of the painful abstinence and thrift in our modern communities is practised by the working and poorer trading and professional classes, the bulk of the 'saving' is effected by the wealthy. The accumulated savings of the manual workers of the country, even if we place to their account the whole of the £200,000,000, which in round figures represents the total capital of savings banks, trade unions, benefit, building, co-operative and mutual societies of every kind, does not amount to more than 2 per cent of the total accumulated wealth of the country. Although we have no means of exactly apportioning the ownership of capital value among the various classes of the community, we know that a large proportion represents the accumulation of the surplus income of the wealthy classes after their wholesome and even their luxurious wants are satisfied. The portentous growth of the capital wielded by a few successful business men in America affords an extreme case of the self-accumulative power of capital. There are on both sides of the Atlantic a small number of families whose most profuse expenditure yet leaves an enormous surplus income to accumulate. 'I can do nothing with my income,' said Mr J. J. Astor, 'but buy more land, build more houses, and lend money on mortgage. In short, I am found with the necessaries of life, and more than that I cannot get out of my money.' The absorption of interest and the specialisation of activities required for the successful practice of money-making are commonly such as to leave undeveloped or to disable the capacities for spending even upon the lower planes of material enjoyment. Hence 'we see as a rule that men who have made money in business are not great spenders of it in the present, and have often no other notion of spending it than to make new businesses to bring them in future returns' [Dr Bonar, *Philosophy and Political Economy*, p. 222].

Turning from these leviathans to the merely wealthy classes, we find most of them living well within their incomes and furnishing large sums for investment. It would, I think, be pretty safe to conclude that a very large percentage of incomes received as rents and interest are not used for current expenditure, but are left to grow by compound interest. Since these elements of income are not earned by present efforts, they are not, as a rule, required to satisfy present desires.

In thus stating my position, I do not wish to be understood as denying the utility or even the 'productive power' of that abstinence which may rightly rank as 'present effort' in the case of the savings of less wealthy members of the community. My point is simply this, that a large proportion of 'new capital' does not represent 'saving' due to painful abstinence, careful postponement of present to future use, but represents the merely automatic accumulation of an idle surplus of income after all genuine and wholesome needs are fully satisfied. Where incomes flow in, yielding a power of consumption wholly disproportionate to the output of personal effort, a natural tendency to 'save' is manifested, which is sharply distinguishable from the reasonable 'saving' made out of legitimate earnings. It is this automatic 'saving' which upsets the balance

109

between consumption and producing-power, and which from the social standpoint may be classed as 'oversaving'. No class of men whose 'savings' are made out of their hard-won earnings is likely to oversave, for each unit of 'capital' will represent a real want, a piece of legitimate consumption deferred. But where 'savings' represent the top portion of large incomes, drawn from economic rents of land, profits of speculation, high interest of capital derived from monopolies, no natural limit is set upon the amount which is saved.

Excess of Capital a Result of 'Unearned' Incomes

If this reasoning is correct, the over-capitalisation which is found to exist is identified with those elements of individual incomes which are unearned in the sense that their 'incoming' is not attended by any corresponding 'outgoing' of effort on the part of the recipient. This is no doubt largely an *a priori* argument, but it contains the only hypothesis which serves to explain the facts. This hypothesis may be formally summarised in the following terms. Modern machinery and methods of production have brought about a vast and continuous increase in the power of producing wealth: the rate of consumption has likewise risen, but less rapidly. This discrepancy in the pace of progress is manifested in the existence of a permanent surplus of producing-power – i.e. though every producing-power implies the existence of a corresponding consuming-power the latter is not fully utilised. This failure to fully utilise consuming-power is due to the fact that much of it is owned by those who, having already satisfied all their strong present desires, have no adequate motive for utilising it in the present, and therefore allow it to accumulate.

The Remedy Lies in a Reformed Distribution of Consuming Power

This is the only rationale of the simultaneous unemployment of labour, land, and capital which forms the problem of the 'unemployed'. Underconsumption is the economic cause of unemployment. The only remedy, therefore, which goes to the root of the evil is a raising of the standard of consumption to the point which shall fully utilise the producing-power, after making due allowance for such present 'saving' as is economically needed to provide for further increase of consumption in the future. If the analysis of causes in the last chapter is correct, this remedy can only be made operative by a line of policy which shall affect the ownership of increased consuming-power.

Unfortunately this last conclusion was not admitted by economic writers whose diagnosis of trade-disease was in close accord with that taken here. The brilliant analysis of Malthus in particular was never rebutted, but it could be disregarded safely by the economists of his day, because he used it in defence of the luxury of the classes. Malthus saw that the oversaving of the wealthy was the direct economic force which kept trade back. His remedy was an increase of luxurious expenditure. But this, even were it otherwise desirable, is wholly impracticable. We have seen that the motives which induce the wealthy to withhold the present use of consuming-power are natural and necessary. A piece of academic advice, unbacked by any economic force, is absolutely futile. The owners of 'unearned' elements of income, as we see, *must* accumulate capital which from the social standpoint is excess. A more natural distribution of consuming-power, under which the power to consume shall be accompanied by the desire to consume – not, as now, severed from it – is the only possible remedial policy.

Lines of Social Policy. Taxation of 'Unearned' Income

Towards this policy, parties of social progress are slowly gravitating. Unfortunately their path is lighted by no clear intellectual conceptions, and they move with hesitant, uneven, staggering steps, often by circuitous routes, along a road which should be recognised as clear, straight, and fairly smooth. The policy of progressive consumption has two direct lines of advance which may here be briefly indicated.

The surplus of consuming-power in the hands of the rich may be 'unearned' by its owners, but it is not, for all that, 'unearned'. Part of it – for example, the growing value of town lands – is earned by public effort, and forms a property designed for public consumption in the support of wholesome public life.

Various Forms of 'Social Property' Amenable to Taxation

'It certainly is true that any increase in the rental value or selling value of land is due, not to the exertions and sacrifices of the owners of the land, but to the exertions and sacrifices of the community. It is certainly true that economic rent tends to increase with the growth of wealth and population, and that thus a larger and larger share of the product of industry tends to pass into the hands of the owners of land, not because they have done more for society, but because society has greater need of that which they control' [Professor Francis Walker, *First Lessons in Political Economy*]. Here then is indicated a large property 'earned' by the work of the community which might be usefully consumed by the community. But these land values by no means exhaust and probably do not form the largest portion of that annual property directly created by public effort or the pressure of public needs. Part of the profits of all monopolies or protected businesses and of many businesses not formally protected but assisted by some dependence upon land, some advantage of position or vicinity to markets, is clearly due to the same social causes as are operative in the direct growth of land values. Profits obtained from various branches of local services, many departments of the transport trades and of retail distribution are often enhanced by this extraneous support. In some cases the profits which thus arise go to swell rent, as is largely the case with the profits of shops in advantageous positions, in other cases sufficient competition, direct or indirect, may survive to enable the consuming public to reap the advantage in lower prices. But anyone who goes over the most remunerative kinds of industry will find that many of these derive their character from dependence upon natural or legal monopoly. The strong position of such a trade as brewing is explained by a combination of natural and legal monopoly. In all such trades elements of profits are apt to emerge which are not the necessary interest upon capital, nor results of skill in production or enterprise in management, but are simply due to a power of monopoly or in other words to the pressure of public needs. Even where no direct assistance is derived from natural or legal monopoly, a combination of capital strong enough to crush out or keep down effective competition may obtain so strong a control of the market through a 'ring', a 'syndicate', 'trust', or other business structure, as to exercise a similar power of taxing the public for its private profit. All this body of rents and profits represents a property made by public efforts and needs which might, wherever it can be discovered, legitimately pass into the public possession.

In many cases it may be difficult, in some perhaps impossible, to discriminate economic rents and monopoly profits from those growths of value which are needed for the maintenance of the private effort and enterprise which co-operated to produce them. But economic analysis discloses the fact that there does exist a large fund of 'unearned' incomes, the private ownership of which is justified neither by natural 'right' nor by expediency, which could economically be taken by the public and used for public purposes. These unearned elements of income are not needed to induce the application of individual effort in those who at present own them; they are needed for the improvement and enlargement of public life.

Our civic and, in general, our public life, is narrow, meagre, inefficient, and undignified in comparison with what it ought to be, if the wealth due to public effort was wisely and economically laid out in the public service. Taxation, or State assumption on equitable terms, of properties whose increasing values are due to public activity and public need, to be administered in the supply of common wants and the enrichment of the common life, is likely to be of material assistance in raising the general standard of consumption. The adoption of progressive taxation of accumulated wealth through the Death Duties is based on an instinctive recognition that this assertion of a public claim is both just and expedient. The same is true of the progressive income tax, so adjusted as to secure for purposes of public use that portion of the income of the well-to-do which otherwise would materially assist to swell the excess of accumulated forms of capital.

The direct and progressive taxation of ground rents and values, so far as they can be ascertained, would accord with this policy. The economist, while insisting upon the necessity of securing to all private investors whose 'saving' is needed to furnish capital, the market price of such saving, i.e. the minimum interest required to draw sufficient capital into the several channels of production, would sanction the taxation of dividends which exceeded that necessary limit. The application of this purely economic principle would of course be liable to be overruled by considerations of practical politics. At present many elements of 'unearned' income accrue in the course of private business which cannot be assessed, and even in the case of public companies, the possibility of evading heavy taxation by watering stock, distributing bonuses and by other means of concealing profits, would have to be considered by statesmen guided by an economic policy. Economists will declare that these elements of income are a legitimate object of taxation wherever they can be reached, in that they are the result of public activities and public needs. How far and in what ways they can best be reached are questions for politics as distinguished from economics.

These practical qualifications do not, however, impair the value of the light which economic analysis throws upon the paths of the progressive policy.

If the public mind once firmly fastens on the economic principle that taxation, in whatever way imposed, tends to settle on the economic rent of land, high profits of monopolies and other 'unearned' elements of individual income, it is likely that the assumption of public property by means of progressive taxation will be more rapid and more systematic than hitherto. [This tendency is of course in many instances thwarted or retarded by the effect of leases and other contracts and by various forms of friction which impede the strictly 'economic' settlement of taxation here indicated, imposing for a time new burdens upon those who are ill able to bear them. The tendency, however, of practical politicians is to over-estimate the length of time taken by a tax to settle on rents.]

Working-Class Movement for Higher Wages

The other line of advance is the organised pressure of the working classes for an increasing proportion of the national income, which they will use in raising their standard of consumption. By effective trade organisation they may raise wages, by co-operation of consumers they may expend their wages more economically, by organised use of the franchise they may secure such equality of educational and economic opportunities as will remove or abate the dangers of ignorance and destitution, which at present bar the progress of the rear-guard of labour. The low rate of interest and profits in many trades is no sufficient barrier to the wisely regulated pressure of trade-organisations for higher wages. Setting aside all consideration of the greater efficiency of higher paid labour, we cannot fail to see that the effective demand for higher wages tends like a tax to settle on unearned elements of income. A rise of wages, in a trade where profits lie at a minimum, tends to lower rents, or, in default of rent, by raising prices, falls upon those consumers whose money incomes will not be affected by a rise of prices.

Increased Consumption Gives Validity to Increased Saving

Let it be clearly understood that this policy of increased consumption by the public and by the working classes of the country contains no repudiation either of the principle or the practice of saving. On the contrary, each rise of general consumption signifies, not merely an increased employment of labour, but of capital as well. A rise in the general standard of consumption is a demand for more saving and it alone can give economic validity to more saving, by enabling it to assist in the satisfaction of increased needs. The very gist of our analysis lay in the disclosure that every increase of effective saving was dependent upon an increase of consumption.

It is in a country where new-felt needs are constantly clamouring for satisfaction, where men spend freely, as in the United States, that the growth of valid forms of capital is largest.

A Summary of the 'High Consumption' Policy

Thus the recognition of 'unemployment' as the labour aspect of a wider economic problem – viz., the excess of productive power over the requirements of current consumption, supplies us for the first time with a sound practical standard by which to test the worth of proposed remedies and palliatives.

It furnishes a strong economic justification for the chief lines of action which modern progressive parties have instinctively taken. The transfer of economic rents and monopoly profits from private owners to the public, whether by taxation of incomes or by direct public assumption of the functions of monopolist industries, is seen to contribute to the enhancement of the aggregate consumption of the community. Similar results attend the well-considered endeavours of working classes, either by direct increase of wages or by increased leisure, to increase the proportion of the total wealth of the community, which falling to them as wages shall be spent in raising the general standard of working-class consumption.

This Policy Involves No Social Danger

But those who are not willing to admit the existence of any large 'unearned' elements of income, or who fear lest this progressive taxation might encroach too far, are needlessly alarmed. Assuming there existed no large unearned elements of income, so long as there exists any quantity of unutilised producing-power, labour, land, and capital, which is under-employed, it does not seem reasonable to suppose that such taxation imposed upon owners of land and capital will reduce the aggregate income derived from such ownership. For since the direct result of this taxation is to increase the general consumption, such increase must in the nature of the case give increased employment to all the requisites of production. Hence it would appear that the quantity of land and capital for which rent, interest, and profit is paid will be larger than before, though the rate of the remuneration for the use of each piece of land or capital may be kept within moderate limits by taxation or by the pressure of labour-organisation. If there were no unearned elements of income they could not be taken by taxation and any attempt to tax socially necessary interest would defeat itself. The complexity of our industrial organism is such as to preclude me from here tracing out the exact *modus operandi* by which a new tax or an effective demand for higher wages must work. But if the principle be once firmly grasped that a demand for commodities is the only ultimate demand for the use of land, labour, and capital, then the existence of 'unemployed' producing-power, is proof that increased consumption is possible without a reduction in the present income of any class of the community. The legitimacy of a 'progressive' consumptive policy is not, therefore, dependent upon a theory of 'economic monopolies', but has a separate justification.

116

3.2 The Economics of Distribution (1900) [pp. 309–15, 334–5]

Turning next to marginal and differential rents, it is convenient first to deal with the element in marginal rents called 'forced gain'. These forced gains issue, as our analysis discloses, in the determination of a price where one of the final pair is able to force the price up, beyond what he would be willing to take, to the utmost that his opponent is willing to give. When markets are small and competition very slight and ineffective, we saw that these forced gains made a large element in prices. Their distinctive character is that they are not earned by any effort of production, but constitute a gratuitous surplus which is obtained by the stronger bargainer. Forming no economic motive to any bargains, they cannot, in theory at any rate, resist taxation. A tax imposed upon them as an element of income could not be transferred to any other element of income.

But these 'forced gains', forming, as we have seen, a part of 'marginal rents', enter into the prices of commodities as portions of the marginal expenses of production. It is therefore important to consider whether a tax levied upon the price of commodities with which they enter will fall upon them.

The commonly accepted theory that taxes upon commodities generally fall upon the consumer is based upon the supposition that their prices only measure the necessary money-costs of producing the portion of supply produced under the least favourable circumstances. Taxes upon commodities, in conformity with this supposition, must normally fall upon the consumer who pays the tax in enhanced prices. Are these 'forced gains' *necessary* money-costs in this sense?

Mill, in his formulation of the principle that a tax upon commodities falls upon the consumer, admits an exception in cases where 'the article is a strict monopoly and at a scarcity price' [*Principles*, p. 515].

'The price in this case being only limited by the desires of the buyer; the sum obtained for the restricted supply being the utmost which the buyers would consent to give rather than go without it; if the treasury intercepts a part of this, the price cannot be further raised to compensate for the tax, and it must be paid from the monopoly profits.' Now it will be evident, if our analysis of price is correct, that every commodity will be sold at a price, which, however subject to the keenest competition in its final retail market, will contain monopoly elements derived from the scarcity of one or other of the requisites of production at different stages. Now a tax imposed upon commodities will not be represented by a rise of prices until these forced gains have been absorbed. We must admit that the prices of these commodities, however keen the competition of retailers in the final stage, are scarcity prices, and are therefore squeezable by taxation to the extent of the forced element they embody . . .

That a tax on the rent of land or upon house-rents containing a large element of land-rent cannot be shifted, but must be borne by the landowner, is a generally received doctrine of economists. It is also frequently admitted that a tax on wages, so far as it relates to the higher grades of mental or educated labour, which enjoy some monopoly of opportunities, must be borne by these classes and cannot be shifted on to other members of the community [Mill, bk V, ch. III, par. 4]. If the same admission is not made regarding interest of monopolies in capital, it is only because these are regarded either as abnormal things or as the products of fortuitous and passing circumstances. There is, however, ample evidence to show that economists are quite aware that certain kinds of taxes upon articles sold at scarcity or monopoly prices will settle upon and be borne by the owners of these monopolies. If, then, we can discover similar elements of unnecessary gain inherent in all prices, we shall recognise a large surplus which is represented in prices and which forms a fund upon which taxation must naturally settle.

The conclusion suggested by this kind of reasoning is that a tax imposed upon any class of commodities will percolate through the various channels of production, will be rejected from all necessary or subsistence payments of capital and labour, and will, either directly or through the agency of consumers, settle upon 'forced gains' or unearned income . . .

If this analysis be correct, the practical importance of its conclusions is very great. By indicating the existence of a vast 'surplus' of rents analogous to the economic rent of land in its taxability, it strengthens immensely the economic means of social progress. By exploding two fallacious notions, that taxes are paid by the poorer classes of the working population, and that high taxation is injurious to trade, our analysis removes chief barriers to that increase of taxation and of wise public expenditure which are essential to a sound progressive social policy.

3.3   The Industrial System (1909)   [pp. 39–55]

Spending and Saving

(1) In any series of processes directly or indirectly producing any class of goods, a quantitative relation must subsist between the capital and labour employed in the several processes; also between the rate of production and the rate of consumption, or withdrawal. This rule will also hold of industry as a whole. (2) In a stationary society the money spent by consumers, passing up the industrial stream, stimulates the continuous processes of production and furnishes all money incomes. The real income consists of commodities and services, which are consumed as fast as they are produced. (3) In a progressive society some money-income must be saved, i.e. applied to buy more new capital-goods. Saving is a stimulation of certain parts of the industrial system in preparation for enhanced spending and consumption. Individual saving need not cause increase of productive capital, social saving must. (4) There exists at any time an economically right ratio of saving to spending, having regard to the probable growth of future consumption and the changes in industrial arts. This right adjustment may be disturbed by overspending or oversaving.

(1) Our shoe operative or shop assistant expanding his area of knowledge from his two standpoints of producer and consumer, has got a comprehensive view of the industrial system in the world as a great complex organised grouping of trades engaged in converting the raw materials and powers of Nature into commodities for the use of man. He will distinguish a main stream of processes, extractive, manufacturing, commercial, along which these raw materials constantly flow towards consumption, and the number of tributaries which continually feed the processes along the main stream, with the plant and other means which enable them to do this work of forwarding the production of commodities. At each point of production along the main stream and along the tributaries he will see a cluster of trades, each composed of a group of businesses whose structure is built of units of capital, labour, land,

119

and management. So far as this system is working economically it seems evident that there will be a definite relation between the quantity of the capital, labour, and other factors at each of the various processes, both in the main stream and along the tributaries.

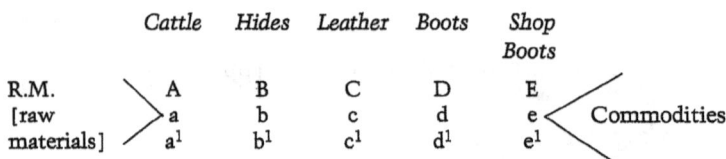

	Cattle	Hides	Leather	Boots	Shop Boots	
R.M.	A	B	C	D	E	
[raw	a	b	c	d	e	Commodities
materials]	a^1	b^1	c^1	d^1	e^1	

Taking the section of industry concerned with production of boots, we shall recognise that some sort of definite quantitative relations must be maintained between the trades along the main series of processes A, B, C, D, E, i.e. there must be some proportion between the rate at which cattle are converted into hides, hides into leather, leather into boots, and boots into consumers' commodities. Shop boots at E cannot be handed over the counter to consumers at a faster rate than the capital and labour at A, B, C, D respectively permits them to be forwarded; nor can hides and leather continue to be produced at a faster pace than boot shops will receive them for supplying customers.

In fact, it is quite evident that if we have a 'system' at all, that system must involve a definite proportion between the quantity of capital, labour, and other factors employed at the several processes of converting cattle into boots.

Confining ourselves, for convenience, to Capital and Labour, we shall say then that the quantity of employment of Capital and Labour at the points A, B, C, D, E will be mutually inter-dependent. It will be equally evident that what applies to the trades in the main current will also apply to the tributaries which supply the plant, machinery, etc., to the main processes. So the quantity of capital and labour employed at a and a^1 will be directly determined by the quantity employed at A, that employed at b and b^1 by the quantity employed at B, and so on, so that the quantitative relation subsisting between the main processes will apply likewise to the subsidiary processes, all the trades directly and indirectly concerned with making boots having their sizes, or their quantity of employment of capital and labour, determined by one another.

Now what holds of the series of boot-making trades will hold equally of bread-making or shirt-making, or of trades in general. Removing, then, our special application to boots, we shall assert the general truth that in the system of industry there will be at any given time a definite relation between the quantity of capital and labour employed in the various sorts of work, extractive, manufacturing, transport, mercantile, retail trade, so far as the system is operating economically. If we take either the most general or the most particular view of industry, we shall recognise that the 'system' involves a delicate provision of adjustment between the amount of energy employed at the several points and between the quantity of the instruments of production giving out this energy.

Applying to general industry our simplified diagram—

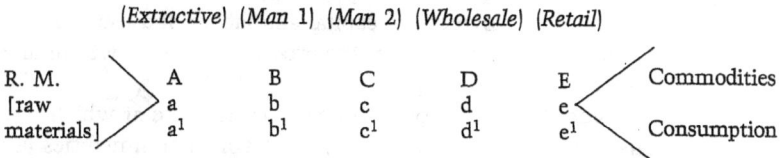

	(*Extractive*)	(*Man* 1)	(*Man* 2)	(*Wholesale*)	(*Retail*)	
R. M.	A	B	C	D	E	Commodities
[raw	a	b	c	d	e	
materials]	a^1	b^1	c^1	d^1	e^1	Consumption

we should first perceive that as the trade groups placed respectively at A, B, C, D, E, and at a, a^1, b, b^1, etc., were all engaged in carrying R. M. (materials) towards consumption, there must be a definite proportion between the work done at these several points and, therefore, between the capital and labour, etc., engaged in doing it.

We should next recognise that the amount of this productive energy given out, both as an aggregate and as apportioned between the several processes, will appear to be directly determined, on the one hand, by the rate at which raw materials (R. M.) are put in at one end of the stream; on the other hand, by the rate at which they are taken out as commodities by consumers at the other end.

A slackening of the rate at which raw materials enter the stream at the source will appear to involve a corresponding slackening of industry (a reduction of employment of capital and labour) at each process of production, and also a corresponding reduction of the pace at which commodities flow out into consumption: a quickening of the inflow of the raw materials will appear to cause a corresponding quickening of industry, for more raw materials cannot continue to enter the stream of production than are capable of being carried forward down the stream. On the other hand, a slackening of the pace of consumption (of the rate at which commodities are withdrawn from the end of the stream) would seem equally to involve a slackening of every process of production, for any attempt to maintain at any point the former pace of production would appear to cause congestion and stoppage: a quickening of the pace of consumption (a more rapid withdrawal of commodities) must involve an increase in the rate of production, for without such increase of the rate of production no increased rate of consumption is possible.

If now we regard the entrance of raw materials into the industrial system as the first stage in production, we shall come to the conclusion that, pooling together all the productive processes, there must be a definite quantitative relation between the rate of production and the rate of consumption, or, in other words, between the quantity of employment of capital and labour and the quantity of commodities withdrawn from the productive stream within any given time.

Recognising this fixed proportion between the rate at which raw materials enter the stream and the rate at which commodities are drawn out, we need not yet concern ourselves with the question how far the one or the other determines or regulates the flow of industry. The law of gravitation, according to which water flows from the high lands towards the sea, seems to exhibit a pushing force as we watch the stream from below, a pulling force as we watch from above. So with the push and pull of the industrial process.

(2) Before we consider what it is that makes the industrial system work, what that energy of push and pull is that corresponds to gravitation in a stream, we need to look a little nearer at the object which this system seems to have set before it, the result or product of all its activity.

As this object for the individual 'producer' is said to be his 'income', so we may say that the *prima facie* object of industry is to produce an income for the industrial society.

Now what is that income? We are accustomed to express income in money, but we are also familiar with the notion that real income is what that money will buy, and in considering the income of industrial society we must begin with this real income. What will be the real income which the industrial system yields? The answer to this question will depend upon our concept of the industrial society. If that society were in an absolutely stationary condition, with a fixed population, fixed wants and fixed methods of industry, the income for each year would consist in the quantity of commodities (goods and services) produced for consumption and handed over to consumers during the year. This, of course, does not mean that all the industrial energy expended that year was represented in these consumption goods, for some industrial energy must go into replacement of plant or provision against wear and tear. This provision against wear and tear does not, however, rank as income, either from the standpoint of social or of individual production. In our fixed or static society all productive energy, after provision for wear and tear fund, would be represented by consumption goods and services. The total output of commodities would be identical with the income: the new boots, loaves, shirts, doctoring, musical performances, governmental care, etc., produced during the year would constitute the real income for the year.

Although there is no real society living in a 'static' condition, it is convenient to examine how such an industrial system would work. We should perceive a constant even flow of raw materials entering the stream of industry, passing through the various processes and emerging as commodities, and the same even flow would take place down the tributary streams engaged in maintaining the plant and other fixed capital in the several processes.

So far we have spoken of the movement of materials and goods as a 'flow', without seeking more closely an explanation of 'how' materials pass from one stage of production to the next stage, and finally pass from retail shopkeepers to consumers.

If we are to retain the 'flow' metaphor, we must supplement our view of the industrial movement by introducing another 'flow' which moves in a reverse direction to the flow of goods. This is the 'flow' or circulation of money. What money is we need not here pause to ask: we may treat anything as money the payment of which enables him who pays to buy what he requires for consumption or for some service of production. Now if, turning to our stream of boot-producing processes, we ask *how* hides pass from the tanner's possession into that of the shoe manufacturer's, we perceive at once that it is because money passes from the shoe manufacturer to the tanner: so with the movement of shoes from the manufacturer to the shop of the merchant, it is attended by a corresponding passage of money the opposite way.

In the stable industrial society we are investigating, it is easy to see how the two streams, the goods flowing from raw materials to commodities, the money flowing from the consumers up the series of industrial processes, inter-act and correspond. The raw material gathers utility, i.e. it reaches a shape or a place where it is nearer towards satisfying some human want than in its earlier shape or place, at each stage in production by the operation of the capital and labour which act upon it, until at the end it takes the finished form of a commodity.

Now follow the course taken by the money which is paid for this commodity, boots or loaves, or other shop goods. The consumer, in buying the commodity, hands over in return a sum of money, the price. What does the shopkeeper at E do with this money? With part of it he defrays the expenses of shopkeeping, he pays his rent, expenses, the wages of his shop assistants, establishment, the interest on his borrowed capital, profits or earnings of management to himself. This disposes of a certain fraction of the money. The rest he passes on to the wholesale merchant at D, or the manufacturer at C, in payment for more goods to replace the boots or shirts he has sold, or more commonly to meet a bill in payment for goods previously received. In fact, then, the merchant who has advanced on credit the boots or flour which the retailer has sold to customers receives a part of the money paid by the customers, handed over to him by the retailer so as to maintain his stock. So a part of the money paid to the retailer at E goes to maintain in productive work the retail capital and labour, etc., the rest is passed on to the merchant at D, stimulating by its passage the flow of goods from the merchant to the retailer. Now the wholesale merchant or importer of shoes or shirts, when he has received the money from the retailer in demand for more shoes or flour, will use this money, partly to defray his current expenses, rent, wages, profit, etc., partly to replenish and maintain his stock by sending more orders to the manufacturer of shoes or shirts at C. Whether he actually pays over the money when he sends the order or receives the goods, or whether he accepts a bill, does not affect the substance of the act: part of the money which, starting from the purse of the consumer, reached him through the retailer, is used to pay the manufacturer for a fresh supply of shoes or shirts. Here, too, the flow of the money from the merchant to the maker (D to C) is the means of driving goods to pass from maker to merchant (C to D). The shoe manufacturer or shirt-maker makes a similar use of the part of the price of shoes or shirts that reaches him, in paying his various expenses and in buying a fresh stock of raw materials, leather or cotton cloth, from the manufacturer of those goods at B. These latter, in their turn, after paying their expenses of production, apply the money thus received in buying a fresh stock of hides or cotton from farmers or growers at A, which latter use the money in maintaining the productive processes by which they 'extract' their raw material (cattle or cotton) from Nature. If we looked a little closer at the payments made at each stage under the head of 'expenses', we should find that some of it went to repair and replace buildings, machinery, and other forms of 'capital' required to assist production, and involved payments to machine-makers and others, who are represented in our diagram by the letters a, b, c, d, e. These makers, as we saw, stand at the head of a series of tributary trades whose flow joins the main current at A, B, C, D, E. A fraction of the consumer's money flows into each of these tributary channels, and causes an onward flow of raw materials towards new finished plant and machinery, corresponding to the flow of goods along the main channel of industry. This illustration makes it evident that in the stationary society we are examining the money paid over the retail counter by the consumer in payment for commodities is the actual source of all money-incomes received throughout the industrial system by the owners of capital, labour, land, etc., and that its flow upward through the main and tributary channels of industry is the stimulus to each movement by which raw materials and goods are carried down the stream towards consumption.

A portion of the money paid over the retail counter is then deposited at each stage in payments to owners of labour, capital, land there employed, then the rest flows on to the next stage. These payments are the direct industrial stimuli of the continued production; though in form they represent work already done by some factor, they are in fact material conditions and moral inducements to the owners of labour, capital, and land, to apply these factors in further industrial work. The money thus paid in wages to labour, expended in food, etc., replaces the labour-power that has been depleted, and furnishes a new supply of productive energy: though paid for work already done, this payment evokes further work by supporting the conviction that this work also will in due course receive payment. So with the owner of capital, the money paid him for the past service rendered by his capital goes partly to replace its wear and tear, partly to induce him to continue its industrial employment. The same holds likewise of the landowner's rent. [The question of the necessity of these payments remains for later and more appropriate discussion. It is not germane to the present inquiry.]

The money-income received by any person engaged at any point in the industrial process as worker, capitalist, landowner is composed of these payments made to him for single uses of some factor of production, and is seen to come out of a fund which flows from the consumer. The total money-income of this industrial community would in this case be equivalent to the aggregate of money expended by consumers for commodities which would be distributed, as we see, throughout the industrial world in payments for the use of labour, capital, and land so as to maintain these factors and keep them in productive operation. The real income of the community would consist of the aggregate of commodities which passed into the hands of the consumers, or, in other words, the goods purchased for consumption by the recipients of the money-incomes.

The meaning of income is, however, somewhat confused by other circumstances which require notice. So far we have treated the industrial mechanism as engaged in producing material commodities only. But political economy is concerned with all forms of marketable wealth, services as well as material wares. Now the production and consumption of services differ in no essential point, so far as the structure and working of industry is concerned, from the production and consumption of material goods.

If I pay half a crown to attend a lecture or 5s. for a doctor's advice, these payments must be treated as equivalent to the payments of another half-crown for the text book I use at the lecture, and of another 5s. which I pay to a chemist for the drugs the doctor orders me to take. Just as there exists a series of industries engaged in forwarding the production of books and drugs, there exists a series of processes engaged in putting into the lecture and the doctor the serviceable information which is bought from them. Schools and colleges, laboratories, hospitals, and work of professional research are all processes which go to produce the skilled information that is sold, and though the continuity of the chain of productive processes is less visible, and in some regards less regular, it is there, and is maintained from the payments for retail services. Though the individual fee you pay a doctor or a lawyer cannot often be traced back in distribution to the earlier stages of production of medical and legal skill, it is none the less true that a demand for medical advice is a demand for medical schools, hospitals, and scientific research, and that any increase of expenditure on litigation tends to swell the profession, and to react along the paths of professional and general education. Moreover, it must be remembered that a demand for services is not only a demand for the teaching of their forms of skill, but for various material instruments subsidiary to these services: offices, books, surgical instruments, and other tools of the craft are 'demanded' by the demand for professional services. The real income of a nation will, therefore, include all professional and other personal services valued, as material commodities are valued, according to their selling prices. So, too, in reckoning the money-income of the nation we shall reckon the incomes of professional men, officials, domestic servants, etc., not as derived from or paid out of the incomes of those who employ them, but as directly representing non-material wealth produced by them which forms part of the real income of the nation. It may seem a hard saying, but a gamekeeper or a secretary of state must be considered to produce real wealth in the preservation of game or of empire, which is the equivalent of the salary they respectively receive. The questions whether such work is socially desirable or is overpaid are entirely irrelevant in such an analysis.

A scientific theory which includes, under wealth, all marketable things, must include all paid services in this national income, and the payment for them as independent items of the money-income of the nation.

Our diagram of industry, with its main and subsidiary streams of production, its statements of the quantitative relations between the factors of production and the rate of consumption, will be just as applicable to the production and consumption of non-material as of material wealth, except that material factors of land and capital play a smaller and a less direct part in the processes of production or preparation of most saleable services, and that the series of processes of production may be shorter and less regular.

The raw material of some rude human faculty is selected from a mass of human faculties, trained, informed, and adapted to the rendering of some special service in a profession, art, or office, by the application of a carefully ordered machinery of education employing various forms of intellectual labour wielding material tools of instruction: the result of these processes is to refine a raw human capacity of small utility and value into a powerful and finely serviceable capacity with high market value. So far as the intellectual, and even the moral and spiritual, activities of man are bought and sold, the laws of their production and consumption do not differ from those of material goods as regards the application of these fundamental laws.

If we are dealing with a community fixed in its numbers and its modes, alike of production and consumption – an absolutely stable industrial society – our simple analysis of production and consumption would suffice. The whole of the money-income paid as rent, profits, wages, etc., to members of the society would be spent in demanding commodities for personal consumption.

The net real income of the community would consist of the aggregate of the finished commodities and services produced and consumed in the year, the net money-income of the money values which these commodities and services represented. The prices which described their money values would include payments made to the owners of capital and labour who replaced the waste of fixed capital and land. Thus the two currents, the stream of production from raw materials to commodities, and the reverse flow of money from the consumer down the channels of production, would maintain a regular amount of production and consumption. In such an industrial society as we have been considering, statical in population, in the arts of production and in standard of consumption, the entire real income would be consumed in material commodities and services, and the entire money-income of all its members would be spent in paying for them. No saving would be necessary or possible.

(3) But this is not the actual industrial system in which our inquiring workman will find himself living. The industrial community, whether he regards it as a nation, or more accurately as the industrial world, must be regarded not as stationary but as changing, and the change is, on the whole, a growth. The structure and working of the actual industrial system must take account of growth of population, a rising standard of consumption and improved economies in the arts of production.

These changes involve some important modifications in our plan of the industrial system. If provision is to be made for commodities to meet the growing needs of an increasing population, the industrial system must be enabled to set up along all its productive channels an increased quantity of the instruments of production; before a larger variety of shop goods can be sold at a faster pace over the retail counter to an increasing number of customers, more capital and labour must previously have been set in operation at each of the processes of production.

Now in the modern industrial world there is only one way of bringing this about. The whole money-income of the community must not be expended in buying finished commodities at the end of the industrial process for consumption; some of it instead must be expended in paying workers to make and set up more plant, machinery, etc., than existed before at the various points in the main stream and the tributaries of production, and to use this increased capital to work up raw materials in the different productive processes, so as to be able to put into the shops of retailers a larger flow of commodities to be sold by them to consumers.

So whereas in a stable industrial society all the money-income received for productive services by capitalists, labourers, land-owners, etc., was applied at E in purchase of consumption goods, in a progressive society some of it will be applied at A, B, C, and D, and down the tributary channels a, a^1, b, b^1, etc., to set up new instruments of production and to work them. In the stable society the money which circulated through the industrial system, stimulating productive activity at each point, and causing the movement of goods down the stream of industry, was inserted entirely at the end of the industrial process in purchase of retail goods. In the actual progressive society some of this money is inserted directly at the different points of production, and serves to stimulate production at these points beyond the rate needed to maintain the former activity of production.

How it operates is quite clear. If we suppose the stable society illustrated in our diagram to become progressive, saving so as to provide for increased consumption in the future, what will happen is this. Some of the money which was regularly applied at E in bringing retail goods will no longer be applied there; and the retailers at E, having less custom, will reduce, as far as they can, their expenses, employing less capital and labour, etc., and handing on less money to wholesale merchants in fresh orders. The merchants at D, finding their business similarly slack, will also curtail expenses and reduce their orders from makers; and so the reduction of spending at E will cause a general slowing down of all the industrial processes, both along the main stream and down the tributaries. This is what happens as the direct effect of a reduction of spending upon commodities. But, as we have recognised, saving (as distinct from hoarding) does not mean a refusal to apply the money stimulus, but only a refusal to apply it at the retail stage in 'demand' for commodities. The 'saving' persons who reduce the 'demand' for commodities apply the same quantity of 'demand' at various interim points in the industrial process. They pay more money for developing new mines, they place contracts for putting up more mills and workshops, they give more orders for machinery. In other words, instead of applying all their money at E, they apply some of it directly at A, B, or C, so as to set up more forms of plant, etc., at these points in production.

The money thus applied at A, B, or C not only stimulates their increased activity of capital and labour, but some of it is passed on to the trades on the tributaries, a, a^1, b, b^1, etc., stimulating industry there. If the saving be taken as a general process, it will flow in regular proportions through the building, machinery-making, and other trades, which set up plant, and the stimulus will then pass through the early processes of the extractive and manufacturing industries, so that a fuller flow of raw materials than before will begin to pass down the main stream towards the consumer.

The first effect of saving, which alone concerns us just now, is thus seen to be a slackening of the former even circulation of money and stimulation of industrial energy, and a substitution of an enhanced circulation and stimulation in certain parts of the industrial system in preparation for a general increased flow of productive energy towards commodities.

In the stable society the only productive energy applied to making the forms of capital was confined to providing against wear and tear, so as to maintain the existing stock of capital, and this is not saving. In the progressive society productive energy is applied to making more forms of capital, setting up more mills, foundries, workshops, machines, and passing through them larger quantities of raw materials than before: this is saving.

Spending means buying commodities with income; saving means

buying productive goods or instruments with income. Spending causes more commodities to be produced; saving causes more forms of capital to be produced.

The sort of stimulus applied by spending and by saving is the same: in each case the application of the money circulating down the series of productive processes from the point where it is applied sets up or maintains industrial activity in all the preceding processes, and causes material to flow from one stage of production to another. In spending, however, the net result is to withdraw some commodities from the industrial system for consumption, replacing what was withdrawn by another set of similar commodities, so that the general stream of industry remains as before: in saving, the net result is to add some new forms of capital (buildings, machines, material, goods), leaving the productive apparatus of the system larger than before in the various processes of industry, and so stimulating production, not from the end of the whole process, but from various interim points. Spending means buying consumption goods; saving means buying production goods.

That all saving implies demand for creation of more forms of fixed or circulating capital is not at first obvious. From the standpoint of the individual who saves, his action consists in a refusal to demand commodities, a not-spending, or, more strictly, a postponement of spending. In primitive industrial societies, or in disturbed conditions of more advanced societies, much refusal to spend takes the form of hoarding money. Though hoarding may be fully justified as an individual precaution, its effect in industry as compared with spending is to check the flow of the industrial stream, causing a smaller employment of capital, labour, and land than would be afforded by the spending of the money that was hoarded. An increase of hoarding inevitably tends to depress trade, though the subsequent spending of hoarded treasure will ultimately redress the balance by affording a corresponding stimulus.

In modern industrial societies, however, hoarding is abnormal. A person who, instead of spending, saves, invests his savings. Now there are two ways in which he may invest his savings. He may hand over the money to someone who wishes to spend it on commodities, buying property which the other sells, or loaning it on mortgage. This is the saving effected when a money-lender advances money to a spendthrift. In this case A, not wishing to spend himself, simply transfers for a consideration the power to spend to B, who does wish to spend. Though A saves and invests his saving, no effect is produced upon the total volume of spending or saving: all that has happened is that B spends instead of A, and that some 'capital' which existed before in B's hands now belongs to A.

(This is not quite all, for A does not hand over to B *all* his power of spending which he saves; he keeps back a certain share, say 5 per cent, which he receives as interest. Thus A, who has saved £100 and 'invests' it with spendthrift B, receiving from B a mortgage deed and £5 per annum, really hands over £95 of spending power, which B uses. If A does not save but spends his £5 interest, the total amount of spending is just as much as if A had not 'saved', for B spends £95 and A spends £5 instead of A spending the whole £100.)

Neither 'hoarding' nor this sort of saving makes provision for expansion of production and of consumption in a progressive community. But if, instead of lending money to a spendthrift, A invests it in his own business or in someone else's business, so as to extend industrial operations, what becomes of the money? Though saved, it is nevertheless spent. But instead of being spent in demanding commodities which, when demanded, are destroyed in consumption, it is spent in demanding productive goods, e.g. new mills, machines, warehouses, raw materials, etc., which, when demanded, are not straightway destroyed, but form an addition to the amount of material wealth in the community. Whereas spending means paying capital and labour to produce finished commodities which are immediately withdrawn from the industrial stream and destroyed, saving means paying the same amount of capital and labour to produce additional productive goods (i.e. forms of capital) which are not withdrawn, but remain an addition to the producing power of the community. Such acts of saving employ, directly, just the same amount of capital and labour as if the money were spent on commodities [J. S. Mill, in one of his most confused passages, argued that they employed more], the difference being that in the former case the capital and labour are employed in producing more productive goods, in the latter in producing more consumptive goods.

(4) It is sometimes assumed that any proportion of the income of a community can advantageously be saved. But this is not the case. We saw how in a stable community a fixed proportion was maintained between the amount of productive energy employed at the various processes, and only a given aggregate of capital could be

employed in forwarding the work of turning out the fixed output of commodities.

Of course, this limitation of useful capital no longer holds of a progressive community; a larger amount of saving is continually wanted to supply capital to meet not only the current but the prospective increase of consumption. But, though the limits of saving are made more elastic, they are not entirely cancelled. In a primitive industrial community, however progressive in population and in needs, the quantity of 'saving' that can usefully be done will be restricted by the simple methods of industry in vogue. Where almost all production is by hand labour with simple tools, the limit of saving as compared with spending must remain very narrow.

In the modern capitalist society there is, of course, an enormously extended possibility of socially useful saving. A large proportion of the modern social income can be saved because it is possible to put it into costly forms of capital, the services of which will fructify in the shape of consumption of goods a long time hence: railroads may be made, opening new tracts of the earth in distant lands, new harbours, mining explorations, afforestation, drainage, and other vast public or private enterprises, destined at some distant future to facilitate the production of actual commodities. Such investments may swallow up large masses of new savings. But while it thus might seem that the opportunities of useful saving were infinite, i.e. that any proportion of the current general income could serviceably be saved *provided* that at some distant time society increased correspondingly its rate of consumption, this is not truly the case. Those alterations in the arts of industry which give so much importance to capital applied in various direct and indirect processes of production, while greatly extending the limits of saving as compared with more primitive production, still leave some limits. Two important considerations maintain these limits. In the first place, most forms of new capital, even in this age of elaborated indirect production by machinery, very soon result in promoting an increased flow of finished goods, and unless the proportion of spending to saving were speedily readjusted so as to take off this increased flow by freer spending, at the same time checking the 'saving' which sets up these sorts of capital, the machinery of industry must become congested and clogged by excessive goods and commodities unable to find an exit in consumption. Secondly, the proportion of new saving which can be so applied as to fructify at some far distant date is necessarily small, restricted principally by our inability to forecast far ahead either the needs of coming men or the most economical modes of providing for them.

Though the amount of saving that can take material shape in new railroads, harbours, and other great capitalist enterprises of a foundational character is large in itself, it constitutes a small proportion of the total saving, nor is it capable of indefinite expansion.

The very pace at which mechanical improvements are taking place, the rapidity of shifts of population and of industry, the swift transformation in methods of living, form considerable checks upon the more enduring shapes of capital. It seldom pays to put up a city building timed to last more than a few decades, the feasibility of rail-less locomotion is cutting down railroad investment, manufacturers attribute an ever-shortening life to their most expensive machinery.

The great bulk of capital fructifies in an early increase of commodities, and so the saving embodied in it is only socially useful on condition that an early increase of consumption proportionate to the increased saving takes place.

A little reflection will make it evident that this implies the maintenance of a definite proportion between the aggregate of saving and of spending over a term of years. An individual may, of course, continue to save any proportion of his income: a class of persons, or even a whole nation, may do the same provided they can find other classes or other nations ready to borrow and to spend what they are saving. But the industrial community as a whole cannot save at any given time more than a certain proportion of its income: that proportion is never accurately known, and it is always shifting with changes in the arts of production and consumption, but it imposes as real a limit on the economy of saving for the industrial community to-day as there was for Robinson Crusoe on his island or for a primitive isolated tribe of men before the era of machine production.

If this proportion is exceeded one year it must be curtailed the next, so that over a term of years a real proportion must be maintained between saving and spending. It is only by taking the partial standpoint of an individual or a group of individuals, or some other part of the industrial whole, that it seems plausible to hold that there is no limit to efficacious saving.

Though the proportion of efficacious saving to spending is always slowly changing, at any given time it must rightly be regarded as fixed in the sense that there is an exact proportion of the current income which, in accordance with existing arts of production and existing foresight, is required to set up new capital so as to make provision for the maximum consumption throughout the near future. Any miscalculation or other play of social forces which disturbs this proportion, including either too much saving or too much spending, causes a waste of productive power and a restriction in aggregate consumption.

In a stable society, as we saw, all the income is spent: there is no place for saving. But in a progressive society where the future rate of consumption is to exceed the present, for a larger population with a higher standard of comfort saving is essential. A little saving will only make provision for a slight rise in the volume of consumption; more saving is needed for a larger rise. The right amount of saving out of a given income, i.e. the right proportion of saving, will be determined by the amount of new capital economically needed to furnish a given increase of consumption goods. Over a period of years there will be a rate of saving which will assist to produce the maximum quantity of consumption goods.

Any spending which reduces the rate of saving is over-spending, and involves a waste of general productive power analogous to that which was attributed to over-saving. Over-spending retards the rate of progress in production and consumption of commodities, sacrificing the future to the present. It does not, however, imply 'getting into debt' or 'living upon capital'. These terms are only applicable to the over-spending of individuals, classes, or other parts of the industrial community. The community as a whole cannot get into debt, for there is no 'outside' to borrow from. Nor can it 'live upon its capital', for that, too, implies borrowing. Even if the industrial community became so reckless in its expenditure as not merely to make no 'saving', but to refuse to provide against 'wear and tear' of existing forms of capital, such extravagance could only be momentary; it would be checked at once by the slackened pace at which raw materials and production goods would pass through the processes of industry into the retail shops. It is manifestly impossible for society to spend more than its actual current income, i.e. to take out at the end of the productive process more commodities than flow through the stream of industry. An individual may exceed his current income by his expenditure, a nation may do the same, but the industrial community as a whole cannot do so. Over-spending on the part of the community does not mean spending more than its income: it means a refusal to spend less now, so as to provide for an increased future rate of expenditure.

We saw, then, that just as in a stable society there was a fixed ratio between the quantity of capital and labour at the various points of production, and also between the aggregate of capital and the aggregate of consumption, so in a progressive society there is at any given time a similar ratio.

There exists at the present moment a right proportion between saving and spending in the income of the industrial community, yielding the maximum rate of consumption over such a period of time as is open by reasonable foresight to capitalist investment. Industrial progress, or the economical working of the industrial system, consists largely in the ascertainment of this proportion and the adjustment of industry to it: any disregard or disturbance of this proportion involves industrial waste.

How far these considerations of the limits of saving and spending, strictly applicable only to the industrial world as a whole, can be held to have a valid bearing upon the industrial life of Great Britain or any other single nation, is a question which may be reserved for later discussion.

Thus we recognise that the annual income of industrial society means two things. First, the net yield of goods (capital goods and commodities) and services from processes of industry during the year.

Second, the addition of the money payments made as rent, salaries, wages, and profits to owners of factors of production taking part in industry. This annual income is partly spent, partly saved. Spending signifies a removal from the industrial system of goods and services which are consumed by those who remove them. Saving signifies an increase of capital-forms which remain within the industrial system, representing an increased power of production.

While in any given year (or short period) there is no limit to the proportion of income that may be spent, and no limit to the proportion which may be saved, except as regards expenditure on necessaries of working life, over a longer period of time a quantitative relation exists between spending and saving so as to secure the maximum productivity over the whole period.

The right proportion of saving to spending at any given time depends upon the present condition of the arts of production and consumption, and the probabilities of such changes in modes of work or living as shall provide social utility for new forms of capital within the near or calculable future.

3.4   The Science of Wealth (1911)   [pp. 64–86]

Costs and Surplus

The product of industry, which constitutes the real income of a community, is, as we see, entirely distributed in payments to the owners of labour, land, capital and ability for the use of these factors. These payments made at the several stages of production are 'expenses of production'.

These payments, we recognize, must make provision in a stationary industrial system for the maintenance of the fabric of industry, i.e. the various factors in their existing size and efficiency. In a progressive industrial system, such as that with which we are familiar, they must in addition evoke an increase and an improvement of the fabric. In a stationary system the whole of the payments, which formed the money income of the owners of the factors, would be spent in buying commodities, the retail goods and services turned out by the different series of productive processes. These goods and services when bought would be withdrawn from the industrial system and consumed.

In a progressive system a part of the income of the owners of the factors would be applied not to buy commodities but to buy new plant and other forms of productive goods capital, which when bought would remain as a permanent addition to the structure of industry, representing an increased power of producing commodities.

But if the size and efficiency of the industrial system is to be increased, provision must be made not only for increased size and efficiency of capital but for some corresponding increase in labour and ability. Now this increase of labour and ability is procured by buying consumable goods which by their consumption promote economic efficiency in preference to buying those which do not, i.e.

by what is called 'productive' instead of 'unproductive' expenditure. If saving persons furnish increased or improved machinery of production, the full advantage of their action can only be reaped on condition that the general expenditure upon commodities is such as to provide an increased quantity and an improved quality of labour and ability.

This does not imply that all expenditure on luxuries or upon comforts and amusements which do not make directly for economic efficiency is absolutely wasteful and injurious. For there are other purposes of life besides the economic. But it does imply that the expenditure shall be such as to provide such increase and improvement of labour and ability as shall keep pace with the increase and improvement of the capital structure. (The increased application of land, the other factor, being procured by an application of new capital, e.g. by road-making, does not require separate recognition here.) In an advancing industrial community, then, the income will be applied in three ways. One part will go to costs of maintenance for the several factors, one to costs of increase, and a third to unproductive expenditure. Now each factor of production has its own costs of maintenance. First let us look at labour. The costs of maintenance mean provision of necessaries of life for the various grades of workers, with any further expenditure for keeping up the supply of labour at the existing level of efficiency. This is commonly known as a subsistence wage. It just suffices to enable and induce a worker to keep on working and to bring up a family large enough to supply another worker to take his place when he is done. For various grades and qualities of labour the amount of this subsistence, of course, will differ. There will be some difference for individual workers in every occupation, according with their particular physique and their circumstances. This provision may be regarded as a 'wear and tear' fund, the minimum towards which wages were always supposed to tend according to 'the iron law'.

Where higher elements of skill or intelligence are involved in work, this bare subsistence may rise considerably higher than the mere maintenance of physical life, containing some provision for education, recreation and other forms of expenditure, so far as they are needed to maintain the existing fund of physical and mental energy. Managerial or professional ability may thus, even if we ignore the conventional part of a standard of comfort, require a relatively high salary as pay for bare subsistence.

To this subsistence wage of the human factors must be added a corresponding provision for capital and land. Here an important distinction comes out. The provision for maintenance of labour forms a part, usually the largest part, of Wages. But the payment for the maintenance of capital is not included under interest, nor the payment for maintenance of land under rent. The maintenance of the capital is furnished by a depreciation fund applied to replacing worn-out or obsolete forms of plant, etc. Interest is an additional payment to owners of capital after this depreciation has been met. Similarly in the case of land, the provision for the replacement of productive powers taken out of the land is not rent: a tenant must engage to 'keep up' the land and to pay rent as well. Economic rent, like interest, is a payment over and above the provision for maintenance of the factor of production.

The costs of maintenance of the industrial system consist, then, of (1) a number of subsistence wages and salaries for the various sorts of labour and ability, (2) a number of 'wear and tear' funds for the upkeep of the various sorts of capital and land. These may be considered a first charge upon the industrial product. Unless adequate provision is made for all of them, the system is starved, its fabric is 'let down' and its productive power reduced. Such starvation sometimes occurs, even in countries where upon the whole a high development of industry has been attained. Under a bad mode of tenancy farmers may let down the land. Under the pressure of shareholders for dividends a railway or an industrial company may not make a sufficient payment out of gross profits into the depreciation and insurance funds; or a telephone or tramways business, about to pass under public ownership upon agreed terms, may fail to maintain its plant in full efficiency. Such incidents, however, are abnormal. In general the obvious self-interest of the controllers and managers of industry secures the payment of the costs of maintenance.

If the whole of the industrial product were absorbed in these costs of maintenance there could be no industrial progress. But if there remains some surplus, after this provision has been made, the whole or part of it may be applied to increasing the size or improving the quality of the industrial system. The payments made for this purpose may be called 'costs of progress'. They will consist of the minimum payments needed to call into industrial use the various sorts and quantities of additional labour, land, capital and ability needed for effective co-operation in the enlarged structure of industry. Each of these additions involves the application of an extra stimulus beyond that required to secure the mere maintenance of the existing factors. More or better labour power can only be obtained by the payment of a wage higher than the bare subsistence wage. This 'wage of progressive efficiency' will operate in several ways to increase and improve the supply of labour in any trade to which it is applied, or in the industrial system as a whole. By the higher standard of life which it admits, it will evoke and maintain a better physique and morale among the workers. Better food, housing and clothing will improve the 'home', raise the standard of personal dignity and intelligence for the worker, enable the seeds of higher education to take root and to bear fruit in a better use of money and leisure, and in the development and satisfaction of higher wants. All these improvements of the mind and body of the worker have their economic significance in the larger quantity or better quality of labour power he is enabled and induced to give out. Perhaps the most important direct result is the better care and education of the children, giving them a more favourable start in life and thus raising the efficiency of the next generation. This 'economy of high wages' is, of course, attended by certain wastes, due to individual defects of character or bad customs, which impair the rate of progress and efficiency. But the familiar instance of a quick rise of wages resulting in an increased expenditure on drink need not be regarded as other than a passing and exceptional effect.

Although in more civilized countries a general rise of wages is not now attended by an increase in the birth-rate, nevertheless, by reducing the still high infant mortality, by lengthening the effective working life, and by securing that larger mobility of labour which brings workers from all parts of the world to the place where their work is most productive, it increases the quantity and efficiency of the supply of labour in a progressive industrial system. The amount of income needed to evoke and sustain the enlarged and improved supply will, of course, differ in different industries, countries and conditions of the arts of industry. But these varying wages of progressive efficiency are necessary 'costs of progress'. If the wages of any class of labour, or the salaries of any class of ability, are increased at a pace so rapid that the increase is not absorbed in higher efficiency, or even evokes a smaller or a worse output of energy, as sometimes happens, such payment comes under a different head, to which reference will be made lower down.

We have seen that the payment of interest is not required to maintain the existing fabric of actual capital. [This does not, however, imply that the payment of such interest is illegitimate or inadvisable. It is both legitimate and advisable. For if payment of interest on existing capital were sought to be suspended, it is likely that the owners of the capital would cease to make provision against depreciation, using this fund instead for temporary payment of interest while the plant was being 'let down'.] The depreciation fund suffices for that. But if more or better plant, machinery and other forms of capital are wanted, as they are in a progressive society, some positive payment of interest is usually necessary. For though the time may come when a sufficient number of persons can be got to 'save', and put new industrial capital into the system, on condition that when later on they want to spend what they have saved, they can do so, without requiring that interest shall be paid them in the meantime for the use of their capital, that time has not yet arrived. A sufficient quantity of new plant and other capital goods can only be got by paying individuals to save, instead of spending, some part of their incomes. The notion sometimes entertained that all interest is an unnecessary or a wrongful payment because the new plant and other forms of capital are 'produced by labour', involves a double error. In the first place, labour does not by itself, unaided and unorganized, produce anything in modern industry; it is only one of several co-operating factors. In the second place, reflection shows that saving involves among a large proportion of savers an effort or sacrifice (sometimes called 'abstinence', sometimes 'waiting') which is necessary to the creation and functioning of new capital. This effort or sacrifice, like other productive services, must be bought and paid for. The necessary payment is interest. Though some saving would be done were no interest obtainable, the full amount of new capital needed and its apportionment among the several industries cannot be procured in a competitive industrial society without interest. [A Socialistic society, were such otherwise feasible, though it too must practise abstinence and 'save' for any increase in its capital, need not pay interest to any one. It will pay 'real interest' to itself in the gains accruing from its enlarged fund of public capital.]

The payment, then, of the minimum interest needed to evoke the saving that shall supply fresh capital to feed the growing industrial system, is a necessary cost of progress . . .

What now of Land? We have seen that out of the product a provision must be made for the 'upkeep' of land, but that this 'cost of maintenance' is not rent. In a growing industrial system more use of land will be required to co-operate with the larger quantity of labour and capital. The land already employed must be cultivated more intensely or otherwise put to better use, or else land not hitherto used at all must be brought into requisition. Both these processes involve expenditure. In order to bring into use more land, roads must be made, land must be cleared, drained, fenced and otherwise equipped for use. If land already in use is to be cultivated more intensely, more expenditure of capital in so cultivating it is incurred, and a larger provision may be required to meet the more rapid exhaustion of the soil. In both cases, however, the 'cost' involved is a capital expenditure. It is not rent. So far as maintenance and improvements are concerned land is capital. The payment called Rent belongs to a different category.

We are now in a position to make a preliminary reckoning of the payments or provisions to be made out of the annual product for maintenance and growth of the industrial system. First, there are the costs of maintenance, or wear and tear fund, for the different factors of production.

Secondly, there are the costs of growth, operating in two ways: (1) by evoking a better or intenser use of the labour, land, capital, or ability already in use, (2) by calling into use new supplies of these factors.

If the whole product were compelled by some necessary law of Nature to apportion itself among these several uses so accurately that it was wholly absorbed in these costs of maintenance and growth, we should have a completely rational and socially satisfactory system of production and distribution of Wealth.

So far as mere maintenance and its 'costs of production' are concerned, powerful laws of necessity do compel a fairly full and accurate provision. For though workers in a trade may be 'sweated', in the sense that they are not paid a true subsistence wage, this can only occur where either these workers are subsidized from some other source, or where this worn-out labour power can be replaced out of a reserve of 'waiting' or unemployed labour kept alive out of some public or private charity. Apart from these abnormal circumstances . . . 'sweating' does not pay, and a trade habitually practising it cannot live. The case is even clearer as regards the costs of maintenance of capital and land. A failure to make regular and adequate provision against wear and tear means nothing else than the starvation of the business. Individual unsuccessful businesses suffer this starvation, but trades do not thus perish, unless some change in the needs or tastes of consumers render them no longer useful. A provision which may be regarded as almost automatic is thus made for the maintenance of the industrial fabric.

But as regards costs of growth there is no such security for adequate provision. The surplus of wealth remaining after costs of maintenance are defrayed does not automatically distribute itself among the owners of the several factors of production in such proportions as to stimulate the new productive energies required to promote the maximum growth of production. Instead of disposing itself in these proper proportions, the surplus may be so divided as to furnish excessive stimuli to some factors and defective stimuli to others, thus retarding that full progress of industry which requires a proportionate growth of all the factors.

In other words, portions of the 'Surplus' may be wasted, or, what is the same thing, employed 'unproductively'. Whenever any owner of a factor of production receives a payment for its use in excess of what is needed to evoke its full use he receives 'unproductive surplus'. The simplest instance is the rent of land. We have seen that rent is neither a cost of maintenance nor a cost of growth. Its payment does not affect the supply of land available for use in an industrial society. It is, of course, true that where private property in land exists, the payment of various rents may be necessary in the sense that the landowners may succeed in demanding them as a condition of giving the use of their land. But they are not necessary in the sense in which costs of maintenance or costs of growth are necessary, i.e. as payments for some voluntary effort or sacrifice. Their payment evokes no productive power. A general rise of rent does not bring into use an increased supply of land nor does a fall of rent put land out of use. (A rise of rent for a particular use of land, e.g. wheat growing, will, of course, increase the supply for that use, but by diverting some land from other uses.) If a landowner can get a high rent he takes it, if he can only get a low rent he takes that: so long as he can get some rent, however little, he will not refuse the use of his land. He will, of course, apply his land to that use for which he can get most rent. So long, therefore, as land remains in private ownership, it may be contended that, in order to induce

143

owners to choose the use for their land which is most productive, they must be paid some trifling premium. To this extent only can rent be deemed necessary in the sense in which wages or interest are necessary.

The same is true, however, of any payment of interest in excess of the minimum, say 3 per cent, required to evoke the quantity of saving needed for the growth of the industrial system. If capitalists, willing to apply capital at 3 per cent, receive 6 per cent, the extra 3 per cent stands precisely on the same level with rent. It is unproductive surplus, stimulating and supporting no useful effort. It is taken because it can be got; if it could not be got the capital would be supplied just the same. The same is true of any element of salary or of wages in excess of the needs of progressive efficiency for ability or labour.

Any payment to a factor of production in excess of the costs of maintenance and progress thus ranks as unproductive surplus. It is a source of industrial waste and damage in three ways. First, it furnishes no stimulus to production. Secondly, it takes away a portion of the income, or annual wealth, which might have been productively applied, if it had passed to some other factor. Excessive payments to some factors involve deficient payments to others, and since industrial progress depends upon proportionate growth of all the factors, the receipt of unproductive surplus must be considered an obstacle to industrial progress. Finally, in its effect upon the factor to which it provides excessive payment, it not merely does not promote activity, it depresses it. For as the receipt of rent, or excessive interest or any other form of unproductive surplus, enables the recipient to satisfy his wants without any output of personal productive energy, it must be held to have a negative influence upon production, retarding the growth of industry. It acts simply as a demand for idleness.

So far as the industrial system provides for the regular distribution of the product in payments which stimulate the factors to maintain or to increase their output of productive energy, industrial health is secured, and complete harmony prevails between the several factors. As it is not to the advantage of employers or capitalists to refuse to labour such share of the product as is necessary to sustain labourers and their families in the level of efficiency needed to co-operate with capital, so it is not to the advantage of labour to beat down interest or profits below the level needed to evoke the fullest use of capital and managing ability. Not merely as regards the maintenance fund, but as regards the application of the productive surplus, there is a harmony between the respective interests of labour, capital and ability. Friction, even violent conflicts, may sometimes arise through the failure of one or both parties to understand or to interpret correctly this harmony of the three factors. Industrial progress, doubtless, has often been retarded by endeavours of unenlightened employers, to beat down wages at the expense of the efficiency of labour, or of unenlightened workers to attempt to secure for labour higher wages or shorter hours or other improvements which the 'profits' cannot bear. But so far as the industrial situation is clearly seen by all the parties concerned, there is a solidarity of interests in the proper apportionment of the costs of maintenance and the costs of surplus.

Discord arises over the emergence of 'unproductive surplus'. It is not to the interest either of the labour or the capital in any trade that a share of the product should be paid in rent. Both are *prima facie* gainers by a reduction of rent, even to extinction, though we shall see that both do not stand an equal chance of securing and holding the gain. The same is true of any other payment of unproductive surplus, e.g. abnormally high interests or salaries or fees. The only true bone of contention, the only valid cause of conflict between capital and labour, land, ability, is the unproductive surplus. It lies in the industrial system a source of continual disturbance, breeding economic maladies.

For this surplus of rents and other unearned and unproductive elements of income represents a large and growing volume of industrial energy diverted from its socially useful purposes and put to positively noxious uses. A large part of this injury consists, as we have seen, in the mal-distribution of the product as between the claims of the several factors to a share. Rent or excessive profits to certain forms of capital imply that labour and other forms of capital are inadequately fed for purposes of industrial growth.

But there is another injury, sometimes even graver, which the taking of unproductive surplus causes. In our simple picture of the industrial system we have, in conformity with usage, left out of consideration one factor which plays an important part in modern industry, namely, the State. For though the State exists to perform other than merely economic functions, a large and a growing part of the work of government is concerned with the protection and

145

promotion of industry. The defensive services of the army, navy and police, a large part of criminal and civil administration, are concerned with the protection of private property and of the economic activities of the people. Directly or indirectly, the public expenditure on sanitation, education and other services for improving the physique and morale of the people, must be considered as contributing to economic efficiency. Much legislation and administration, central and local, is industrial in its express intent, concerned with improving the conditions of labour, regulating the conduct of business and safeguarding the interests of the consumer.

So far as this work of the State contributes to the security and progress of industry, it is rightly regarded as a factor of production, co-operating with the labour, land, capital and ability of the individuals who engage in industry. Although the State is not recognized as standing at each stage in the processes of industry, demanding its payment for work done, like the owners of the other factors, it is none the less true that the State must have its share. It also needs its costs of maintenance, and of progress, to be paid out of the only ultimate source of all payments, the product of industry. We shall concern ourselves later on with the methods by which the State comes to take her share. It is here sufficient to recognize that she takes it by the same natural or reasonable right by which the other factors of production take theirs, on the ground that she assists to produce it and cannot render this assistance properly unless she is paid her share. For unless proper provision is made out of the industrial product for the upkeep and improvement of the State, defective public services may bring such insecurity and inefficiency as will stop the flow of capital and labour to the industries where they are needed, or prevent them co-operating effectively for the production of Wealth.

The reason why it has been necessary to make this passing reference to the economic work of the State is that without doing so the full measure of the waste and damages involved in the unproductive surplus would not be understood. For the surplus consists only in part of wealth diverted to owners of land and of favoured forms of capital and ability from other private factors of production. It consists in part also of wealth rightly regarded as belonging to the State, because it is needed for the efficient operation of the public services. When unproductive surplus forms a large proportion of the wealth that is distributed, it entails starvation alike of the other factors in the private industrial system and of the State.

Taking account, then, of the claims of the various factors of production, public as well as private, and of the scheme of distribution by which the industrial product is apportioned among the owners of these factors, we may thus summarize the result—

Maintenance (cost of subsistence)   A
Productive Surplus (cost of growth)   B
Unproductive Surplus (waste)   C

A. Maintenance includes (1) minimum wages necessary to support the various sorts of labour and ability required for the regular working of the industries in their present size and efficiency; (2) depreciation for wear and tear of plant and other fixed capital; (3) a wear and tear provision for land; (4) a provision for the upkeep of the public services which the State renders to industry.

B. The Productive Surplus includes (1) minimum wages of progressive efficiency, to evoke a larger quantity and better quality of labour and ability for the enlargement and improvement of the industrial system; (2) such a minimum of interest as suffices to evoke the supply of new capital needed to co-operate with the enlarged and improved supply of labour; (3) a provision for the improved size and efficiency of the public services rendered by the State to industry.

C. The Unproductive Surplus consists of (1) economic rents of land and of other natural resources; (2) all interest in excess of the rate laid down in B; (3) all profits, salaries and other payments for ability or labour in excess of what would, under equal terms of competition, suffice to evoke the sufficient use of these factors.

3.5 Rationalisation and Unemployment (1930)
[pp. 62–73]

Rationalisation and Productivity

Our argument thus far has established two propositions. First, there exists a general tendency in the economic system for the productive capacity to outrun the expansion of markets. Secondly, this is attributable to a distribution of money-income which upsets the true balance between saving and spending, productivity and markets. It is now desirable to relate this argument to the processes included under the term 'Rationalisation', to which many business men, politicians, and economists are looking as a remedy for our present economic troubles. Improved plant and mechanical power, accelerated labour, better organisation of business personnel, and better marketing arrangements are the main factors in rationalisation. A single business in an industry of competing businesses, pursuing such a policy, may effect considerable economies that lead to a reduction in costs of production per unit of its output. If its output was no larger than before, this would mean a reduction in the number of employees. Labour would be 'saved'. But, since a business employing this policy would be able to undersell other competing businesses which carried on in the older wasteful ways, it might take a large enough share of the market to enable it to expand its output sufficiently to employ as many workers as before, or even to increase the number. The displacement of workers would then be thrown upon the other businesses whose markets it had taken. There would probably be some enlargement of total supply and some fall in selling price resulting from this policy. But if a similar rationalisation were not undertaken by the other competing businesses, an expansion of the rationalised business, perhaps accompanied by an absorption of some of the competitors and a suppression of others, would almost necessarily occur. In this way rationalisation usually extends to all or most of the strong businesses in a trade. Indeed, its full economies can only be realised when it signifies organisation of a whole industry for pursuing a common policy in methods of production and marketing. Though early experiments in such an organisation may leave much independence to individual businesses in production and finance, confining their federal policy to agreements upon output and selling prices, the normal development is towards the closer union of a cartel. Now, while there are many differences in the structure and working of cartels, their normal method is the regulation of the total supply in a national or a world-market so as to secure a profitable price, buying up or putting out of business firms with inferior equipment, management, or position, imposing specialisation of productive processes, with organised bulk buying of materials, power, and labour.

Now the first effect of this process carried on in a whole industry is generally understood to be a reduction in the number of workers, i.e. unemployment. Less labour is put into each unit of the product. More use of automatic machinery, higher standardisation, less waste in buying and selling, imply a reduction in employment, especially of the skilled and higher-paid workers. Wages seem hit in three ways: by a reduced number of wage-earners, by a reduced proportion of skilled and relatively highly-paid workers, and by wage-cuts pressed on Trade Unions when weakened by unemployment.

But these bad reactions upon wages and employment are based upon the assumption that the business organisers of this policy will adopt a selling price that will require them to restrict production so as to secure the full gains of their economy in high profits on a limited sale. This, however, is not the necessary effect of a rationalising policy. The large increase of productive power, in the form of capital and better organisation, which attends a successful rationalisation would not be utilised in most industries without an actual enlargement of the product, and this enlargement can only be sold by lowering prices so as to enlarge the market. This will not apply equally to all cases. Where rationalisation involves no considerable capital expenditure in new plant or other technical improvements, but consists chiefly in economies of a monopolised market, and where, as in the case of some prime requisites of life or trade, the elasticity of demand is low, it may pay a cartel or other combine severely to restrict output and even to raise prices. [Restriction of output, indeed, is regarded as a normal economy in the rationalising process. Lord Melchett, for example, gives it the first place in his analysis. 'Basically (writes Lord Melchett), rationalisation is simply the rational control of industry to ensure that as far as possible you do not produce more than your market can absorb . . . It means the closing down of obsolete plant and machinery and of unprofitable mines and factories, and the allocation of production to those mines and factories most favourably situated and equipped. It involves the use of every labour-saving and every fuel- and power-saving device which, together with the elimination of every unnecessary link in the chain of distribution, results in a vital saving in the ratio of costs to output. It means concentration on scientific research, the employment of the latest plant and inventions, and the scrapping of obsolete equipment. In the purchasing of raw materials, in transport, and in the chain of distribution and of merchanting abroad it means unification and centralisation, with all the corresponding economies and enhanced efficiency.'] But more usually mass production under a cartel policy will find it profitable to increase production by some reduction of selling prices, earning a larger aggregate profit out of a somewhat reduced profit per item of the larger output. In so far as this policy is pursued, the reduction of employment and of the wage-bill will evidently be less than where a more rigorous reduction of output is imposed. Indeed, when the elasticity of demand is great, the whole of the workers who would have been displaced under the former market conditions may be retained, and an addition may be made to the total volume of employment in the trade.

But even where some net reduction of employment and of wages occurs within the rationalised trade, it may be compensated by considerations affecting other workers. When heavy expenditure is incurred in replacement of obsolete or inferior plant a stimulus will be given to employment and wages in metals, machine-making, mining, and other fundamental industries which, though temporary in each case of rationalisation, may count considerably when a more enlightened scrapping policy (on the American scale) comes to be adopted.

Further, when rationalisation is followed by a planned reduction of selling prices to satisfy an expanding market, the real wage throughout the whole consuming community is raised by the fall in price of an item in its standard of living. Even if the product is not itself a final consumable article, but a semi-manufactured article that is utilised in other trades, the lowering of costs of production in these other trades will normally be followed by a reduction of prices in some markets for consumable goods, so raising the purchasing power of a given income. When the product of a rationalised trade is thus sold at a lower price, either that lower price greatly stimulates effective demand (in which case employment and wages in the particular industry may be as high as, or even higher than, before) or else the lower price paid for what is bought may leave a larger quantity of purchasing power available for more demand in other markets, stimulating employment and wages in these.

In a word, when considering the effects of rationalisation, we must not confine our attention to the immediate results and the

150

rationalised industry, but to the further effects upon volume of employment and of real wages in the industrial community as a whole. Regarding, as we must, rationalisation as the most recent and progressive type of Capitalism, does its advance in the industrial world, though primarily motived by the pursuit of profits, involve an increase of the rates of real wages and of employment in the rationalised industries and in the economic system as a whole, and in the proportion of the aggregate product which comes directly and indirectly to the wage-earners?

The full validity of rationalisation as a policy for maximising production and raising the general standard of consumption depends upon an adequate expansion of markets. Does this take place? The evidence of the last few years, especially in the United States, where the rationalising process has gone farthest and fastest, does not support a favourable answer to this question.

There are at present no [employment/payroll/production] statistics available from Germany and England representing the whole body of manufacturing employment. In certain particular industries, e.g. the boot and shoe trade in this country, the statistics appear to show that in 1924 a smaller number of operatives working a forty-hour week produced a larger number of boots than a greater number of operatives in 1907 working at least fifty hours a week. But no valid conclusions as to the general effect of rationalisation upon employment or wages can be based upon the statistics of a single trade or a single group of trades. For there are trades where labour-saving devices do not produce any considerable expansion of market. Boots seem to be such a trade. Though retail prices show less increase than the average retail price for commodities as compared with the pre-War level, no large expansion of the home market has occurred. Rubber soles are perhaps largely responsible for this. But the export market shows a large actual shrinkage in volume of exports since the War, though the latest figures show some recovery. Here is a case where a net displacement of labour may be attributed to improved machinery and organisation. But, taken by itself, it cannot be regarded as indicative of a reduction in the general volume of employment. For apart from some increase of employment that may have taken place in the shoe-machinery manufacturing and the rubber trade, the reduced proportion of national expenditure on shoes (if it has occurred) will signify some

151

increased expenditure on other articles and increased employment in the trades which have not been taking on labour-saving methods.

It is these indirect effects of labour-saving in particular businesses or trades that preclude us from measuring the general effects upon volume of employment. The broader basis of the American statistics, supported as it is by evidence from other great productive industries such as agriculture and mining, does, however, go far to warrant the conviction that rationalisation is not able to get full play for its economies because of the failure of an adequate expansion of home or foreign markets. Though we have not the same amount of statistical support for the effects of labour-saving rationalisation in Germany and England and other highly industrialised countries, the large and persistent body of unemployment is a powerful *prima facie* testimony to a similar failure of expansion of markets, or, put otherwise, a failure of the application of enough purchasing power to buy the larger output which the 'rationalised' processes could supply. The amazing exhibition of a world economic system which is continually tending to produce too much wheat, wool, cotton, leather, coal, steel, shipping, and the manufactured goods into which these materials and services enter, is testimony to the fundamental irrationality in the economy of rationalisation itself. Everywhere, in most trades, extractive, manufacturing, transport, commercial, so much technical and organising power exists that a large and growing proportion is devoted to producing the bad sort of leisure termed unemployment. Yet, as we have shown, the economic wants of man are illimitable. There are would-be consumers for all the wheat, wool, cotton, steel, and other goods that cannot under existing circumstances get produced. There is not any lack of purchasing power or money to buy these goods. Is there any other possible explanation of this irrationality except a maldistribution of income (purchasing power), which puts a disproportionate amount in the hands of those who desire to buy capital goods (to invest) and are unable to achieve their desire because the final commodities which these capital goods are intended to supply cannot secure a full reliable market owing to the too small share of the total income vested in the would-be consumer?

— 4 —

Imperialism and the International World

Hobson's *Imperialism: A Study* was undoubtedly his most famous work, and one frequently resurrected into print. The excerpt reproduced here is taken from the 1938 version of its best-known chapter (hardly changed from the original) – 'The economic taproot of imperialism' – and largely based on Hobson's 1898 article in the *Fortnightly Review*. It reflects his combination of economic and social analysis with immediate conclusions for radical political action. Utilizing his knowledge of the United States, Hobson contested the dominant view of the supposed advantages of imperialism, attacking trustification and maldistribution of income as responsible for the outward-looking vent-for-surplus pressure. The danger of imperialism was not only economic; it was a 'political revolution' that subordinated national politics to financial magnates. Hobson also furnishes a clear instance when Say's Law (that production creates its own demand), to which he so objected, could apply. Although it did not have .general validity, the law would obtain in a rational society where consuming power was distributed according to needs. The section further exemplifies how Hobson linked his analysis of imperialism to social reform as an economic, social and ethical alternative. In 1906, Hobson published a second edition of his historical survey *The Evolution of Modern Capitalism* (first published 1894), a book he later described as his 'first solid piece of economic writing'. In it he added a chapter that amplified his frosty view of financiers.

The New Protectionism, written during the First World War, illustrates Hobson's deep commitment to free trade, despite recognizing the flaws in Cobden's position. Arguing against the current, Hobson denied the usefulness of protection against Germany because it would weaken the British economy. But he also displayed considerable foresight in warning the Allies against the spirit of German revenge that a punitive economic policy would encourage. Free trade would remain valuable when it served genuine communal ends, inviting co-operation of governments and transcending particular national and international interests.

Hobson frequently resorted to thoughtful historical discussion, as in *Problems of a New World*, published in 1921 and incorporating some of his immediate postwar essays. He exposed the old belief in an immanent reason in history, though this did not mean that he now subscribed to irrationalism. Rather, nationalism bereft of democratic control was a recipe for an aggressive self-seeking class-interest that was the antithesis of rational communitarian self-regulation. Moreover, democratic control was meaningless unless economic equality was joined to political participation, and unless a responsible state was guided by humanitarian ends. Hobson's organicism once again dismissed the separation of politics and economics. Nineteenth-century theorists and practitioners, who ignored this, were culpable of an error that exacerbated class war and failed to protect their peoples from an impending cataclysm.

In the affairs among states the only solution that, in Hobson's opinion, stood a chance was pacific internationalism. His approach, though connected in practice with the activities of a number of British pressure groups, was but another variant of his social theories, incorporating the notion of ever-extending circles from the individual to humanity. Crucial to Hobson's analysis was the attempt to preserve the integrity of the unit – in this case the nation-state – while ultimately enveloping it in a cocoon of overriding considerations of supernational import, political, social and economic. *Democracy and a Changing Civilisation*, published in 1934 during the early days of a snowballing and ominous crisis, was one of a long list of works in which Hobson addressed those issues, but unlike his immediate post-war writings, it benefited from a sadder and wiser view of the efficacy of organizations such as the League of Nations.

4.1 Imperialism: A Study (1938; 1st edn. 1902)
[pp. 71–93]

The Economic Taproot of Imperialism

No mere array of facts and figures adduced to illustrate the economic nature of the new Imperialism will suffice to dispel the popular delusion that the use of national force to secure new markets by annexing fresh tracts of territory is a sound and a necessary policy for an advanced industrial country like Great Britain [written in 1905]. It has indeed been proved that recent annexations of tropical countries, procured at great expense, have furnished poor and precarious markets, that our aggregate trade with our colonial possessions is virtually stationary, and that our most profitable and progressive trade is with rival industrial nations, whose territories we have no desire to annex, whose markets we cannot force, and whose active antagonism we are provoking by our expansive policy.

But these arguments are not conclusive. It is open to Imperialists to argue thus: 'We must have markets for our growing manufactures, we must have new outlets for the investment of our surplus capital and for the energies of the adventurous surplus of our population: such expansion is a necessity of life to a nation with our great and growing powers of production. An ever larger share of our population is devoted to the manufactures and commerce of towns, and is thus dependent for life and work upon food and raw materials from foreign lands. In order to buy and pay for these things we must sell our goods abroad. During the first three-quarters of the nineteenth century we could do so without difficulty by a natural expansion of commerce with continental nations and our colonies, all of which were far behind us in the main arts of manufacture and the carrying trades. So long as England held a virtual monopoly of the world markets for certain important classes of manufactured goods, Imperialism was unnecessary. After 1870 this manufacturing and trading supremacy was greatly impaired: other nations, especially Germany, the United States, and Belgium, advanced with great rapidity, and while they have not crushed or even stayed the increase of our external trade, their competition made it more and more difficult to dispose of the full surplus of our manufactures at a profit. The encroachments made by these nations upon our old markets, even in our own possessions, made it most urgent that we should take energetic means to secure new markets. These new markets had to lie in hitherto undeveloped countries, chiefly in the tropics, where vast populations lived capable of growing economic needs which our manufacturers and merchants could supply. Our rivals were seizing and annexing territories for similar purposes, and when they had annexed them closed them to our trade. The diplomacy and the arms of Great Britain had to be used in order to compel the owners of the new markets to deal with us: and experience showed that the safest means of securing and developing such markets is by establishing 'protectorates' or by annexation. The value in 1905 of these markets must not be taken as a final test of the economy of such a policy; the process of educating civilized needs which we can supply is of necessity a gradual one, and the cost of such Imperialism must be regarded as a capital outlay, the fruits of which posterity would reap. The new markets might not be large, but they formed serviceable outlets for the overflow of our great textile and metal industries, and, when the vast Asiatic and African populations of the interior were reached, a rapid expansion of trade was expected to result.

'Far larger and more important is the pressure of capital for external fields of investment. Moreover, while the manufacturer and trader are well content to trade with foreign nations, the tendency for investors to work towards the political annexation of countries which contain their more speculative investments is very powerful. Of the fact of this pressure of capital there can be no question. Large savings are made which cannot find any profitable investment in this country; they must find employment elsewhere, and it is to the advantage of the nation that they should be employed as largely as possible in lands where they can be utilized in opening up markets for British trade and employment for British enterprise.

'However costly, however perilous, this process of imperial expansion may be, it is necessary to the continued existence and progress of our nation ['And why, indeed, are wars undertaken, if not to conquer colonies which permit the employment of fresh capital, to acquire commercial monopolies, or to obtain the exclusive use of certain highways of commerce?' (Loria, *Economic Foundations of Society*, p. 267)]; if we abandoned it we must be content to leave the development of the world to other nations, who will everywhere cut into our trade, and even impair our means of securing the food and raw materials we require to support our population. Imperialism is thus seen to be, not a choice, but a necessity.

The practical force of this economic argument in politics is strikingly illustrated by the later history of the United States. Here is a country which suddenly broke through a conservative policy, strongly held by both political parties, bound up with every popular instinct and tradition, and flung itself into a rapid imperial career for which it possessed neither the material nor the moral equipment, risking the principles and practices of liberty and equality by the establishment of militarism and the forcible subjugation of peoples which it could not safely admit to the condition of American citizenship.

Was this a mere wild freak of spread-eaglism, a burst of political ambition on the part of a nation coming to a sudden realization of its destiny? Not at all. The spirit of adventure, the American 'mission of civilization', were as forces making for Imperialism, clearly subordinate to the driving force of the economic factor. The dramatic character of the change is due to the unprecedented rapidity of the industrial revolution in the United States from the eighties onwards. During that period the United States, with her unrivalled natural resources, her immense resources of skilled and unskilled labour, and her genius for invention and organization, developed the best equipped and most productive manufacturing economy the world has yet seen. Fostered by rigid protective tariffs, her metal, textile, tool, clothing, furniture, and other manufactures shot up in a single generation from infancy to full maturity, and, having passed through a period of intense competition, attained, under the able control of great trust-makers, a power of production greater than has been attained in the most advanced industrial countries of Europe.

An era of cut-throat competition, followed by a rapid process of amalgamation, threw an enormous quantity of wealth into the hands of a small number of captains of industry. No luxury of living to which this class could attain kept pace with its rise of income, and a process of automatic saving set in upon an unprecedented scale. The investment of these savings in other industries helped to bring these under the same concentrative forces. Thus a great increase of savings seeking profitable investment is synchronous with a stricter economy of the use of existing capital. No doubt the rapid growth of a population, accustomed to a high and an always ascending standard of comfort, absorbs in the satisfaction of its wants a large quantity of new capital. But the actual rate of saving, conjoined with a more economical application of forms of existing capital, exceeded considerably the rise of the national consumption of manufactures. The power of production far outstripped the actual rate of consumption, and, contrary to the older economic theory, was unable to force a corresponding increase of consumption by lowering prices.

This is no mere theory. The history of any of the numerous trusts or combinations in the United States sets out the facts with complete distinctness. In the free competition of manufactures preceding combination the chronic condition is one of 'overproduction', in the sense that all the mills or factories can only be kept at work by cutting prices down towards a point where the weaker competitors are forced to close down, because they cannot sell their goods at a price which covers the true cost of production. The first result of the successful formation of a trust or combine is to close down the worse equipped or worse placed mills, and supply the entire market from the better equipped and better placed ones. This course may or may not be attended by a rise of price and some restriction of consumption: in some cases trusts take most of their profits by raising prices, in other cases by reducing the costs of production through employing only the best mills and stopping the waste of competition.

For the present argument it matters not which course is taken; the point is that this concentration of industry in 'trusts', 'combines', etc., at once limits the quantity of capital which can be effectively employed and increases the share of profits out of which fresh savings and fresh capital will spring. It is quite evident that a trust which is motived by cut-throat competition, due to an excess of capital, cannot normally find inside the 'trusted' industry employment for that portion of the profits which the trust-makers desire to save and to invest. New inventions and other economies of production or distribution within the trade may absorb some of the new capital, but there are rigid limits to this absorption. The trust-maker in oil or sugar must find other investments for his savings: if he is early in the application of the combination principles to his trade, he will naturally apply his surplus capital to establish similar combinations in other industries, economising capital still further, and rendering it ever harder for ordinary saving men to find investments for their savings.

It is not indeed necessary to own a country in order to do trade with it or to invest capital in it, and doubtless the United States could find some vent for their surplus goods and capital in European countries. But these countries were for the most part able to make provision for themselves: most of them erected tariffs against manufacturing imports, and even Great Britain was urged to defend herself by reverting to Protection. The big American manufacturers and financiers were compelled to look to China and the Pacific and to South America for their most profitable chances; Protectionists by principle and practice, they would insist upon getting as close a monopoly of these markets as they can secure, and the competition of Germany, England, and other trading nations would drive them to the establishment of special political relations with the markets they most prize. Cuba, the Philippines, and Hawaii were but the *hors d'œuvre* to whet an appetite for an ampler banquet. Moreover, the powerful hold upon politics which these industrial and financial magnates possessed formed a separate stimulus, which, as we have shown, was operative in Great Britain and elsewhere; the public expenditure in pursuit of an imperial career would be a separate immense source of profit to these men, as financiers negotiating loans, shipbuilders and owners handling subsidies, contractors and manufacturers of armaments and other imperialist appliances.

The suddenness of this political revolution is due to the rapid manifestation of the need. In the last years of the nineteenth century the United States nearly trebled the value of its manufacturing export trade, and it was to be expected that, if the rate of progress of those years continued, within a decade it would overtake our more slowly advancing export trade, and stand first in the list of manufacture-exporting nations.

This was the avowed ambition, and no idle one, of the keenest business men of America; and with the natural resources, the labour and the administrative talents at their disposal, it was quite likely they would achieve their object. The stronger and more direct control over politics exercised in America by business men enabled them to drive more quickly and more straightly along the line of their economic interests than in Great Britain. American Imperialism was the natural product of the economic pressure of a sudden advance of capitalism which could not find occupation at home and needed foreign markets for goods and for investments.

The same needs existed in European countries, and, as is admitted, drove Governments along the same path. Over-production in the sense of an excessive manufacturing plant, and surplus capital which could not find sound investments within the country, forced Great Britain, Germany, Holland, France to place larger and larger portions of their economic resources outside the area of their present political domain, and then stimulate a policy of political expansion so as to take in the new areas. The economic sources of this movement are laid bare by periodic trade-depressions due to an inability of producers to find adequate and profitable markets for what they can produce. The Majority Report of the Commission upon the Depression of Trade in 1885 put the matter in a nutshell. 'That, owing to the nature of the times, the demand for our commodities does not increase at the same rate as formerly; that our capacity for production is consequently in excess of our requirements, and could be considerably increased at short notice; that this is due partly to the competition of the capital which is being steadily accumulated in the country.' The Minority Report straightly imputed the condition of affairs to 'over-production'. Germany was in the early 1900s suffering severely from what is called a glut of capital and of manufacturing power: she had to have new markets; her Consuls all over the world were 'hustling' for trade; trading settlements were forced upon Asia Minor; in East and West Africa, in China and elsewhere the German Empire was impelled to a policy of colonization and protectorates as outlets for German commercial energy.

Every improvement of methods of production, every concentration of ownership and control, seems to accentuate the tendency. As one nation after another enters the machine economy and adopts advanced industrial methods, it becomes more difficult for its manufacturers, merchants, and financiers to dispose profitably of their economic resources, and they are tempted more and more to use their Governments in order to secure for their particular use some distant undeveloped country by annexation and protection.

The process, we may be told, is inevitable, and so it seems upon a superficial inspection. Everywhere appear excessive powers of production, excessive capital in search of investment. It is admitted by all business men that the growth of the powers of production in their country exceeds the growth in consumption, that more goods can be produced than can be sold at a profit, and that more capital exists than can find remunerative investment.

It is this economic condition of affairs that forms the taproot of Imperialism. If the consuming public in this country raised its standard of consumption to keep pace with every rise of productive powers, there could be no excess of goods or capital clamorous to use Imperialism in order to find markets: foreign trade would indeed exist, but there would be no difficulty in exchanging a small surplus of our manufactures for the food and raw material we annually absorbed, and all the savings that we made could find employment, if we chose, in home industries.

There is nothing inherently irrational in such a supposition. Whatever is, or can be, produced, can be consumed, for a claim upon it, as rent, profit, or wages, forms part of the real income of some member of the community, and he can consume it, or else exchange it for some other consumable with some one else who will consume it. With everything that is produced a consuming power is born. If then there are goods which cannot get consumed, or which cannot even get produced because it is evident they cannot get consumed, and if there is a quantity of capital and labour which cannot get full employment because its products cannot get consumed, the only possible explanation of this paradox is the refusal of owners of consuming power to apply that power in effective demand for commodities.

It is, of course, possible that an excess of producing power might exist in particular industries by misdirection, being engaged in certain manufactures, whereas it ought to have been engaged in agriculture or some other use. But no one can seriously contend that such misdirection explains the recurrent gluts and consequent depressions of modern industry, or that, when overproduction is manifest in the leading manufactures, ample avenues are open for the surplus capital and labour in other industries. The general character of the excess of producing power is proved by the existence at such times of large bank stocks of idle money seeking any sort of profitable investment and finding none.

The root questions underlying the phenomena are clearly these:'Why is it that consumption fails to keep pace automatically in a community with power of production?' 'Why does

161

under-consumption or over-saving occur?' For it is evident that the consuming power, which, if exercised, would keep tense the reins of production, is in part withheld, or in other words is 'saved' and stored up for investment. All saving for investment does not imply slackness of production; quite the contrary. Saving is economically justified, from the social standpoint, when the capital in which it takes material shape finds full employment in helping to produce commodities which, when produced, will be consumed. It is saving in excess of this amount that causes mischief, taking shape in surplus capital which is not needed to assist current consumption, and which either lies idle, or tries to oust existing capital from its employment, or else seeks speculative use abroad under the protection of the Government.

But it may be asked, 'Why should there be any tendency to over-saving? Why should the owners of consuming power withhold a larger quantity for savings than can be serviceably employed?' Another way of putting the same question is this, 'Why should not the pressure of present wants keep pace with every possibility of satisfying them?' The answer to these pertinent questions carries us to the broadest issue of the distribution of wealth. If a tendency to distribute income or consuming power according to needs were operative, it is evident that consumption would rise with every rise of producing power, for human needs are illimitable, and there could be no excess of saving. But it is quite otherwise in a state of economic society where distribution has no fixed relation to needs, but is determined by other conditions which assign to some people a consuming power vastly in excess of needs or possible uses, while others are destitute of consuming power enough to satisfy even the full demands of physical efficiency.

Where competition remains free, the result is a chronic congestion of productive power and of production, forcing down home prices, wasting large sums in advertising and in pushing for orders, and periodically causing a crisis followed by a collapse, during which quantities of capital and labour lie unemployed and unremunerated. The prime object of the trust or other combine is to remedy this waste and loss by substituting regulation of output for reckless over-production. In achieving this it actually narrows or even dams up the old channels of investment, limiting the overflow stream to the exact amount required to maintain the normal current of output. But this rigid limitation of trade, though required for the separate economy of each trust, does not suit the trust-maker, who is driven to compensate for strictly regulated industry at home by cutting new foreign channels as outlets for his productive power and his excessive savings. Thus we reach the conclusion that Imperialism is the endeavour of the great controllers of industry to broaden the channel for the flow of their surplus wealth by seeking foreign markets and foreign investments to take off the goods and capital they cannot sell or use at home.

The fallacy of the supposed inevitability of imperial expansion as a necessary outlet for progressive industry is now manifest. It is not industrial progress that demands the opening up of new markets and areas of investment, but mal-distribution of consuming power which prevents the absorption of commodities and capital within the country. The over-saving which is the economic root of Imperialism is found by analysis to consist of rents, monopoly profits, and other unearned or excessive elements of income, which, not being earned by labour of head or hand, have no legitimate *raison d'être*. Having no natural relation to effort of production, they impel their recipients to no corresponding satisfaction of consumption: they form a surplus wealth, which, having no proper place in the normal economy of production and consumption, tends to accumulate as excessive savings. Let any turn in the tide of politico-economic forces divert from these owners their excess of income and make it flow, either to the workers in higher wages, or to the community in taxes, so that it will be spent instead of being saved, serving in either of these ways to swell the tide of consumption – there will be no need to fight for foreign markets or foreign areas of investment.

Many have carried their analysis so far as to realize the absurdity of spending half our financial resources in fighting to secure foreign markets at times when hungry mouths, ill-clad backs, ill-furnished houses indicate countless unsatisfied material wants among our own population. If we may take the careful statistics of Mr Rowntree [*Poverty: A Study of Town Life*] for our guide, we shall be aware that more than one-fourth of the population of our towns is living at a standard which is below bare physical efficiency. If, by some economic readjustment, the products which flow from the surplus saving of the rich to swell the overflow streams could be diverted so as to raise the incomes and the standard of consumption of .this inefficient fourth, there would be no need for pushful Imperialism, and the cause of social reform would have won its greatest victory.

It is not inherent in the nature of things that we should spend our natural resources on militarism, war, and risky, unscrupulous diplomacy, in order to find markets for our goods and surplus capital. An intelligent progressive community, based upon substantial equality of economic and educational opportunities, will raise its standard of consumption to correspond with every increased power of production, and can find full employment for an unlimited quantity of capital and labour within the limits of the country which it occupies. Where the distribution of incomes is such as to enable all classes of the nation to convert their felt wants into an effective demand for commodities, there can be no over-production, no under-employment of capital and labour, and no necessity to fight for foreign markets.

If the apportionment of income were such as to evoke no excessive saving, full constant employment for capital and labour would be furnished at home. This, of course, does not imply that there would be no foreign trade. Goods that could not be produced at home, or produced as well or as cheaply, would still be purchased by ordinary process of international exchange, but here again the pressure would be the wholesome pressure of the consumer anxious to buy abroad what he could not buy at home, not the blind eagerness of the producer to use every force or trick of trade or politics to find markets for his 'surplus' goods.

The struggle for markets, the greater eagerness of producers to sell than of consumers to buy, is the crowning proof of a false economy of distribution. Imperialism is the fruit of this false economy; 'social reform' is its remedy. The primary purpose of 'social reform', using the term in its economic signification, is to raise the wholesome standard of private and public consumption for a nation, so as to enable the nation to live up to its highest standard of production. Even those social reformers who aim directly at abolishing or reducing some bad form of consumption, as in the Temperance Movement, generally recognise the necessity of substituting some better form of current consumption which is more educative and stimulative of other tastes, and will assist to raise the general standard of consumption.

There is no necessity to open up new foreign markets; the home markets are capable of indefinite expansion. Whatever is produced in England can be consumed in England, provided that the 'income' or power to demand commodities, is properly distributed. This only appears untrue because of the unnatural and unwholesome specialisation to which this country has been subjected, based upon a bad distribution of economic resources, which has induced an overgrowth of certain manufacturing trades for the express purpose of effecting foreign sales. If the industrial revolution had taken place in an England founded upon equal access by all classes to land, education and legislation, specialisation in manufactures would not have gone so far (though more intelligent progress would have been made, by reason of a widening of the area of selection of inventive and organising talents); foreign trade would have been less important, though more steady; the standard of life for all portions of the population would have been high, and the present rate of national consumption would probably have given full, constant, remunerative employment to a far larger quantity of private and public capital than is now employed. [The classical economists of England, forbidden by their theories of parsimony and of the growth of capital to entertain the notion of an indefinite expansion of home markets by reason of a constantly rising standard of national comfort, were early driven to countenance a doctrine of the necessity of finding external markets for the investment of capital. So J. S. Mill: 'The expansion of capital would soon reach its ultimate boundary if the boundary itself did not continually open and leave more space' (*Political Economy*). And before him Ricardo (in a letter to Malthus): 'If with every accumulation of capital we could take a piece of fresh fertile land to our island, profits would never fall.'] For the over-saving or wider consumption that is traced to excessive incomes of the rich is a suicidal economy, even from the exclusive standpoint of capital; for consumption alone vitalises capital and makes it capable of yielding profits. An economy that assigns to the 'possessing' classes an excess of consuming power which they cannot use, and cannot convert into really serviceable capital, is a dog-in-the-manger policy. The social reforms which deprive the possessing classes of their surplus will not, therefore, inflict upon them the real injury they dread; they can only use this surplus by forcing on their country a wrecking policy of Imperialism.

165

Everywhere the issue of quantitative *versus* qualitative growth comes up. This is the entire issue of empire. A people limited in number and energy and in the land they occupy have the choice of improving to the utmost the political and economic management of their own land, confining themselves to such accessions of territory as are justified by the most economical disposition of a growing population; or they may proceed, like the slovenly farmer, to spread their power and energy over the whole earth, tempted by the speculative value or the quick profits of some new market, or else by mere greed of territorial acquisition, and ignoring the political and economic wastes and risks involved by this imperial career. It must be clearly understood that this is essentially a choice of alternatives; a full simultaneous application of intensive and extensive cultivation is impossible. A nation may either, following the example of Denmark or Switzerland, put brains into agriculture, develop a finely varied system of public education, general and technical, apply the ripest science to its special manufacturing industries, and so support in progressive comfort and character a considerable population upon a strictly limited area; or it may, like Great Britain, neglect its agriculture, allowing its lands to go out of cultivation and its population to grow up in towns, fall behind other nations in its methods of education and in the capacity of adapting to its uses the latest scientific knowledge, in order that it may squander its pecuniary and military resources in forcing bad markets and finding speculative fields of investment in distant corners of the earth, adding millions of square miles and of unassimilable population to the area of the Empire.

The driving forces of class interest which stimulate and support this false economy we have explained. No remedy will serve which permits the future operation of these forces. It is idle to attack Imperialism or Militarism as political expedients or policies unless the axe is laid at the economic root of the tree, and the classes for whose interest Imperialism works are shorn of the surplus revenues which seek this outlet.

4.2 The Evolution of Modern Capitalism (1906; 1st edn 1894) [pp. 235–6, 251–2]

The Financier

The structure of modern Capitalism tends to throw an ever-increasing power into the hands of the men who operate the monetary machinery of industrial communities, the financial class. For large enterprises the financier has always been a necessary man: in the ancient and the mediæval world he found large sums of money to meet the emergencies of kings and great nobles, ecclesiastical or civil, to furnish military or naval expeditions, and to facilitate the larger forms of commercial enterprises which needed capital. Small financiers, as usurers or money-lenders, have at all times lived upon the irregularities and misfortunes of the farming, artisan, and small trading classes. But not until the development of modern industrial methods required a large, free, various flow of capital into many channels of productive employment did the financier show signs of assuming the seat of authority he now occupies in our economic system. Every important step which we have traced in the growth of industrial structure has favoured the segregation of a financial from a more general capitalist class, and has given it a larger and a more profitable control over the course of industry.

The financial class, then, as distinguished from the main body of capitalists or amateur investors, grafts upon its legitimate and useful function of determining and directing the most productive flow of capital, three methods of private gain, each of which is a corruption and abuse of its true function.

Planning and promoting Companies based, not upon economy of industrial or financial working, but upon an artfully enhanced vendibility of shares, they cause a waste of general capital by obtaining an excessive subscription to the Company and diverting the excess into their own pockets, thus imparting insecurity to otherwise sound businesses, damaging their credit and impeding their productive operations. To this waste must, of course, be added the injury wrought by floating 'bogus' Companies which have no actual foundation in the business world; the wide prevalence of these criminal adventures not only wastes capital, but, disturbing public confidence, further impedes the easy, natural flow of capital throughout the industrial organism.

Creating or stimulating fluctuations of prices in order to contrive corners or to practise concerted *coups* is an even more injurious dislocation of the social machinery of finance: it is a falsification of the automatic register of values expressly designed to determine the most productive application of capital.

Finally, the creation, absorption, and supreme control of the most profitable forms of natural monopoly and other abnormally prosperous businesses impart a strength and solidity to the new financial oligarchy which enable it to fasten its hold still more firmly on the necks of the proletariat of capital, who thus, cut off more and more from secure investments, are driven into the 'gambling hells' of speculative stocks and shares kept by these masters of finance.

4.3 The New Protectionism (1916) [pp. 55–9, 116–22]

A protective tariff here can do nothing to check or impede German economic aggression. It can only make it more successfully aggressive. Would it, on the other hand, strengthen our national resistance to this aggression? How should it? It can have only two chief and inevitable effects.

1. It would reduce our aggregate national income, and so our resources alike for armed defence upon the one hand, economic defence upon the other. How can the advocates of a policy which diminishes our funds alike for education, scientific experimentation, and technical equipment (the supreme needs for successful competition with Germany) plead 'defence'?

2. It wastes the sources of public revenue. A large proportion of the gross yield of a tariff is consumed in expenses of collection. By enabling protected industries to raise their prices it throws on consumers a burden of payment vastly greater than the gain to public revenue. The incidence of this burden is heaviest on the poorer working classes, for the prices of the necessaries of life are subject to the greatest increase. Thus the standard of living of the workers is depressed and their productive efficiency impaired.

It thus appears how bad a weapon of defence a general tariff is. But it has an even worse defect. No other policy could do so much to make another early war inevitable. The superficial notion that by hindering the economic recuperation and the commercial development of the Central Powers it would cripple their projects of 'revenge' will bear no investigation. It could have no such tendency. The announcement of the intention of the Allies to pursue a punitive economic policy after the war must confirm the false statements made in Germany that England in making war was actuated by feelings of commercial jealousy. This would feed the spirit of hate and revenge, and would help to maintain in Germany the Prussian militarism we are seeking to crush. This militarism would animate the new economic system of 'Middle Europe'. Tariff wars would keep alive everywhere the memories of the military struggle, and would be recognized as preparations and incentives to an early renewal of the struggle, as soon as one of the two parties found a 'favourable' opportunity. The 'balance of power' policy in the economic world would be clearly understood to be an instrument and an index of the terrible military struggle waiting in the background. Not only Europe but the whole world would tend to be drawn into the new battle-array, as members of one economic group or the other. A breaking of Europe into two hostile commercial systems would be an even greater crime against civilization than the war itself. For it would be an open-eyed prostitution of peaceful commerce to the purposes of international hostility. It would be the perpetuation of a trench warfare in which Customs officers would take the place of soldiers. The mode of fighting would be different, the aim and the animating principle would be the same. The net effect would be to reverse the great and fruitful processes of human co-operation, not only in the mutually profitable interchange of goods, but in every other mode of intercourse. International law, so much battered and enfeebled by the experiences of war, would be unable to raise its head again in such an atmosphere, or to begin to recover that authority which is indispensable to any hope for European civilization. All that elaborate and delicate network of communications by which, not only for business and personal relations, but for the common tasks of humanity in the world of thought and science, art, literature, and philanthropy, men of all nations have laboured together regardless of political boundaries, would suffer wreckage by this subversive enterprise.

The full pacific virtues of Free Trade and the constructive policy which it requires have seldom yet been recognized, even by professed Free Traders. This is due to a failure fully to appreciate the profound change that has come about in the economic internationalism of the last half-century. Trade, in its simple meaning of exchange of goods for goods, does not cover the new industrial, commercial, and financial relations between members of different countries. Cobden was admittedly mistaken in thinking that the perception of their obvious self-interest must rapidly lead all other nations in the world to liberate their trade as we had done, and that this universal Free Trade would afford security against future war. His error lay in failing to perceive that, though the interest of each people as a whole lay in freedom of commerce, the interests of special groups of traders or producers within each country would continue to lie along the lines of privilege and protection, and that until democracy became a political reality these organized group interests might continue to mould the fiscal policy of their several States.

But though this consideration has retarded the pacific influence of commerce, it has not been a direct and potent influence for international dissension. While the refusal of nations to open their markets on equal terms to foreigners retards and chills friendship, it does not normally promote hostility. It is the struggle for colonies, protectorates, and concessions in undeveloped countries, that has been the most disturbing feature in modern politics and economics. Foreign policy in recent decades has more and more turned upon the acquisition of business advantages in backward parts of the world, spheres of commerce, influence, and exploitation, leases, concessions, and other privileges, partly for commerce, but mainly for the profitable investment of capital. For it is the export of capital, the wider and more adventurous overflow of the savings of the capitalists of the developed Western countries, that constitutes the new and dominant factor in the modern situation. Larger and larger quantities of capital are available for overseas investment, and powerful, highly organized firms and groups of financiers seek to plant out these savings in distant lands, where they can be loaned to spendthrift monarchs or ambitious Governments, or applied to build railways, harbours, or other public works, to open and work mines, plant tea, rubber, or sugar, or to serve the general money-lending operations which pass under the name of banking. Many hundreds of millions of pounds during recent years have been flowing from the creditor nations of Europe into this work of 'development', which forms the main material ingredient in what is sometimes called the 'march', sometimes the 'mission', of civilization among backward peoples.

It is the competition between groups of business men, financiers, and traders, in the several nations, using the offices of their respective Governments to assist them in promoting these profitable business enterprises, that has underlain most of the friction in modern diplomacy and foreign policy, and has brought powerful nations so often into dangerous conflict. To prove this statement, one has only to name the countries which have been the recent danger-areas: Egypt, Morocco, Tripoli, Transvaal, Persia, Mexico, China, the Balkans. Though in every case other considerations, racial, political, dynastic, or religious, are also involved, sometimes more potent in the passions they evoke, the moving and directing influences have come from traders, financiers, and bondholders. Through the entanglements of Anglo-French political policy in Egypt runs the clear, determinant streak of bondholding interests. The kernel of the Moroccan trouble was the competition of the Mannesmann and the Schneider firms over the 'richest iron ores in the world'. Mining financiers moulded the policy of South Africa towards annexation of the gold reef. Tripoli was in essence a gigantic business coup of the Banco di Roma. In Mexico history will find a leading clue to recent disturbances in the contest of two commercial potentates for the control of oil-fields. Persia came into modern politics as an arena of struggle between Russian and British bankers, seeking areas of profitable concessions and spheres of financial influence. In China it was the competition for railroads and for leases and concessions, followed by forced pressures, now competing, now combining to plant profitable loans. Turkey and the Balkans became an incendiary issue to Western Europe because they lay along the route of German economic penetration in Asia, a project fatally antagonized by Russian needs for 'free' Southern waters.

The pressure of demand from organized business interests for preferential economic opportunities in backward countries is the driving force behind the grievances and aspirations of thwarted nationalism, political ambition, and imperialistic megalomania. A recent writer [Mr Lippmann, *The Stakes of Diplomacy*, p. 93] has thus condensed these facts of history: 'It is essential to remember that what turns a territory into a diplomatic problem is the combination of natural resources, cheap labour, markets, defencelessness, corrupt and inefficient government.'

If the Free Trade policy is to fulfil its mission as a civilizing, pacifying agency, it must adapt itself to the larger needs of this modern situation. Free Trade is indeed the nucleus of the larger constructive economic internationalism; but it needs a conversion from the negative conception of *laissez faire, laissez aller*, to a positive constructive one. The required policy must direct itself to secure economic liberty and equality not for trade alone, but for the capital, the enterprise, and the labour, which are required to do the work of development in all the backward countries of the earth, whether those countries 'belong to' some civilized State or are as yet independent countries. This fuller doctrine of the Open Door, or equality of economic opportunity, cannot, however, be applied without definite co-operative action on the part of nations and their Governments.

4.4 Problems of a New World (1921) [pp. 13–32]

We are opportunists on principle. That principle implies a generally favourable drift or tendency, or even providence, upon which we may rely to see us through and which dispenses with the obligation to practise much forethought. In America this is called the doctrine of manifest destiny. But we feel that even to make a conscious doctrine of it interferes with its spontaneity. The great historical example of this way of life is our Empire, rightly described as built up in a 'fit of absence of mind'. To Teutonic statecraft such a statement ranks as sheer hypocrisy, but none the less it is the truth. Individual builders there have been, and bits of personal planning, but never has the edifice of empire presented itself as an object of policy or even of desire to our government or people. Its general purpose can only be found in terms of drift or tendency. It will no doubt be urged that irrationalism is a more appropriate term than rationalism to describe this state of mind. But my point is that the state of mind implies a belief in the existence of some immanent reason in history working towards harmony and justifying optimism. Reason in the nature of things happily dispenses with the painful toil of clear individual thinking.

These general reflections may help to explain the universal surprise at the collapse of our world in 1914. For whether we regard the theorizing few or the many content with practice, we find no perception of the formidable nature of the antagonisms which for several generations had been gathering strength for open conflict. Even the historical commentators of to-day, as they survey and group into general movements the large happenings of the nineteenth century, often exhibit the same blindness which I have imputed to the current theorists. The smooth bourgeois optimism which characterized the liberal thinkers of the mid-century in their championship of nationalism, parliamentary institutions, broad franchise, free trade, capitalistic industry and internationalism, is discernible in the present-day interpreters of these movements. Take, for example, that widest stream of political events in Europe designated as the movement for national self-government. Historians distinguish its two currents or impulses, one making for national unity or government, the nation-State in its completeness, and another seeking to establish democratic rule within the State. Correct in regarding this common flow and tendency of events as of profound significance, they have usually overvalued the achievements. On the one hand they have taken too formal a view of the liberative processes with which they deal, and on the other they have failed to appreciate the flaws in the working of the so-called democratic institutions.

The reign of machinery, the outward and visible sign of nineteenth-century progress, has annexed our very minds and processes of thinking. Mechanical metaphors have secretly imposd themselves upon our politics and squeezed out the humanity. That willing communion of intelligences which should constitute a party has become in name and in substance a 'machine', politics are 'engineered', and divergent interests are reconciled by 'balances of power'. I should be far from describing the great nationalist movement of the nineteenth century as mechanical. It was the product of passionate enthusiasms as well as of the play of reasonable interests. The struggle for liberation on the part of subject nationalities and for the gains of unification in the place of division broke out in a dozen different quarters during the first half of the century, and the two following decades saw the movement not

173

indeed completed, but brought to a long halt in which splendid successes were recorded. In some cases, as in Germany and to a less extent in Italy, dynastic, military, fiscal and transport considerations were powerful propellers towards unification. But everywhere a genuinely national sentiment, based on a varying blend of racial, religious, linguistic and territorial community, gave force and nourishment to the new national structure. Its liberative and self-realizing virtues were garnered not in Europe alone. The foundations of the nationhood of our great overseas dominions were laid in the colonial policy of this epoch, while the breaking away of the Spanish-American colonies from their European attachment gave a great expansion of national self-government in the New World. But nationalism, regarded as the spirit and the practice of racial and territorial autonomy, has borne an exceedingly precarious relation to democracy. It has been consistent with the tyrannous domination of a dynasty, a caste or class, within the area of the nation. Indeed, at all times the spirit of nationality has been subject to exploitation by a dominant class for the suppression of internal discontents and the defence of privileges. Stein, Hardenberg, Bismarck and Treitschke used the enthusiasm of nationalism to fasten the fetters of a dominant Prussian caste upon the Germanic peoples. The struggles for the maintenance or the recovery of Polish and Hungarian national independence were directed by the ruling ambitions of an oppressive racial and economic oligarchy . . .

The conviction that political security and progress are made effective by the union of national independence with representative government rests upon a totally defective analysis that was responsible in no small measure for the failure to forecast and to prevent the collapse of 1914. The nature of the flaw in this polity is slow to emerge to the middle-class intelligence, necessarily approaching public affairs with the prepossession of its class. We can best discover it by turning once more to the defects of nationalism. The first we have already indicated, e.g. the masking of the interests or ambitions of a ruling, owning class or caste in the national movement. Nationalism is often internally oppressive. But a second vice bred of struggle and the intensity of self-realization is an exclusiveness which easily lends itself to fiscal or military policies of national defence, through which dangerous separatist interests are fostered within the national State. The spirit of nationalism, stimulated by the struggle for independence, easily becomes so self-centred as to make its devotees reckless of the vital interests of the entire outside world. To Irish Nationalists, Czecho-Slovaks, or Poles, this vast world struggle has been apt to figure merely or mainly as their great opportunity for the achievement of a national aim to which they are willing to sacrifice the lives, property and rights of all other peoples without a qualm. This absorbing passion, like others, is exploited for various ends and is the spiritual sustenance of the protectionism that always brings grist to the commercial mill. But there is a third defect which partakes of the nature of excess. Nationalism may become swell-headed and express itself in territorial aggrandizement. Imperialism is nationalism run riot and turned from self-possession to aggression. No modern nation can pursue a policy of isolation. It must have foreign relations, and its foreign policy may become a 'spirited' one, passing rashly into schemes of conquest and annexation.

These three perversions of nationalism, the oppressive, the exclusive and the aggressive, are all grounded in the usurpation of a nation by a predominant class or set of interests. This class-power is rooted often in traditional prestige, but this prestige itself rests upon solid economic supports. Landlordism and serfdom, capitalism and wagedom, money-lending and indebtedness – such have been the distinctive cleavages which have so often made a mockery of the boasted national freedom.

If we turn from this survey of ninteenth-century nationalism to a consideration of the democratic movement with which it has been associated, we discover that 'democracy' is vitiated by the same defects. It either signifies Parliamentarism upon an utterly inadequate franchise, by which the majority of the governed have no electoral voice, or else the formal government by the people is a machinery controlled for all essential purposes by small powerful groups and interests. Political democracy based upon economic equality is as yet an unattained ideal.

The liberal political philosophers of the Victorian era failed entirely to comprehend this vital flaw in the movement of nationalism and democracy. That failure was chiefly due to their underlying assumption that politics and business were independent spheres. It was in their view as illicit for business interests to handle politics as for government to encroach upon or hamper business interests. Such interference from either side appeared to them unnecessary and injurious. They failed to perceive that the evolution of modern industry, commerce and finance, had two important bearings upon politics. In the first place, it impelled business interests to exercise political pressure upon government for tariff aids, lucrative public contracts, and for favourable access to foreign markets and areas of development. Secondly, it evoked a growing demand for the protection of weaker industries, the workers and the consuming public from the oppressive power of strong corporations and combinations, which in many of the essential trades were displacing competition.

In other words, history was playing havoc with the economic harmonies upon which Bastiat and Cobden relied for the peaceful and fruitful co-operation of capital and labour within the nation, and of commerce between the different countries of the world. Cobden valiantly assailed the militarism, protectionism and imperialism of his day, and recognized their affinity of spirit and certain of their common business aims, but without any full perception of their economic taproot, or of the rapid domination over foreign policy which they were soon destined to attain. The grave social-economic problems which have lately loomed so large in the statecraft of every country lay then unrecognized. Throughout the long public career of two such genuinely liberal statesmen as Cobden and Gladstone neither evinced the slightest recognition that the state had any interest or obligation in respect of health and housing, the wages, hours and tenure of employment, the settlement of issues between capital and labour, or in any drastic reforms of our feudal land system. So far as they recognized these economic grievances at all, they deemed individual or privately associated effort to be the proper and adequate mode of redress. Where government was called upon to intervene for liberative or constructive work, the superficiality of its treatment showed a quite abysmal ignorance of social structure. A generation in which the Artisans' Dwellings Act of 1875, the Ground Game and Small Holdings Act of the early eighties, and the Factory Acts of 1870 and 1878 ranked as serious contributions to a new social policy, is self-condemned for utter incapacity to see, much less to solve, the social problem. Such statecraft failed to perceive that the new conditions of modern capitalist trade and finance had poisoned the policies of nationality and democratic self-government, and were breeding antagonisms that would bring class war within each nation and international war in its train.

Not until the eighties did these antagonisms begin to become

176

evident to those with eyes to see. During the period 1850 to 1880, Britain had still remained so far ahead of other countries in her industrial development, her foreign trade, her shipping and her finance as to entertain no fears of serious rivalry. Though our markets and those of our world-wide Empire were formally open upon equal terms to foreign merchants, our traders held the field, and British enterprise and capital met little competition in European markets or in loans for the great railroad development in North and South America. Not until the industrial countries of the Continent had reconstituted their industries upon British models and had furnished themselves with steam transport, while the United States, recovered from the Civil War, was advancing rapidly along the same road, was any check put upon the optimism which held that England was designed by Providence to be the abiding workshop of the world. Throughout the mid-Victorian era our economists and social prophets, with a few exceptions, were satisfied with a national prosperity and progress which enriched business classes, while the level of comfort among the skilled artisans showed a fairly constant and considerable rise.

Internally the economic harmony appeared, at any rate to well-to-do observers, justified by events. Externally there seemed no reason for suspecting any gathering conflict from the fact that one great nation after another was entering the path of industrial capitalism. Why should the rising productivity and trade of Germany, the United States and other developing nations be any source of enmity or injury to us? The economic harmonies were clear in their insistence that free intercourse would bring about an international division of labour as profitable to all the participating nations as the similar division of labour within each nation was to its individual members. It was impossible for the world to produce too much wealth or too rapidly for the satisfaction of the expanding wants of its customers. Foolish persons prated of over-production and pointed to recurrent periods of trade depression and unemployment. But the harmonists saw nothing in these phenomena but such friction, miscalculation and maladjustment as were involved in the processes of structural change and the elasticity of markets. As a noted economist of the eighties put it, 'the modern system of industry will not work without a margin of unemployment'.

All the same, several notable occurrences in the eighties ruffled the complacency of the mid-Victorian optimism. One was the revelation of the massed poverty and degradation of the slum-dwellers in our towns, and the searchlight turned upon working-class conditions in this and other lands by the competing criticisms of Henry George and the newly formed socialist organizations. The second was the rise in the United States of those Trusts and other formidable combinations which emerged as the culmination and the cancelment of that competition upon which the harmonists relied for the salutary operation of their economic laws.

The third event did not assume at first sight an economic face. It was the testimony to competing Imperialism furnished by the Berlin Conference for the partition of Central Africa. This was the first intimation to the world of a new rivalry, the true nature of which lay long concealed under the garb of foreign policy, and in the eighties was by no means plain to the statesmen who were its executants.

Imperialism is not, indeed, a simple policy with a single motive. It is compact of political ambition, military adventure, philanthropic and missionary enterprise and sheer expansionism, partly for settlement, partly for power, partly for legitimate and materially gainful trade. But more and more, as the White man's world has been occupied and colonized, the aggrandizing instincts have turned to those tropical and subtropical countries where genuine white colonization is precluded and where rich natural resources and submissive lower peoples present the opportunity of a new and distinctively economic empire.

Since the compelling pressure from this greed of empire has been the main source of the growing discord in the modern world, it is of the utmost importance to understand how the discord rises, and to see its organic relation to the class war within the several nations which has grown contemporaneously with it. If modern industrial society were closely conformable to the economic harmonies, the mobility and competition of capital and business ability would ensure that no larger share of the product was obtained by the owners of those productive agents than served to promote their useful growth and efficiency, and that the surplus of the fruits of industry would pass to the general body of the working population in their capacity of wage-earners and consumers, through the instrumentality of high wages and low prices. Combinations of workers would be needless and mischievous, for they could not increase the aggregate that would fall to labour, and the gains they might secure for stronger groups of workers would be at the expense of the weaker sections. It was to the interest of labour that capital and business ability should be well remunerated, in order that the increase of savings and of the wage-fund should be as large as possible, and that the arts of invention and business enterprise should be stimulated to the utmost. For labour was the residuary legatee of this fruitful co-operation. It was, again, a manifest impossibility that production should outstrip consumption, for somebody had a lien upon everything that was produced and the wants of men were illimitable. Thus effective demand must keep pace with every increase of supply. The notion that members of the same trade were hostile competitors, in the sense that there was not enough market to go round, and that if some sold their goods others would fail to sell, seemed a palpable absurdity.

Yet it was precisely these impossibilities and absurdities that asserted themselves as dominant facts in the operation of modern capitalist business. Every business man knew from experience that a chronic tendency to produce more goods than could profitably be sold prevailed over large fields of industry, that the wheels of industry had frequently and for long periods to be slowed down in order to prevent overproduction, and that more and more work, money, force and skill had to be put into the selling as distinguished from the productive side of a business. Every instructed worker knew that wealth was not, in fact, distributed in accordance with the economic harmonies, that much of it stuck in the form of rent and other unearned or excessive payments for well-placed capital and brains, and that the great gains of the technical improvements did not come down to 'the residual legatee'. Where free competition survived, it became cut-throat, leading to unremunerative prices, congested markets and frequent stoppages: when effective combination took its place, restricted output and regulated prices operated both in restraint of production and in the emergence of monopoly. Put otherwise, the weaker bargaining power of labour, pitted against the superior material resources, organization, knowledge and other strategic advantages of the landowning, capitalist and entrepreneur classes, left the former with an effective demand for commodities too small to purchase the products of the machine industries as fast as these were capable of providing them. The habitual underconsumption of the workers, due to the massing of unearned or excessive income in the hands of the master classes, has been the plainest testimony to the reality of that antagonism of

179

interests within each nation which is dramatized as 'class war'. No smooth talk about the real identity of interests between capital and labour disposes of the issue. A real identity does exist within certain limits. It does not pay capitalists, employers, landowners, or other strong bargainers, to drive down wages below the level of efficiency. Nor does it pay labour, even should it possess the power, to force down 'profits' below what is required, under the existing arrangements, to maintain a good flow of capital and technical and business ability into a trade. But, wherever the state of trade is such as to yield a return more than enough to cover these minimum provisions, the surplus is a real 'bone of contention', and lies entirely outside the economic harmonies. It goes to the stronger party as the spoils of actual or potential class war. Strikes and lock-outs are not the wholly irrational and wasteful actions they appear at first sight. In default of any more reasonable or equitable way of distributing the surplus among the claimants, they rank as a natural and necessary process. However much we may deplore class war, it is to this extent a reality, and does testify to an existing class antagonism inside our social-economic system.

. . . what concerns us here is to understand the sources of the blindness which caused the war to break upon us as a horrible surprise. I desire here to show that this blindness lay in a deep-seated misapprehension of the dominant movements of the century, and particularly of the latest outcomes of perverted Nationalism and Capitalism in their joint reactions upon foreign relations.

We have seen these two dominant forces emerging and moulding the course of actual events. Nationalism and Capitalism in secret conjunction produced independent, armed and opposed powers within each country, claiming and wielding a paramountcy, political, social and economic, within the nation, and working for further expansion outside. This competition of what may fairly be called capitalist states, evolving modern forms of militarism and protectionism, laid the powder trains. The dramatic antithesis of aggressive autocracies and pacific democracies in recent history is false, and the failure to discern this falsehood explains the great surprise. Nowhere had the conditions of a pacific democracy been established. Everywhere an inflamed and aggrandizing Nationalism had placed the growing powers of an absolute State (absolute alike in its demands upon its citizens and in its attitude to other States) at the disposal of powerful oligarchies, directed in their operations mainly by clear-sighted business men, using the political machinery of their country for the furtherance of their private interests. This by no means implies that States are equally aggressive, equally absolute, and equally susceptible to business control. Still less does it imply that in the immediate causation of the war conscious economic conflicts of interests were the efficient causes, or that direct causal responsibility is to be distributed equally among the belligerent groups. Indeed, the account of nineteenth-century movements here presented, if correct, explains why the German State became more absolutist in its claims and powers than other States, more consciously aggressive in its external policy, and in recent years more definitely occupied with economic considerations. Its geographical position, its meagre access to the sea, its rapid recent career of industrialism, its growing need of foreign markets, and its late entrance upon the struggle for empire, all contributed to sharpen the sense of antagonism in German state-craft and to make it more aggressive. The pressures for forcible expansion were necessarily stronger in this pent-up nation than in those which enjoyed in a literal sense 'the freedom of the seas' and large dependencies for occupation, government, trade priority and capitalistic exploitation. The ruthless realism of German statecraft, its habitual and successful reliance upon military force, the tough strain of feudal tyranny and servitude surviving in the spirit of Prussian institutions, served to make Germany in a quite peculiar degree the centre of discord, alike in its internal and its external polity. In the nation where Marx and Bismarck had stamped their teaching so forcibly upon the general mind, no great faith in the economic harmonies and pacific internationalism could be expected to survive. To these distinctively realistic forces must be added the subtler but not less significant contributions of Hegel and Darwin, working along widely different channels to give a 'scientific' support to political autocracy, economic domination and an absolutist State striving to enforce its will in a world of rival States contending for survival and supremacy. Out of that devil's brew were concocted the heady doctrines of Treitschke and his school, to whose educative influences such extravagant importance is attached by those who seek to represent the whole German nation as privy to a long preconcerted plan for war. That large romantic theories, claiming scientific or philosophical authority, have had, especially in Germany, a considerable influence in disposing the educated

181

members of the ruling and possessing classes to accept policies of force in the internal and external acts of government that seemed favourable to their interests and prestige, there can be no doubt. We also know that in Germany and elsewhere, among the class-conscious leaders of socialist and labour movements, a sort of semi-scientific sanction for the use of violence in a class war that was an inevitable phase in the evolution of a 'new' society was based upon the same biological misconception.

But we must not be misled by ideologists or heated pamphleteers into imputing an excessive value to these theories regarded as actual forces in conduct. Were this value what it is pretended in some quarters, the war would not have come as a surprise. It would have been expected. The wide prevalence of doctrines of 'force', rivalry of nations, and struggles for survival on a basis of social efficiency, were not in any real sense determinant factors in bringing about the war. Nor did they do more than mitigate in more reflecting minds the profound astonishment which accompanied the outbreak of war. The really operative causes were the deep antagonisms of interest and feeling which this analysis has disclosed, or, conversely, the feebleness of the safeguards upon which liberal and humane thinkers had relied, viz. economic internationalism, democracy and the restricted functions of the State.

4.5 Democracy and a Changing Civilisation (1934) [pp. 133–46]

Democracy and Internationalism

Pacific internationalism, not merely in the sense of disarmament and political co-operation, but expressed in a growing solidarity of economic institutions, is not merely in the long run but even in the short run essential to the survival and revival of democracy within each State. This judgment does not, however, signify that we must wait for an international solidarity, which now seems remoter than in 1918, before attempting seriously such national planning as is needed to replace the fumbling wastes and failures of a capitalism which can no longer be operated so as to secure its prime object, profit.

A revival of democracy upon a reformed basis will need a simultaneous activity upon the national and international fronts. The planning of economic life must be taken out of the hands of dictators and placed in the hands of the freely elected representatives of the people. This conscious struggle for economic democracy, with its equality of opportunity and standard of living, must be fought out within each nation. For only within the national area is the democratic sentiment strong enough and the concrete gains of victory clearly envisaged. And yet the separatist policy of 'setting your own house in order first' is not adequate to the solution. For we have seen that this sentiment and policy are weapons utilised by capitalists and their politicians for the defence of their economic dominance. Militarism and protectionism are the direct products of this nationalism, and the newly developed arts of propaganda are even more skilfully applied to the production of 'emergencies' which shall keep 'the people' under discipline. While, therefore, the areas of this democratic struggle are primarily national, the need for the wider appeal to constructive internationalism is very urgent. For though there seems little likelihood of international co-operation along the free-trade line, the pacific and efficient exploitation of natural and human resources of production on a reliable basis of agreement must become the prime economic objective of a League of Nations or any other form of international government. For the danger and waste of economic isolation, with competitive struggles for limited markets, are so manifest that no leader of democracy can believe in confining the struggle to his own country, with a view to some distant future when the national democracies shall come together in a common cause of humanity. The economic separatism to which each nation has committed itself must, therefore, give way to active practical policies of international co-operation, as the only way of salvation. The policy of independent sovereign States, that was compatible with some limited measure of peace and security so long as governments kept their economic functions within narrow limits, is no longer possible when every government is committed to a planning and control of all essential business processes, including the regulation of foreign trade and the money that finances it. International democracy is the only road to peace and prosperity, however difficult to travel. But international democracy does not signify the scrapping of national democracy in favour of cosmopolitanism. Territorial, racial, linguistic, sentimental bonds guarantee the continued existence of national governments. Even Mr Wells in his latest utterance [*The Shape of Things to Come* (Hutchinson)] has to evoke a cataclysmic epoch of collapse, in order to provide the chaos out of which his cosmopolitan government can emerge. National interest and sentiment, with the political and other social institutions they have produced, though they may and should be weakened as the wider areas of interest and sentiment acquire importance, will retain a strong hold as essential units of internationalism. In fact, that very term is a pledge of their survival.

A completely cosmopolitan government as a development from the existing system of national States is not merely impracticable. It is undesirable. For effective self-government requires that the area of such government shall be related to the particular groups interested in the objects of such government. This principle is applicable through every sphere of human conduct. There are many issues so closely associated with what we rightly term the private personality of each human being that they are left to that rational self-government which consists in correlating the diverse and sometimes contending urges and interests within the personal life under a single self-control. It is of vital importance that such self-control shall be left free from the interference or dictation of the wider or narrower group in which such a person lives and the social customs and institutions which under the name of morality, respectability, propriety, 'good form', would interfere within this area of free personal self-government.

I here introduce for the first time in this argument a term which is fundamental to the practical technique of democracy, the term federal. Federalism implies everywhere the subordination of the absolute sovereignty of one political area to the claims of a wider rule on the ground that certain aspects of local or national government vitally affect the wider area. It may be regarded as an economy of government, each area, from the family through the widening areas of local and national government to internationalism, practising free self-government in such matters as fall predominantly within the compass of its own knowledge, interest and capacity. But the term economy does not do justice to the full value of the federal principle. Its moral root lies in the basic concept of fraternity, interpreted in various phases and areas of the common life, the humanity which binds man to man ever more closely as civilisation furnishes closer and more numerous modes of communication, material, intellectual and moral.

This, it may be said, sounds specious talk, but what does it all come to? Let us then apply it to the special field of international relations. What are the governmental relations between the different countries and populations that make up the world? The basic relation between most of them is the negative one of absolute sovereign independence. This independence is, however, qualified in several ways. A loose code of international law has long been in operation, dealing with the customary rights of intercourse between citizens of different States travelling or resident outside their national area or owning property in foreign countries. A good deal of this law is concerned with shipping and other maritime relations in the open seas. Such laws have been constituted by the voluntary recognition of community of interest among peoples of different States and the mutual advantage of putting these interests on a stable basis of co-operation. But though a Court now exists at The Hague for the equitable pacific adjustment by arbitral or judicial procedure of differences between member nations, no adequate powers exist either to compel recourse to this Court or to enable the Court to execute its awards.

Outside the area of so-called international law, international co-operation has in recent times been making important advances along the lines of postal, railway, telegraphic, telephonic and radio arrangements, and for certain hygienic and other humane policies. Before the War international governmental conferences were making a timid advance towards a common standard of conditions for labour in different countries. But none of this internationalism contained a surrender of sovereign independence, or the acceptance of any effective sanctions for the fulfilment of any obligations which the member governments in such arrangements might have undertaken.

Though the League of Nations has furnished a more continuous set of instruments for such positive co-operation, in its various Commissions and its supplementary bodies such as the I.L.O. and the Bank of International Settlement, regarded as a basis for world government in the true sense, it is defective alike in membership, methods and authority. The slowness of this advance is attributable to two conspicuous defects of nationalism. On one of them, the insistence upon sovereign independence, the vicious temper of

185

isolated nationalism, I have already touched. The other lies in that imperialism which is the denial of legitimate nationalism to weaker countries held as Colonial possessions, protectorates, mandated areas, or 'spheres of influence'. The history of modern imperialism makes it evident that, whether this power is acquired and exerted for political or for purely economic ends, it is obstructive to international democracy, on the one hand by the denial of self-government to the subject peoples, on the other, by poisoning the democratic atmosphere of the country wielding this coercive power over the life and labour of weaker peoples.

For the personal freedom which is the breath of national democracy is inconsistent with the claims of imperialism to limit freedom in its subject empire. The worst symptom of this evil spirit is the pretence that this imperial power is 'a white man's burden' undertaken for the elevation of the subject races, to teach them the 'dignity of labour' and to lead them towards self-government. This moral corrosion necessarily accompanies the political corrosion which makes national democracy incompatible with imperialism. That an advanced people is able to help a backward people in many serviceable arts of civilisation for their own good, may well be admitted. The form of a mandate under the Covenant of the League was a true profession of this service. It was, however, marred in its application by the allotment of these mandates in accordance with the respective claims and 'pulls' of the recipient nations, and the lack of any adequate international safeguards either for the rights of the inhabitants of mandated areas or for the equal enjoyment of rights of trade and settlement by other nations.

But though the 'mandate' principle is imperfectly applied, it must none the less be regarded as a right and necessary adjunct of federal democracy in internationalism. For there exist certain countries whose populations are too backward in the arts of civilisation for equal participation in democratic federalism but which none the less cannot be left out of any scheme of world-government. For such countries may contain material resources the development of which is of prime importance for world prosperity, and the claim that the people in occupation of a country are the absolute owners of those resources, and entitled to leave them undeveloped, is a quite inadmissible assertion of national sovereignty. So likewise a backward country which, by its position, affords the only or the easiest access for the peoples of adjoining countries to communicate with one another, is not entitled to refuse or to impede such access. Such claims of absolute ownership and of isolation are of course equally applicable to civilised countries, and any democratic world-government would deal with them. Here I cite them as conclusive evidence against the view that the injustice and tyranny of imperialism can properly be cured by the complete liberation of such areas from external rule. But if it is neither to the interest of the world, nor of the backward peoples, that they should be left entirely to their own devices, a federal democracy must be accorded some powers of intervention primarily directed to the welfare of those backward populations, but also to the commercial and other rights of the outside world. A specific mandate to perform such services may be given to a civilised country whose position and knowledge render it best fitted for this performance, or else a body more directly representative of the Society of Nations may undertake it.

In this necessarily brief indication of a democratic world-government, the vital questions are two, first, what are the functions which must be handed over by the national democracies, secondly, how should the international government be constituted. As to the main functions of such a world federation there can, I think, be little doubt. The maintenance of peace by the requisite machinery of international law, with the judiciary and police powers needed to enforce such a law, is the first essential. The lamentable failure of recent disarmament attempts is manifestly due to the insistence of each national power upon its right to make its own provisions for its national security and to set its own qualifications upon each practical proposal to disarm. A Society of Nations is impossible until those elementary powers to maintain world order are placed in its hands.

Hardly less important are the powers to secure the world against the economic disorders and conflicts which have been the causes and precursors of actual war. The federal government must here have firm control over the instruments of international trade and communications. International trade can only be secure and prosperous on condition that the finance through which it is conducted is internationally controlled. Therefore, the supply of currency, credit, investments and loans, outside the needs of the several national areas, must be regulated by the federal government.

The network of communications by land, sea and air is likewise an essential of international government. The development of national resources in backward countries, and the finance connected with it, is, as we have already indicated, a proper task of internationalism.

A fully developed Society of Nations on a democratic socialistic basis would, no doubt, go much further in the expansion of its economic functions. It would organise the material and human productive resources of each country in relation, not exclusively to the needs and gains of its own inhabitants, but to those of humanity at large. Such a task would, of course, involve far larger cessions of national sovereignty than we have here contemplated. But even if each nation member of a world federation were socialised for internal government, it is unlikely that they would all consent to a world-pooling of the national resources. At any rate such a consummation is too distant for consideration here. The economic application of the democratic principle to the functions of world-federalism would be unlikely, for some generations, to proceed to so strict a limitation of national self-government. But it would be foolish, even at the outset of the experiment, to limit the powers ceded to the international government so closely as to place difficulties in the way of their enlargement to meet the new requirements of a changing world.

CHAPTER

— 5 —

British Politics

The Psychology of Jingoism was published in 1901 at the height of
the agitation against 'Little Englanders' – those who opposed the
aims and conduct of the war in South Africa. Hobson joined the
moral crusade intended not only to criticize the policy of the
Conservative Government but to warn Liberals against the pitfalls
of imperialism. This early sociological and psychological analysis
showed Hobson as an intrepid reformer whose main concern was to
expose the internal dangers Britain was facing as greater than any
external threat, but it also revealed his prejudices against 'herd-
tendencies' among the working class.

Lloyd George's 1909 Budget, thrown out by the Lords only to be
reconfirmed after a general election, was a fundamental challenge to
the existing social, political and economic order. The new liberals
could hardly have hoped for more at that stage, and Hobson joined
them in hailing it as the implementation of the political theories
they had been formulating for half a generation. Among its more
radical proposals were the imposition of a supertax on high incomes,
land value duties and a development grant set aside for organizing
national resources. In 'The significance of the Budget' Hobson
triumphantly saw it as vindicating his economic arguments,
endorsing as it did the imposition of the 'ability to pay' principle on
surplus incomes.

During the First World War many liberals expressed growing
anxieties about governmental intervention, and even new liberals
such as Hobson retreated from their previous enthusiasm for the
state. Their hostility to the war aims influenced their objection to
compulsory conscription as an assault on civil liberty and individual
conscience. But they were also perturbed by the vast powers of
the Defence of the Realm Act, with its censorship and powers of

arrest, and by various restrictions on industrial activity. For Hobson, these were features he identified with the 'Prussian' state Britain was fighting against, and they were imbued with what he and Hobhouse regarded as the pernicious heritage of German Idealism. Hobson's alarm at similar reactionary manifestations within the British state prompted his 'rediscovery' of the importance of liberty, his reformulation of a liberal organicism and his renewed insistence on the democratization of the modern state.

In 1926 Hobson participated as senior advisor in the drafting of a report commissioned by the Independent Labour Party that appeared in popular form under the name *The Living Wage*. Its policies were much publicized and discussed over the next few years, although its demand for an immediate minimum wage was considered to be too radical for the Labour party leadership, including Hobson's erstwhile Rainbow Circle colleague, Ramsay MacDonald. Hobson's intellectual influence was unmistakable: underconsumption and the surplus took their pride of place as justifications for Labour's claim on the national income.

The year 1929 saw a partial revival of the fortunes of liberalism. The concerted activities of the Liberal summer schools since the early years of the decade had combined with the re-radicalized Lloyd George to produce the Yellow Book of 1928. That document incorporated a large measure of state regulation of industry together with the safeguarding of individual liberty and private enterprise. For Hobson this was a 'new era of Liberalism'; it also reinforced the views of many former new liberals that a combined platform of the Liberal and Labour parties was the only feasible way forward for progressives. Hobson, by then a member of the Labour Party, endorsed this position in a series of articles published by the *Manchester Guardian* in 1929 shortly before the general election, when he envisaged the possibility of a 'practicable socialism'. The political parties in question had other considerations, however, but Hobson did not desist. The 'British socialism' he wrote about in 1936 in the *New Statesman*, with the depression still in mind, had all the characteristics of the fused liberal progressivism he had always promoted, even if by now the Labour Party seemed its only vehicle.

5.1 The Psychology of Jingoism (1901) [pp. 1–4, 8–9, 29–31]

That inverted patriotism whereby the love of one's own nation is transformed into the hatred of another nation, and the fierce craving to destroy the individual members of that other nation, is no new thing. Wars have not always, or perhaps commonly, demanded for their origin and support the pervasion of such a frenzy among the body of the people. The will of a king, of a statesman, or of a small caste of nobles, soldiers, priests, has often sufficed to breed and to maintain bloody conflicts between nations, without any full or fierce participation in the war-spirit by the lay multitude. Only in recent times, and even now over but a small part of the world, has the great mass of the individuals of any nation been placed in such quick touch with great political events that their opinions, their passion, and their will, have played an appreciable part in originating strife, or in determining by sanction or by criticism any important turn in the political conduct of a war. In a long-continued war, the passion of a whole people has, even in old times, been gradually inflamed against another people's, with whom, for reasons usually known to few, a state of war existed; and such martial animus, once roused, has lasted far beyond the limits of the strife, sometimes smouldering for decades or for centuries.

The quick ebullition of national hate termed Jingoism is a particular form of this primitive passion, modified and intensified by certain conditions of modern civilization. One who is curious of etymological origins will find true significance in the mode by which the word Jingo first came into vogue as an expression of popular pugnacity.

The oft-quoted saying of Fletcher of Saltoun, 'Let me make the ballads of a people, and let who will make the laws', ever finds fresh illustration. A gradual debasement of popular art attending the new industrial era of congested, ugly, manufacturing towns has raised up the music-hall to be the most powerful instrument of such musical and literary culture as the people are open to receive.

Among large sections of the middle and the labouring classes, the music-hall, and the recreative public-house into which it shades off by imperceptible degrees, are a more potent educator than the church, the school, the political meeting, or even than the press.

191

Into this 'lighter self' of the city populace the artiste conveys by song or recitation crude notions upon morals and politics, appealing by coarse humour or exaggerated pathos to the animal lusts of an audience stimulated by alcohol into appreciative hilarity.

In ordinary times politics plays no important part in these feasts of sensationalism, but the glorification of brute force and an ignorant contempt for foreigners are ever-present factors which at great political crises make the music-hall a very serviceable engine for generating military passion. The art of the music-hall is the only 'popular' art of the present day: its words and melodies pass by quick magic from the Empire or the Alhambra over the length and breadth of the land, re-echoed in a thousand provincial halls, clubs and drinking saloons, until the remotest village is familiar with air and sentiment. By such process of artistic suggestion the fervour of Jingoism has been widely fed, and it is worthy of note that the present meaning of the word was fastened upon it by the popularity of a single verse . . . 'We don't want to fight, / But by Jingo, if we do, / We've got the men, / We've got the ships, / We've got the money too' . . .

The neurotic temperament generated by town life seeks natural relief in stormy sensational appeals, and the crowded life of the streets, or other public gatherings, gives the best medium for communicating them. This is the very atmosphere of Jingoism. A coarse patriotism, fed by the wildest rumours and the most violent appeals to hate and the animal lust of blood, passes by quick contagion through the crowded life of cities, and recommends itself everywhere by the satisfaction it affords to sensational cravings. It is less the savage yearning for personal participation in the fray than the feeding of a neurotic imagination that marks Jingoism. The actual rage of the combat is of a different and a more individual order. Jingoism is the passion of the spectator, the inciter, the backer, not of the fighter; it is a collective or mob passion which, in as far as it prevails, makes the individual mind subject to a control that joins him irresistibly to his fellows.

The modern newspaper is a Roman arena, a Spanish bull-ring, and an English prize-fight rolled into one. The popularization of the power to read has made the press the chief instrument of brutality. For a halfpenny every man, woman, or child can stimulate and feed those lusts of blood and physical cruelty which it is the chief aim of civilization and of government to repress, and which, in their literal modes of realization, have been assigned by modern specialization to soldiers, butchers, sportsmen, and a few other trained professions. The business man, the weaver, the clerk, the clergyman, the shop assistant, can no longer satisfy these savage cravings, either in personal activity or in direct spectacular display; but the art of reading print enables them to indulge *ad libitum* in ghoulish gloating over scenes of human suffering, outrage, and destruction. Blended with the root-passion of sheer brutality are certain other feelings, more complex in origin and composition – admiration of courage and adroitness, the zest of sport, curiosity, the interest in swift change and the unusual: all these serve to conceal and decorate the dominant force of brutality, that Yahoo passion which revels in material disorder and destruction, with carnage for its centre-piece. That this passion, like other phases of the war fever, is of social origin, and grows by swift, unseen contagion and communication, is made evident by the character and behaviour of its victims. Mild and aged clergymen; gently bred, refined English ladies; quiet, sober, unimaginative business men, long to point a rifle at the Boers, and to dabble their fingers in the carnage. The basic character of the passion is disclosed by the fact that death and destruction by fire-arms do not satisfy; it is the cold steel and the twist of the British bayonet in the body of the now defenceless foe that brings the keenest thrill of exultation. Many will deny this subjection to sheer animalism – in some cases a revulsion of pity, or some better human feeling, hides it; but, wherever the dissecting-knife is honestly applied, the essential brutality which underlies the glow of patriotic triumph in 'another British victory' is discernible.

5.2 'The Significance of the Budget' (1909) [*English Review*, pp. 794–805]

The audacity of the Budget has put a new spirit into English politics. The nature and magnitude of its financial proposals have come upon our people as a surprise. This ought not to have been the case. For when this Government was entrusted with the policy of reconciling social reconstruction with the maintenance of Free Trade, it was evident that this task would impose the necessity of a radical finance, providing a large increase of revenue by taxing the incomes and property of those with large ability to pay. No conscious theory of taxation but sheer political necessity has driven the Liberal Party along the road which many of its members tread reluctantly. To such an extent has blind short-range opportunism become the ruling principle of English politics that any measure which, like this Budget, brings into the foreground of debate vital issues of political theory is staggering to the intelligence . . .

But if we are to realise either the magnitude of the issue or the inner nature of the fight, we must look a little closer at the novel tendency embodied in the Finance Bill. This novelty consists in an interpretation of the canon of 'ability to pay' which is rightly recognised as an attack upon certain orthodox rights of property . . .

Liberal statesmen do not like to admit that any Socialistic principle, or indeed any unity of principle, underlies their finance, preferring to fall back upon the need of taking money wherever it can be obtained without great disturbance of industry. But the Socialistic doctrine, and none other, implicitly inspires and justifies this opportunism. In other words, unless the large properties and incomes of the rich did in fact contain elements of unearned increment similar in origin and nature to the rent of land, the increased taxation put upon them would be an unwarrantable disturbance of the incentives to apply capital and ability in their most productive ways, and would affect injuriously the general production of wealth and the future taxing ability of the State. Thus, though the new graduation of the income tax with the sur-tax and the increase of estate duties do not constitute a novel policy, their inclusion with the land and liquor duties in a single integral finance gives them a new significance. The moral and intellectual defence of the Budget rests on the validity of a general distinction between earned and unearned wealth, that is, between those elements of income which are necessary to evoke the powers of mental or physical labour and the application of capital, and those which are not necessary but which constitute surplus incomes taken because they can be got. The historic importance of this Budget is thus derived from the fact that it is the first half-conscious recognition that taxation rightly means the assumption by the State of a socially earned income which in the operations of industry passes as unearned income to private individuals, unless the State enforces its rightful claim . . .

The reality and intensity of this new spirit of positive progress, definitely transcending the orthodox limits of past Liberalism, is a revelation of this session. The exposures made during the last few years of the signal defects and dangers of our national life are now bearing fruit in confident demands that we shall set our house in order.

The claims of this finance may be thus summarised. (1) It presents a defence and a justification of Free Trade by showing that a large increase of revenue can be obtained without recourse to protective duties. (2) It furnishes an instrument of growing revenue to meet the expenses of a policy of social reform. (3) It affords a sound application of the canon of 'ability to pay' by the discovery and taxation of unearned increments and incomes. (4) It promotes the cause of temperance and imposes checks upon expenditure on luxuries. (5) It stimulates the improved use of the natural resources of the country, and furnishes a fund destined to their further development. (6) By requiring the valuation of site values and of all interests in real property, and by securing a full return of all incomes assessible for income tax, it furnishes an instrument of economic survey indispensable to the provident conduct of public finance.

5.3 'The War and British Liberties: The Claims of the State upon the Individual' (*Nation*, 10 June 1916)

We are told that these restrictions of liberty are necessary to preserve the unity of the nation and to make its full resources available for the emergency of war. In a war of self-defence the State is entitled to override all personal rights of life, liberty, and property, and to compel all citizens to perform such personal services as it requires. *Salus reipublicæ suprema lex.* Upon every criticism of these inroads upon liberty falls the retort, 'Don't you want to win the war?' which conveniently dispenses with the necessity of proving that the burden or the sacrifice required does help to win the war.

But what validity attaches to the assertion or assumption that in a struggle for national safety the State has a right, and even a duty, to cancel all personal rights of individual citizens and to enforce their surrender? No reasonable person would deny that many of the emergency measures taken by our Government during the period of the war are salutary. But the question remains, 'Are there no right or reasonable limits to the encroachment of the State on personal liberties?' Or, to put it conversely, 'Does the individual owe an absolute and unlimited obedience to the State at such a time?' Now, if these questions were put to a 'good' German citizen, his answer would be that there were no limits to the power of the State or the submission of the individual. This is the orthodox theory and practice of the Prussian State, not only in war, but in peace. The individual citizen exists there only as a servant of the State, and his value consists only in contributing to the power and purposes of the State. In war-time this power and purpose are expressed primarily in terms of military energy, and the citizen is merely cannon-food. Must we, ought we, and can we adopt this principle of State for the period of the war? Those who reply in the affirmative should have the honesty to admit that in a war for the 'idea' of liberty they are throwing away the substance of liberty, and that in order to destroy the body of Prussianism they are taking on its soul. For British liberty does not consist merely in the negative condition of not being subject to a foreign power, but in the positive enjoyment of those personal rights which are now passing. Prussianism again consists, not in the rule of the Kaiser and his army, but in the spirit of the Prussian State, its absolute control over the will of its citizens. It is consistent with the German conception of the State to impose military obedience upon all its citizens in all their actions. 'Theirs not to reason why, theirs but to do or die' is as applicable there to the citizen in his workshop or his home, as to the soldier in the trenches. The State has imposed itself as a super-personality upon the individual citizen, who is taught and compelled to regard himself, his activity, and his very will, as mere instruments of this higher personality.

Now the doctrine of the absolute State is no modern one. Tyrannical thinkers and rulers have always maintained it. It has not lacked intellectual support in this country. Hobbes's *Leviathan* was a full-blooded expression of the doctrine, and seventeenth-century political controversy reeked with its arrogance. But the modern conception and policy of the British State has definitely repudiated this absolutism. It has steadfastly refused to regard the individual as a mere means to the power and purpose of the State. In the British conception of the State, the individual citizen figures as an end, with indefeasible rights attaching to his own personality. Indeed, the

British conception regards the State itself as the means or instrument to subserve and to promote the personal ends of its citizens. Although modern Socialism and the doctrine of the general or collective will have modified or confused this simpler individualism, it still remains the case that in the British idea of the State the individual is an end as well as a means. Now this admission is fatal to the contention that even in war-time the power of the State to coerce the individual is unlimited. For such unrestricted power, such claim to reduce the citizen to a dumb subservient tool, is a commission of political suicide. Whereas the Prussian State exacts implicit blind obedience, the British State rests on a basis of personal free-will. Our ideal of self-government requires that the right of the individual to consult his own good and make his own choice, even to the extent of refusing private sacrifices to the public good, shall be preserved at all costs. In opposition to the Prussian State, which is absolutely centralized in its power and control, the British State is organic in the sense that it is a free corporation of cells and organs which, while contributing to the life of the organism, preserve also their private liberties and ends . . . We maintain that there is a net economy of political strength and progress in encouraging the free play of personal views and sentiments, even when they impede the smooth activity of some particular State function. For this sort of free-will, with all its elements of faction and perversity, nourishes a sounder social system and gives more vitality and adaptability to political institutions than the submissive unity that prevails in Germany.

5.4 The Living Wage [with H. N. Brailsford, A. Creech Jones and E. F. Wise] (1926) [pp. 8–10, 27–30]

We produce less wealth than our technical resources would enable us to create, because the mass of the wage-earners lack 'effective demand'. The owning class has misused the advantage of its position. Too much, proportionately, of the product of industry, has been accumulated and applied to the creation of fresh instruments of production: too little, proportionately, has gone in wages to make a market for the product of these new machines . . .

In thinking out any constructive policy, we would urge that the

Labour Movement must base itself upon this fact of 'under-consumption' . . .

It is not sufficient to ensure that the nation's total purchasing power shall be increased. Care must be taken, in distributing it, to ensure that a due proportion shall be observed, in its probable destination, between saving and spending, or in other words between expenditure on reproductive instruments and on consumable goods and services. This means that a higher proportion than is customary in our society must go to the wage-earning masses, and a lower proportion to the owning and investing class.

The root idea governing any Socialist policy of distribution is, we take it, that Labour has a claim upon the total pool of the national income. This pool we regard as the result of the co-operative effort of all the connected activities of the community. It is not possible to isolate the contribution of any industry, firm, or individual worker. The cotton cloth which a weaving shed produces, is not the product of the workers in that shed alone; coal miners, engineers, transport workers and many others, contributed towards it, and behind them lay the contribution of the whole civilisation around them, through its science, its education, and its social and legal organisation.

It follows from this familiar view, which regards the production of wealth as an indivisible activity of the whole community, that we reject the qualification commonly attached to the accepted doctrine of the Living Wage. 'A living wage by all means,' is the usual reply to the demands of Labour, 'but you cannot take from the industry more than it is producing. The money to meet your demand is not in the industry.'

Assuredly, there must be a reference to some divisible total. But the haphazard arrangements of the market give no assurance that the income drawn by an industry, or by the workers in an industry, from the national pool, shall be a fair measure of their share. Some groups are in a fortunate, others in an unfavourable position, and the varying 'pulls' which scarcity and strategic accidents enable the several groups to exert upon national income, have no necessary or even usual relation to effort, skill, or risk, and even less to need. One group can combine to create a slight artificial scarcity in the product which it brings to the market: another group is exposed to world-wide competition.

Little progress can be made in raising the level of the depressed workers, or in securing some nearer approach to equal justice between trade and trade, until we are prepared to define what we mean by a Living Wage. We would urge that even now, while Labour lacks the power to take political action, the whole Movement acting through the Trade Union Congress and the Labour Party, might take the first step, by setting up a Labour Commission to formulate in precise terms and figures the vague claim which is in all our minds. If this Enquiry, which should be public, resulted in the suggestion of some minimum figure, the task of the General Council would then be to direct and co-ordinate the whole of the industrial struggle, with the purpose of rendering effective support to bodies of workers who sought to raise their wages to this figure. We believe that a struggle conducted for a purpose so manifestly just would give a new sense of unity and direction to the whole Labour Movement. The argument over this claim would soon dominate public life, and focus political and economic discussion. The Living Wage, with all its far-reaching implications, would become the central question before the nation, and might hasten a general election in which it would be the leading issue. A Labour Government, when it took office, would, we assume, conduct an enquiry of its own, by the most expeditious methods, in order to supplement the work of the Labour Commission, by a full use of official data, for the purpose of ratifying or adjusting the figure at which it had estimated the Living Wage.

5.5 'Liberalism and Labour: Lines of Co-operation'
(*Manchester Guardian*, 9 February 1929)

While Liberals conceive economic progress primarily in terms of increased productivity, Labour conceives it in terms of better distribution. Labour sees large unearned incomes owned and squandered by a small rich class, and is disposed to think that political devices for tapping this surplus wealth and diverting it into higher working-class incomes and improved social services could secure a high standard of living for the whole community.

As Liberal economists have shown, this is a delusion. Large as may be the surplus wealth, the part disposable for raising current standards of living is not nearly large enough to give satisfaction. More must be produced; the national income must be raised to a higher level. But Liberal economists are also under a delusion when they argue that higher productivity must precede a better distribution, failing to recognise that a better distribution is an indispensable condition of the higher productivity . . .

Labour and Liberalism have here something important to learn from one another. There is no incompatibility between higher production and better distribution; on the contrary, they are the two interacting conditions of economic reform . . .

While, therefore, it would be foolish to contend that there is no diversity of interests and outlook between Liberalism and Labour in their economics, the diversity is less than it was before the new industrial revolution, and amicable contacts between the two parties would promote a better understanding of opposed viewpoints, the first prerequisite for reconcilement . . .

New alignments of power and interest have displaced the older crude opposition of capital and labour, while the clearer revelation of the intricate interactions of different industries in the national economy is compelling all parties to look with favour upon some representative economic Government where the relations between national economy and national politics may be amicably settled . . .

This argument in favour of now considering co-operation between Liberalism and Labour is addressed to those who acknowledge allegiance to good citizenship first, then to party. It follows two main lines. It first explores those fields of policy which are not primarily or directly economic in significance, though fraught sometimes with grave economic consequences, and finds in them a close and avowed agreement between the two parties. This includes not only the whole area of imperial and foreign policy, in Europe and elsewhere, especially questions of peace, trade, disarmament, arbitration, and constructive internationalism, but a whole series of social reforms in health, education, insurance, and other improvements of 'the condition of the people'. There is substantial agreement also in constitutional policy and in developmental work by State aid and enterprise. The argument then explores those fields of definitely economic policy in which it is often supposed that the gulf between Liberalism and Labour is impassable. It shows how modern alterations of industrial structure involve a necessary recasting of Liberal doctrines and ideas, involving methods and measures of public control and interference which are distinctively 'socialistic'.

On the other hand, it dispels the notion that the Labour party is committed to wholesale schemes of State bureaucracy, and shows how little is the substantial difference between the 'nationalisation' which Labour contemplates and the divided controls and directorate reforms which figure in the New Liberalism.

5.6 'A British Socialism' (*New Statesman and Nation*: 25 January 1936; 1 February 1936)

At a time when depression and unemployment of all the factors of production attest the failure of competitive and monopolist capitalism to keep pace with the powers of modern productivity for the supply of consumers' needs, the Socialist Labour Party in this country has experienced a signal setback to its political advance . . . I think that must be found in the failure of Socialism to make a sufficiently intelligible and equitable impress upon the minds of the mass of the wage-earners on the one hand, and of the salaried, professional and public employees upon the other. For what is rightly called 'the practical common sense' of our people repudiates both the desirability and the possibility of a successful class-war for Socialism conducted by the proletariat, and demands the co-operation of the brain workers in an effective policy of social-economic reconstruction. What is needed first of all is a clear presentation of a new social-economic structure which shall seem reasonable, equitable and attainable.

Socialism as preached in this country seems to suffer from three incompatible and undesirable appeals, sentimentalism, over-regimentation and revolutionary force. What is most urgently wanted is perhaps a clear conception of what individuals and what society actually do in the making of economic products and the determination of their values. And here we must, in dealing with British mentality, put aside the rigorous and difficult logic of Marxism, eschew the more abstract considerations of justice and humanity, and appeal to the accepted British standards of 'fair play'. If a person can truly be said to make a thing, it belongs to him. It is his 'property'. If a group of persons co-operate to make a thing, it is 'theirs'. Of course, it may be said that this view cannot be strictly applicable even to a peasant, a craftsman, or an artist. For no person has made the raw materials on which he spends his labour, or the traditional or acquired knowledge and skill he applies. These must be regarded as social properties and carry some limitation upon individual property, even when equal access to materials and knowledge exists. But, all the same, in such kinds of production 'fair play' and 'common sense' endorse a private personal property which does not apply to industry or even agriculture in general.

That economic planning is essential to Socialism goes without saying. But if the planning is to be conducted in the interests of the people, as workers and consumers, it must not be left to the control of the owning classes. This signifies that the practical business men and the technical managers, those in possession of the necessary expert knowledge required for skilled planning, must be detached from their subservience to the owners of capital and pass into the service of the community. This in its turn will signify the transfer of the control of the capital from private hands to the public.

This statement plunges us at once into the turmoil of fears and misconceptions which befog the minds of men brought up in the old Liberal tradition – the attack on liberty and property. It is not necessary here to discuss at length the wild charge – that Socialism means the abolition or confiscation of private property. If well-conducted, it would bring a wide extension of private ownership of all sorts of goods for personal use, including such tools and materials as persons want for private working purposes.

. . . a Socialism which should win the needed co-operation of the mental working classes and avert the violence of class-war must confine its early efforts to the nationalisation of key industries. How much farther should it seek to go? Is there any natural limit to the public ownership and planned operation of the economic system? Most 'orthodox' Socialists would say 'No.' Planning, socially ordered production and consumption, must be applied to all economic processes, or waste and dislocation will take place. Now this view seems to me based upon a fundamental misconception of human equality and of the liberty related thereto. The validity of a planned economy, whether democratically or autocratically ordered, is based on the two assumptions that the plan is directed to the supply of needs which are common to all consumers and that the

202

planner knows what these needs are. Now, those assumptions are valid just in so far as human beings are the same in their needs and wants and can, therefore, be supplied by standard goods produced by routine methods. Most of the necessaries and conveniences of life would conform to those conditions. In so far as such economic requirements are concerned the members of a community are closely similar, if not identical, in their needs and wants. But outside this identity there are important differences, numerous and various, which cannot be properly provided for by routine standardised processes. These personal individual qualities have higher conscious values than the common qualities, and, if they require economic nourishment, its provision demands the personal freedom of production outside the compass of collective planning.

Selected Bibliography

(Hobson wrote over fifty books and pamphlets and hundreds of articles and reviews; some of the more important are listed below. For additional information see the books by Nemmers and Allett and the thesis by Lee.)

1 Works by Hobson (in chronological order)

A Books and Pamphlets

The Physiology of Industry [with A. F. Mummery] (London: 1889).
Problems of Poverty (London: 1891).
The Evolution of Modern Capitalism (London: 1894; rev. edns 1906, 1917, 1926).
The Problem of the Unemployed (London: 1896; rev. edns 1904, 1906).
John Ruskin Social Reformer (London: 1898).
The War in South Africa (London: 1900).
The Economics of Distribution (New York: 1900).
The Psychology of Jingoism (London: 1901).
The Social Problem (London: 1901).
Imperialism: A Study (London: 1902; rev. edns 1905, 1938).
International Trade (London: 1904).
Canada Today (London: 1906).
The Industrial System (London: 1909).
The Crisis of Liberalism (London: 1909).
A Modern Outlook (London: 1910).
The Science of Wealth (London: 1911; rev. edns 1914, 1934, 1950).
An Economic Interpretation of Investment (London: 1911).
The German Panic (London: 1913).
Gold, Prices and Wages (London: 1913).
Work and Wealth: A Human Valuation (London: 1914).
Traffic in Treason (London: 1914).
Towards International Government (London: 1915).
The New Protectionism (London: 1916).
Democracy After the War (London: 1917).
1920: Dips into the Near Future [by Lucian] (London: 1918).
Richard Cobden: The International Man (London: 1919).
Taxation in the New State (London: 1919).
The Morals of Economic Internationalism (Boston and New York: 1920).
The Economics of Reparation (London: 1921).

Problems of a New World (London: 1921).
Incentives in the New Industrial Order (London: 1922).
The Economics of Unemployment (London: 1922).
Notes on Law and Order (London: 1926).
Free-Thought in the Social Sciences (London: 1926).
The Living Wage [with H. N. Brailsford, A. Creech Jones, E. F. Wise] (London: 1926).
The Conditions of Industrial Peace (London: 1927).
Wealth and Life (London: 1929).
Rationalisation and Unemployment (London: 1930).
Towards Social Equality (London: 1931).
The Modern State (London: 1931).
Poverty in Plenty (London: 1931).
God and Mammon (London: 1931).
L. T. Hobhouse: His Life and Work [with Morris Ginsberg] (London: 1931).
The Recording Angel (London: 1932).
From Capitalism to Socialism (London: 1932).
Rationalism and Humanism (London: 1933).
Democracy and a Changing Civilisation (London: 1934).
Veblen (London: 1936).
Property and Improperty (London: 1937).
Confessions of an Economic Heretic (London: 1938).

B Articles and Chapters in Essay Collections *(excluding articles in daily and weekly newspapers)*

'Law of the three rents', *Quarterly Journal of Economics*, vol. 5 (1891), 263–88.
'Rights of Property', *Free Review*, vol. 1 (1893), 130–49.
'Mr Kidd's "social evolution" ', *American Journal of Sociology*, vol. 1 (1895), 299–312.
'A Living Wage', *Commonwealth*, vol. 1 (1896), 128–9.
'The influence of Henry George in England', *Fortnightly Review*, vol. 62 (1897), 835–44.
'Free trade and foreign policy', *Contemporary Review*, vol. 74 (1898), 167–80.
'On capital' and 'Of labour' in J. E. Hand (ed.), *Good Citizenship* (London: 1899).
'The ethics of industrialism', in S. Coit (ed.), *Ethical Democracy: Essays in Social Dynamics* (London: 1900).
'The approaching abandonment of free trade', *Fortnightly Review*, vol. 71 (1902), 434–44.
'Ruskin and democracy', *Contemporary Review*, vol. 81 (1902), 103–11.
'The re-statement of democracy', *Contemporary Review*, vol. 81 (1902), 262–72.
'Protection as a working-class policy', in H. W. Massingham (ed.), *Labour and Protection* (London: 1903).
'Marginal units in the theory of distribution', *Journal of Political Economy*, vol. 12 (1904), 449–72.

J. A. Hobson: A Reader

'Herbert Spencer', *South Place Magazine*, vol. 9 (1904), 49–55.
'The possibilities of popular progress', *University Review*, vol. 1 (1905), 150–69.
'The taxation of monopolies', *Independent Review*, vol. 9 (1906), 20–33.
'Science and industry', in J. E. Hand (ed.), *Science in Public Affairs* (London: 1906).
'The ethics of internationalism', *International Journal of Ethics*, vol. 17 (1906–7), 16–28.
'Old age pensions. II. The responsibility of the state to the aged poor', *Sociological Review*, vol. 1 (1908), 295–9.
'The passing of private charity', *The International*, vol. 6 (1909), 3–10.
'Eugenics as an art of social progress', *South Place Magazine*, vol. 14 (1909), 168–70.
'The significance of the Budget', *English Review*, vol. 2 (1909), 794–805.
'The General Election: a sociological interpretation', *Sociological Review*, vol. 3 (1910), 105–17.
'Character and society', in P. L. Parker (ed.), *Character and Life* (London: 1912).
'The open door', in C. R. Buxton (ed.), *Towards a Lasting Settlement* (London: 1915).
'Ruskin as political economist', in J. H. Whitehouse (ed.), *Ruskin the Prophet* (London: 1920).
'The new industrial revolution', *Contemporary Review*, vol. 118 (1920), 638–45.
'The Ethical Movement and the natural man', *Hibbert Journal*, vol. 20 (1922), 667–79.
'The reformation of politics', *Contemporary Review*, vol. 129 (1925), 430–6.
'Economics and ethics', in W. F. Ogden and A. Goldweiser (eds), *The Social Sciences and their Interrelations* (Boston: 1927).
'Social thinkers in nineteenth-century England', *Contemporary Review*, vol. 137 (1930), 453–61.
'The state as an organ of Rationalisation', *Political Quarterly*, vol. 2 (1931), 30–45.
'Force necessary to government', *Hibbert Journal*, vol. 33 (1934), 331–42.
'Democracy, liberty and force', *Hibbert Journal*, vol. 34 (1935), 35–44.
'Thoughts on our present discontents', *Political Quarterly*, vol. 9 (1938), 47–57.

2 Works on Hobson

Allett, J., *New Liberalism: The Political Economy of J. A. Hobson* (Toronto: University of Toronto Press, 1981).
Brailsford, H. N., *The Life-Work of J. A. Hobson* (London: 1948).
Cain, P. J., 'J. A. Hobson, Cobdenism, and the radical theory of economic imperialism, 1898–1914', *Economic History Review*, vol. 31 (1978), 565–84.
Cain, P. J., 'International trade and economic development in the work of

J. A. Hobson before 1914', *History of Political Economy*, vol. 11 (1979), 406–24.

Cain, P. J., 'Hobson's developing theory of imperialism', *Economic History Review*, vol. 34 (1981), 313–16.

Cain, P. J., 'J. A. Hobson, financial capitalism and imperialism in late Victorian and Edwardian England', *Journal of Imperial and Commonwealth History*, vol. 13 (May 1985), 1–27.

Clarke, P. F., 'Hobson, free trade, and imperialism', *Economic History Review*, vol. 34 (1981), 308–12.

Clarke, P., *Liberals and Social Democrats* (Cambridge: Cambridge University Press, 1978) [paperback edn 1981].

Cole, G. D. H., 'J. A. Hobson (1858–1940)', *Economic Journal*, vol. 50 (1940), 351–60.

Coppock, D. J. 'A reconsideration of Hobson's theory of unemployment', *Manchester School of Economic and Social Studies*, vol. 21 (1953), 1–21.

Davis, H. B., 'Hobson and human welfare', *Science and Society*, vol. 21 (1957), 291–318.

Etherington, N., *Theories of Imperialism: War, Conquest and Capital* (London, 1984).

Freeden, M., 'J. A. Hobson as a New Liberal theorist: some aspects of his social thought until 1914', *Journal of the History of Ideas*, vol. 34 (1973), 421–43.

Freeden, M., *The New Liberalism* (Oxford: Clarendon Press, 1978) [paperback edn 1986].

Freeden, M., *Liberalism Divided* (Oxford: Clarendon Press, 1986)

Hamilton, D., 'Hobson with a Keynesian twist', *American Journal of Economics and Sociology*, vol. 13 (1953–4), 273–82.

Homan, P. T., *Contemporary Economic Thought* (New York: 1928), pp. 283–374.

Hutchison, T. W., *A Review of Economic Doctrines, 1870–1929* (Oxford: 1953), pp. 319–28.

Lee, A. J., 'The social and economic thought of J. A. Hobson', (unpublished PhD thesis, London: 1970).

Lee, A., 'J. A. Hobson', in J. M. Bellamy and J. Saville (eds), *Dictionary of Labour Biography*, Vol. I (London: 1972), pp. 176–81.

Lloyd, T., 'Africa and Hobson's imperialism', *Past and Present*, no. 55 (1972), 130–53.

Mitchell, H., 'Hobson revisited', *Journal of the History of Ideas*, vol. 26 (1965), 397–416.

Nemmers, E. E., *Hobson and Underconsumption* (Amsterdam: 1956).

Porter, B., *Critics of Empire* (London: 1968).

Soffer, R. N., *Ethics and Society in England: The Revolution in the Social Sciences* (Berkeley and Los Angeles: University of California Press, 1978).

Tawney, R. H., 'Hobson, John Atkinson', in *Dictionary of National Biography*, 1931–40 (London: 1949), pp. 435–6.

Wood, J. C., *British Economists and the Empire* (London: 1983).

Index

Index

Index

Price, L. L. 3
private
 enterprise 85, 103, 179, 190
 ownership 12, 79, 143
 property 57–9, 146, 202
Problem of the Unemployed, The 106–7, 110–16
Problems of a New World 154, 172–82
producing class 108
production/consumption relationship 121, 128, 151, 158, 161–4, 179, 202
productive
 capacity 147
 expenditure 138
productivity 54, 148–9, 177
progressive
 efficiency, wage of 140, 144
 socialism 60
 society 164; capital/labour relationship 136; money circulation in 129–30, 133, 135, 137
protectionism 17, 21, 106, 154, 159–60, 168, 170, 175–6, 180, 183
Prussianism 196–7
psychology, Hobson's attitude to 49, 94–7
Psychology of Jingoism, The 19, 189, 191–3
public
 ownership 78, 202
 protection 106
 services 103, 146–7
purchasing power 152
puritan ethics 92, 97

Radical Party 79
radicalism 77, 80–1, 91
Rainbow Circle, the 3, 190
rationalisation 107, 148–52
Rationalisation and Unemployment 147–52
redistributionism 22
Ricardo, D. 165
Ritchie, D. G. 8
Robertson, J. M. 4
Rousseau, J. J. 69
Rousseauist tradition 8
Rowntree, B. S. 163
Ruskin, J. 6, 8, 28–30, 72, 99

sabbatarianism 92
Samuel, Herbert 4

saving 107–11, 115, 119, 130–6, 138, 141, 144, 148, 157–9, 161–3, 179, 198
Say's Law 14, 153
Science of Wealth, The 107, 137–47
Scott, C. P. 4, 19
Scott, Edward 4
shares 167
Sidgwick, H. 36
Significance of the Budget, The 189, 193–5
social
 consciousness 85
 democracy 81
 equality 105
 liberalism 17
 organicism 7–8, 21, 65–74, 83–5, 87–9, 101–2, 107
 productivity 54
 property 48, 50, 55–60, 70, 78, 106, 112, 202
 reform 1, 4–5, 7, 17, 78–81, 89, 106, 153, 164–5
 science 45–6
 theory 49–105
 utility 39
 welfare 64, 90, 99
 will 82–7
Social Problem, The 6, 28, 33–40, 48–60
socialism 11–13, 16, 22, 33, 75, 77, 79, 81, 87, 107, 190, 197–8, 201–2
 continental 79, 81
Society of Nations 187–8
sociology 5–6
Socrates 96
South Africa 19, 31, 189
South America 159
South Place Ethical Society, the 4, 48
Speaker 4
Spencer, Herbert 5, 8, 48, 50, 53, 59, 61–5
spending 107, 119, 130–1, 134–6, 148, 198
stable society
 capital/labour relationship 136
 money circulation in 129–30, 132, 135, 137
State
 British idea of the 197
 economic work of the 146
 regulation of industry 190
 role in industry 145–7

211

For Product Safety Concerns and Information please contact our EU
representative GPSR@taylorandfrancis.com
Taylor & Francis Verlag GmbH, Kaufingerstraße 24, 80331 München, Germany

www.ingramcontent.com/pod-product-compliance
Lightning Source LLC
Chambersburg PA
CBHW070413270326
41926CB00014B/2799